CICERO

STUDIES IN LATIN LITERATURE
AND ITS INFLUENCE

Editors

D. R. Dudley and T. A. Dorey

CICERO
Chapters by J. P. V. D. Balsdon, M. L. Clarke, T. A. Dorey, A. E. Douglas, R. G. M. Nisbet, H. H. Scullard, G. B. Townend

LUCRETIUS
Chapters by D. R. Dudley, B. Farrington, O. E. Lowenstein, W. S. Maguinness, T. J. B. Spencer, G. B. Townend, D. E. W. Wormell

ROMAN DRAMA
Chapters by W. R. Chalmers, C. D. N. Costa, G. L. Evans, J. A. Hanson, A. Steegman, T. B. L. Webster, T. L. Zinn

LATIN HISTORIANS
Chapters by E. Badian, F. W. Walbank, T. A. Dorey, G. M. Paul, P. G. Walsh, E. A. Thompson, J. Campbell

CICERO

Chapters by

H. H. Scullard   T. A. Dorey

R. G. M. Nisbet   A. E. Douglas

G. B. Townend   M. L. Clarke

J. P. V. D. Balsdon

Edited by

T. A. DOREY

BASIC BOOKS, INC., PUBLISHERS

NEW YORK

Studies in Latin Literature
and its Influence

'ARE the Dons out of touch?' In a series of articles recently published under this heading, Mr. M. I. Finley, of Jesus College, Cambridge, attacked the excessive emphasis placed by Classics teachers on the study of language, and criticized those professional Classicists who 'are turning their profession into a self-contained world of specialists communicating with each other alone'. He ends his contribution in these words: 'If the past is to be more than a dead-weight of tradition it requires active interpretation and re-interpretation, informed, flexible, and relevant to the present.' Mr. Finley's statements attracted a wide measure of agreement, but it was unfortunate that pressure of space prevented the *Sunday Times* from printing those letters that gave some account of the 'active re-interpretation' that is even now going on in a number of universities.

During the past few years there has been a tendency to recognize Latin not merely as one of the two classical languages but also as a vital element, in its own right, in the growth of Western culture. No person of sense would wish to harm or restrict the classical studies so long and fruitfully cultivated in our universities. But an increase in the numbers of students (many of whom, unhappily, have never had the chance to do Greek) has made it possible to provide for the study of Latin in conjunction with English, or one of the Romance languages, or with Medieval and Renaissance authors. There are two aspects of this approach. First, Latin is treated as a language whose use by writers, some of them of the greatest literary eminence, extends at least to the end of the seventeenth century. Viewed in this light, the study of Latin will involve not only Cicero and Virgil, Plautus and Tacitus, but also, amongst others, Augustine, Bede, William of Malmesbury, John of Salisbury, Erasmus, Thomas More, Sepulveda, von Hutten, Cleveland, Gager, and Milton. Secondly, special prominence is given to the influence of classical Latin writers on the vernacular literature of Western Europe in history, poetry, drama, satire, and other literary *genres*; and this must lead on to the evaluation of classical writers by standards relevant to our own day.

Nor, perhaps, has Latin scholarship been quite so esoteric as Mr. Finley would suggest. To name only a few, we have had recent studies of Ovid, Horace, Virgil, and Tacitus in which high scholarship has

v

been finely combined with an appeal to the general intelligent reader. But anyone who feels complacent about the present position of Latin in Britain should have regard to two warning signs. Of the seven new universities recently established, only Kent and Lancaster have, so far, shown signs of treating Latin, or classical studies, as subjects in their own right. At the present moment, it really does look as though at York, city of Constantine and Alcuin, and at Colchester, the Roman *colonia* which is the oldest city in Britain, the students are to know nothing of Latin if the university authorities can prevent it. Reactions to this strange phenomenon may vary. Indignation may lead one to dub some of these new institutions as only too faithful to the spirit of the age, which regards itself as progressive because it has discarded provincialism in space for provincialism in time. Indulgence may reflect that the eyes of new-born infants take some time to come into focus. But Latinists would do well to ask themselves how far their own deficiencies have contributed to the growth of a public opinion which is ready to tolerate such aberrations. Our second warning sign is no less revealing, in its own way. In his recent lectures as Professor of Poetry at Oxford, Mr. Robert Graves chose to deliver a violent onslaught on Virgil. So far as we know, there was no public reply from any classical scholar: the trumpet that blew so loudly for battle drew no answering cry. That Mr. Graves's arguments were ill-founded (as we believe) is not the point. They were certainly not negligible, since they came from one of the leading poets of our day, an accomplished translator, and a man who has spent much time in the study of Roman history and literature. Are our studies so professionalized that we do not care? If so, it shows how much remains to be done before the study of Latin literature stands—as it should, and once did—at the very centre of the humanities. Latinists are still too prone to confine themselves within the traditional classical field, to care little for the influence of Latin literature on later times, and to ignore advances in scholarship in the study of other literatures. Literary criticism, as it is now understood in English studies, has, with a few brilliant exceptions, not been widely applied to Latin: many doubt whether it can be applied at all.

Historians and archaeologists have shown that there is a wide audience of the general intelligent public prepared to be interested in Rome; very little of it has been captured for Latin literature. There is also the problem of the Latinate reading public, defined as all those who read Latin for their own pleasure and profit. No one knows how large this public is, either in Britain or the United States. It is on record that a distinguished Lowell lecturer once drew up a reading-list for his audience, based on the assumption that they would devote to Latin literature at least half an hour every day. Was he assuming too much, even in Boston? What is certain, at any rate, is that this Latinate reading public is vital for the health of Latin studies, for on it depends their prospects of continuing to influence the culture of the West. It will wither away if scholars write only for scholars, and will leave Latin in a worse position than Hebrew.

In short, there is an urgent need to fertilize Latin studies by bringing in scholars from other fields, and to encourage Latinists at all levels to enlarge their interests and to write for a wider audience. The present project is meant as a contribution to these ends. It proposes the publication of a series of books under the general title of STUDIES IN LATIN LITERATURE AND ITS INFLUENCE. Each volume will be devoted to a single major theme—a Latin author, a literary genre, an important period of literary history. Each will contain a number of essays specially commissioned for the purpose. Scholars from other disciplines, especially English and other modern literatures, will be brought in. Most contributors will be from the United Kingdom or North America; chapters by Continental scholars will be included from time to time, but all contributions will be in English. The series will be free to explore the whole range of Latin literature, from the earliest writers of the Republic to the neo-Latin authors of the Renaissance. The Greek background will be dealt with wherever appropriate, and a portion of each volume will always be devoted to a study of the influence of Latin literature on later times.

This volume will be followed by others on Lucretius, Latin Historians, and Roman Drama.

D. R. DUDLEY

T. A. DOREY

Contents

To

LORD COUTANCHE

who for twenty-five years in the

Island of Jersey was a wise and courageous

GUBERNATOR REI PUBLICAE

Introduction

IT is just over two thousand years since Cicero was executed on the orders of the Triumvirs. In 1959 the bimillenary of his death was celebrated in Rome by the foundation of the Institute of Ciceronian Studies and the holding of an international conference.[1] In England, an attempt to organize a Society for the study of Cicero failed from lack of support. The general antipathy shown towards Cicero in this country is due not to any positive dislike of his weaknesses but rather to the feeling that he was a man who, to put things at their best, devoted all his energies and finally gave his life for a cause that was not worth saving. Yet, even granted the truth of this judgement—a point that many Ciceronian scholars on the Continent would not concede—there is more in Cicero than an unsuccessful politician. We have to consider him not merely for what he did but also for what he wrote, and as a writer he is of pre-eminent importance in four different aspects. First, he was a master of style, and his handling of language had a greater influence on the subsequent use of Latin, for the next two thousand years, than any other Latin prose writer. Secondly, he was one of the outstanding figures in the history of advocacy, and his published speeches contain some of the most brilliant examples of the use of that art. It is easy to decry the advocate's profession, and to throw undue emphasis on the distortion of the truth to which at times it descends, but the art of persuasion is the only alternative to the rule of force, and the more sophisticated a society becomes, the greater the scope there is for the skill of the pleader. In the third place, Cicero had a very wide knowledge of literature, and, although he could not be called a critical thinker, he had not only a thorough grasp of the political and philosophical thought of the ancient world but also the power of lucid expression necessary to transmit to posterity the ideas of the past. Finally, Cicero lived at a period of history in which radical changes were taking place in the system of government of the civilized world, and in his Correspondence he provides first-hand contemporary information about the great events that were occurring and the men by whom they were performed. It is thanks to him that we can get such vivid pictures of men like the stern, uncompromising Cato, Pompey with his day-dreams of greatness, the sinister Crassus, arrogant nobles like Appius Claudius and Metellus Celer, and the whole cross-section of the political society of Rome, corrupt and selfish but vital and loyal to its own ideals, however perverted they may seem.

It is hoped that the present volume will have two results. First, that it will stimulate general interest in Cicero as a speaker and a writer, a scholar and a statesman, and as an individual personality of engaging interest. Secondly, that it will bring together various points of views, sometimes conflicting, on Cicero's life and works, and show more clearly that Cicero deserves to be the subject of a definitive biography in English.

The lack of interest in Cicero shown in this country is made even clearer by the fact that no major full-scale study has been published about him in English since the end of the War. No one has been found to do for Cicero what Syme has done for Tacitus and Walsh for Livy.[2] Leaving on one side the valuable work done by Dacre Balsdon on the historical problems associated with Cicero's career[3] and by Shackleton Bailey on the text of the Correspondence,[4] the following books and articles can be noted, most of them of interest to the non-specialist reader:

H. A. K. HUNT, *The Humanism of Cicero* (Carlton), 1954.

F. R. COWELL, *Cicero and the Roman Republic* (London), 1948.

H. FRISCH, *Cicero's Fight for the Republic* (Copenhagen), 1946.

E. LAUGHTON, 'Cicero and the Greek Orators', *AJPh.*, Jan. 1961.

S. E. SMETHURST, 'Cicero and Isocrates,' *TAPhA*, 1953.

T. W. ALLEN, 'Cicero's Conceit', *TAPhA*, 1954.

S. E. SMETHURST, 'Bibliographical Survey of Cicero's Philosophical and Rhetorical Works', *CW*, 1958, vol. LI.

W. ALLEN, 'Survey of Selected Ciceronian Bibliography', *CW*, 1954, vol. XLVII.

In French there have been:

M. RAMBAUD, *Ciceron et l'histoire romaine* (Paris), 1953.

A. HAURY, *L'ironie et l'humeur chez Ciceron* (Leiden), 1955.

CICERO

R. PONCELET, *Ciceron, traducteur de Platon* (Paris), 1957.

A. MICHEL, *Rhetorique et philosophie chez Ciceron* (Paris), 1960.

R. MONSUEZ, 'Le style epistolaire de Ciceron', AFLT Pallas II; 1952 & 1954.

M. VAN DER BRUWAENE, *Etude sur Ciceron* (Brussels) 1949.

In German:

H. D. MEYER, *Cicero und das Reich* (Cologne), 1957.

K. BÜCHNER, *Cicero* (Wiesbaden), 1962.

O. SEEL, *Cicero* (Stuttgart), 1953.

In Italy, apart from the *Collegium Ciceronianum*, published at Rome in 1959 on the occasion of the Ciceronian Congress, there is now a regular periodical, *Ciceroniana*, devoted to articles on Cicero. So far there have appeared: vol. I, 1; I, 2; II, 1-2.

NOTES

[1] Cf. Greece and Rome, Oct. 1959.

[2] R. Syme, *Tacitus* (Oxford), 1958. P. G. Walsh, *Livy: his historical aims and methods* (Cambridge), 1961.

[3] Cf. *JRS* 1957; 1962.

[4] J. Shackleton Bailey, *Towards a text of the 'ad Atticum'* (Cambridge), 1960.

I

The Political Career of a 'Novus Homo'

H. H. SCULLARD

THE third king of Rome in the seventh century B.C. was named Tullus Hostilius and the sixth king was Servius Tullius, yet the family of the Tullii in later Republican times was plebeian and had not become ennobled because none of its members had attained to the consulship. When M. Tullius Cicero was elected consul for 63 B.C. he thereby ennobled his family, but he was what was known as a 'new man' (*novus homo*). Throughout his life he was conscious of this background. In his earlier days as a rising lawyer and politician he strove to reach the highest honour to which Romans could be elected and thus to force his way into the closed circle of the nobility; but when he had achieved this goal, he remained aware that, although he might be named *Parens Patriae*, he had still not been fully accepted by some of the older families. In order to appreciate what this meant, and indeed in order to understand his life, it is necessary to look at the composition of Roman society as it was in his day and also at the nature of Roman political life.

The aristocracy of Rome in early days had consisted of the patrician clans, who in the fifth and fourth centuries had fought a losing battle with the plebeians in an attempt to keep control over the political, economic, social, and religious life of the community. This 'Struggle of the Orders' had been waged with great bitterness but without bloodshed; by compromise and common-sense a constitution was hammered out in which both Orders shared and many of their differences began to disappear. This was possible because many plebeians had become socially and economically the equals of the patricians. A most significant revolution gradually took place: a new governing class emerged, comprising both patricians and plebeians. At the same time it appeared that Rome might soon develop into a real democracy, but the emergence of this new patricio-plebeian aristocracy prevented this. Although the People had considerable powers of legislation and election, nevertheless a small body of men managed to retain real power in their own hands. They held the chief magistracies especially the consulship, and they dominated the Senate, which became the effective, though not the legal, governing body of Rome. Theoretically the magistrates, who were elected by the people, merely consulted the Senate, which was only an advisory body, but in fact, as the most permanent and experienced organ in the State, the Senate soon exercised an overall control. It was, however, a rather large body of some 300 members (500 or 600 in Cicero's day), and it was likely therefore to be 'run' by a more limited group of its members.

This came about because the new aristocracy was not a homogeneous body with equal privilege for all its members: there emerged an inner circle of *nobiles*. These were the men who reached the highest ('curule') offices; later, in Cicero's time only the consulship would qualify a man. These men became the *nobiles* and they ennobled their descendants for the future. They formed a closed society, drawn from a limited number of families: thus the 200 consuls between 232 and 133 B.C. belonged to 58 families, but 159 of them came from only 26 of the families, and half the total came from only ten. Members of other families might hold the lower offices (e.g. the quaestorship), but only exceptionally could an outsider reach an office, such as the praetorship or consulship, that would allow him to exert much influence on public policy. As a result, members of some 20 families guided senatorial policy, commanded the armies and governed the provinces: they were the 'Few' of whom Sallust wrote, 'regna, provinciae, leges, iura, iudicia, bella atque paces, postremo divina et humana omnia penes paucos erant'.

How then could a man like Cicero, a man of the Equestrian Order in a small hill-town in Italy, hope to break into the charmed circle? Few had succeeded in doing this, but it was made possible for men of exceptional qualities by the nature of political life at Rome. This rested largely on personal relationships: political influence and electoral success depended on the extent of personal support that a man could gain to help him to work the constitutional machinery in his favour. This system, or lack of it, enabled the *nobiles* to keep control of the State, but it also meant that an outsider who won the support of a powerful noble family or families might be pushed up the political ladder higher than his own unaided qualities could ever have raised him. This was because the Romans were a conservative people with a great respect for ancestral custom (*mos maiorum*), and Roman society was bound together by a nexus of personal obligations. Many men were linked by ties that bound patron and client, since in early days the weaker often sought the help and protection of the stronger. Hence developed a relationship with strong reciprocal duties for men bound together by ties of loyalty (*fides*). The form it took would depend on the social or economic needs of the client: the poor man would need help in cash or land, others might need protection in the law courts against oppression, while the more successful and ambitious might seek support if they wanted a political career at Rome. All this helps to explain how the nobles secured votes and political influence, but there is another side to the picture. If a man could get sufficient backing from noble families to start on a political career, he might be able to advance himself further by his own talents in one particular sphere, distinction in oratory and law. This, as Cicero himself tells us, formed with nobility of birth and military service a third channel to the consulship.

Beside depending on the electoral support of their clients, the nobles sought help from their families, their *gentes* and, by means of political friendships or alliances (*amicitiae*), from other *gentes*. Where personal friendship was lacking, practical co-operation could often be arranged: an outstanding example of such an *amicitia*, strengthened, as often, by a marriage alliance, was the so-called First Triumvirate of Pompey, Caesar, and Crassus, who privately agreed to work together for their mutual political benefit. Thus a kind of 'family politics' developed, in which individuals and groups of nobles strove in rivalry with other groups for the electoral success of members of their families. Conditions were not unlike those of eighteenth-century England during the period of the Whig oligarchy under the first two Georges. But at Rome this did not lead to the growth of party politics in the modern sense. Men appealed to the electors on the ground of their family traditions and personal achievements, not necessarily because they advocated any particular policy.

Although electoral struggles between rival coteries might be sharp, they did not shake the solidarity of the aristocracy's control of the State through the Senate. This received a major shock in 133 B.C. when challenged by a group of reforming nobles, led by Tiberius Gracchus; unity was restored, but only at the price of using force to crush the dissidents. Another division within the nobility is now observable; that of the *Optimates* and *Populares*. These words have often been misunderstood, since the *Populares* were not a party of reform or advocates of democracy. The difference lay not in class or even in policies, but in the methods they used. Some of the *Populares* sought personal power (few, like the Gracchi, were genuine reformers), while the *Optimates* tried to uphold the oligarchy that they controlled. In the pursuit of their aims many of the *Populares* used the tribunate and the People in an attempt to break the dominant oligarchy. In the process the influence of the Senate was shaken, but it survived these buffetings, and, when Cicero was a young man, it received a renewal of strength from the reforms of Sulla, who had held a temporary military dictatorship.

The world of Cicero's childhood was changing rapidly. The most serious threat to the control of the Senate was ultimately to come from men whose ambitions led them to seek personal predominance by winning the personal loyalty of Roman armies. But that danger was only dimly foreshadowed, since Marius had employed his military power to advance himself, but had stopped short of using it in a direct challenge to the Senate. At the moment the Senatorial aristocracy was harassed on other fronts, by the Equestrian Order, the class to which Cicero belonged. The *Equites* had originally been the aristocrats who served as cavalry in the Roman armies, but by the second century men of a certain financial status, who were not senators, were classified in what came to be known as the Equestrian Order. This occurred because senators were a landed aristocracy who were precluded by law from taking part in commerce. Thus a distinction developed between land and trade, between the governing and the commercial classes. With the extension of Roman rule overseas, greater opportunities for commercial activities were created, and as Rome failed to create a Civil Service adequate to her growing needs, private businessmen were used as individuals or in companies to transact some of the financial affairs of the state (e.g. to collect certain taxes). It was these rich businessmen that formed the Equestrian Order, and although they avoided political responsibility, they naturally began to seek political influence. They secured this in 122 B.C. when they gained, and the Senate lost, control of the law court in which senatorial provincial governors were tried when charged with maladministration. The issue of whether members of the senatorial or equestrian orders should control this and other courts became a bone of contention between them, and now that the *Equites* could exert more political pressure on the governing senatorial class, a rift tended to widen between them. But this should not be exaggerated: although politically divided, these two groups were not necessarily far apart, since many came from the same class; some men of this social group turned to public life and politics, others preferred business. In one sense the Equestrian Order formed a Third Estate between Senate and People, but it was much closer to the former. Further, by Cicero's day many senators were privately indulging in business deals in disregard of the formal ban on such activities.

Such in brief was the background of Cicero's early life. His father, Marcus Tullius Cicero, was a member of the Roman Equestrian Order, who lived near Arpinum, a hill-town some sixty miles south-east of Rome; owing to poor health he spent most of his life in study there. But this well-to-do family had links with senatorial circles in Rome. The elder Cicero's mother, Gratidia, was sister of M. Gratidius, a friend of the orator M. Antonius; his cousin, M. Marius Gratidianus, reached the praetorship in 86 B.C., while young Cicero's cousin, Visellius Aculeo, became curule aedile about 59 B.C. But young Cicero did not spend all his boyhood in his country home, since his father had another house in Rome on the slopes of the Esquiline, not far from the home of young Julius Caesar. Here he and his younger brother, Quintus, began their education, attending lectures by Epicureans and Academics, while a blind Stoic named Diodotus lived in the house; further, they would study the leading orators of the day. After assuming the *toga virilis* ('coming of age') in 91 or 90 B.C., Cicero attended the legal receptions of one of the greatest jurists of the day, the eighty-year old Scaevola 'Augur', and after the latter's death he attended Q. Scaevola 'Pontifex' (consul in 95).

It was here that he met his life-long friend T. Pomponius Atticus, as well as Sulpicius Rufus, the tribune of 88. This was an important time for Cicero: not only was he laying the foundations for his professional legal career, but he was brought into the circle of the governing class in Rome. Old Scaevola was the step-son of Scipio Aemilianus's intimate friend Laelius, and so Cicero came into personal touch with men who had been linked with statesmen who had shaped Roman policy in the days of the Gracchi. This must have stimulated his imagination and he began to dream of a senatorial career for himself as well as to admire the leading statesmen, the *principes civitatis*. It was the parting of the ways: as he later wrote to his friend Atticus (*ad Att.* i, 17, 5), 'a touch of ambition led me to seek for distinction (*ad honorum studium*), while another perfectly laudible motive led you to honourable ease (*ad honestum otium*)'.[1] Senatorial and Equestrian careers diverged, and the two friends made their choices. Later, when he was defending his client Cluentius, Cicero contrasted the quiet life of the *Equites* with the storms and dangers to which a senator was exposed, but he also listed the alluring rewards that success in a senatorial career might bring: 'locus, auctoritas, domi splendor, apud externas nationes nomen et gratia, toga praetexta,sella curulis, insignia, fasces, exercitus, imperia, provinciae' (*pro Cluent.* 154). These were the prizes that the Roman aristocracy enjoyed: they dazzled and attracted the knight's son from Arpinum.

During the Social War, which led to the extension of Roman citizenship to all Italy, Cicero served in Sulla's army in 89, but he took no active part in the subsequent civil wars that resulted in Sulla's dictatorship. Instead, he devoted himself to his studies and wrote his early work *De Inventione*. After Sulla's victory, when the dictator was trying by constitutional reforms to infuse new life and strength into the senatorial government, Cicero undertook his first case in 81 when he defended P. Quinctius in a civil action about disputed property. Across the court he had to face two formidable nobles, since Quinctius was being prosecuted by Q. Hortensius, one of the greatest lawyers of the day, who was to become consul in 69 and a strong supporter of the supremacy of the Senate. Hortensius was assisted by a man of great eminence and *auctoritas*, L. Marcius Philippus who had been censor in 86.

[1] This and subsequent translations of Cicero are based on those in the Loeb Classical Library.

It is interesting to note Cicero's attitude: he was conscious of the gulf between himself and the nobility; the latter could execute any plan, whether right or wrong, with greater success than one born in his position ('nostro loco natus', *pro Qu.* 31). Thus he showed respect to his noble opponents, though he did criticize Cn. Cornelius Dolabella, one of the praetors; this however did not in fact harm his future, since Dolabella shortly afterwards was condemned for provincial extortion and went into exile. Soon Cicero was involved in his first criminal case when he boldly undertook the defence of Sextus Roscius, an innocent victim of one of Sulla's agents in the civil war: his father had been murdered and his property seized. Here Cicero had to move with care. He made a tactful reference to Sulla's power (*pro S. Roscio*, § 139) and explained that the dictator was too busy to know what his agents were doing. At the same time he showed his pleasure at the victory of the *causa nobilitatis* in the war in which he had taken no part (§§ 135, 142). Roscius's father had been on friendly terms with such distinguished families as the Scipios and Metelli, and Cicero took the opportunity to praise some of their members: Caecilia Metella, wife of Pulcher the consul of 79, who had sheltered young Roscius; P. Scipio (probably later consul in 52); M. Metellus (praetor in 69): such men are 'homines nobilissimi atque integerrimi nostrae civitatis' (§ 119). The success of Cicero's speech not only established his professional reputation but also helped to determine his political position. He had come out strongly on the side of 'optimus et nobilissimus quisque', but he was under no illusions about their future prospects: the restored nobility must be more than 'boni et fortes et misericordes', they must also be vigilant (§ 139).

During the next years (79-77) Cicero's health was not good and he pursued his oratorical studies in Greece and Asia Minor, but on his return to Rome he was active in the Courts, not least in the interest of the equestrian *publicani* (*In Verr.* 2, 3, 181). About this time he married Terentia, who came from a prosperous family and whose half-sister Fabia was a Vestal Virgin (*virgo nobilis*); what political support this marriage may have brought Cicero is not known. Nor unfortunately do we know what families supported him when he stood for the quaestorship in 76, but by this time he had put many men in his debt by the help that he had given them in the Courts and he seems to have antagonized neither the nobles nor the Knights. His quaestorship (75) meant that he now became a senator. He still continued working in the Courts, thereby increasing the size of his *clientela*. Then came his great triumph: he secured the condemnation of Verres in 70, the year when Pompey and Crassus swept away much of Sulla's work. This victory he gained despite the intrigues of Verres's noble friends, Hortensius and three of the Metelli. Now that his influence was increasing, he could clash with the Metelli with less fear of the consequences: indeed he contrasted L. Metellus with an earlier Metellus, Numidicus, who had been a true Metellus ('verus ac germanus Metellus'). Cicero, now a senator and identified with senatorial interests, showed that he had no desire to become a *Popularis*: rather, he wanted to win the good esteem of the *Optimates*. He might criticize some, but he praised men like Catulus (consul in 78) and Servilius (consul in 79) as worthy to rank with the 'antiquissimi clarissimique homines', and indeed 'omnes boni', and he looked back to the days of Scipio Aemilianus as the golden age of aristocratic rule.

Beside his forensic triumph in 70 Cicero also won a considerable political victory. At the elections for 69 Verres's supporters had swept the boards: Hortensius and Q. Metellus (Creticus) had gained the consulship, and M. Metellus a praetorship. Then followed the elections for the plebeian aedileship, at which Cicero was a candidate: despite attempted bribery by Verres, Cicero was successful. The aedileship offered an easy road to popularity, at any rate for the rich, since aediles were responsible for the public Games, and the lavish staging of these would help to win votes when the ex-aedile stood for the praetorship. Cicero later quoted (*de Off.* ii. 57 ff.) examples of such magnificent entertainments given by members of the nobility, but his own expenditure on his Games was moderate: although the grateful Sicilians had sent him many gifts, he preferred to devote these to reducing the price of food (Plutarch, *Cicero*, 8, 1) rather than trying to outbid the nobility in lavishness—or in ostentatious austerity, as L. Philippus (cos. 91), who boasted that he had held all the great offices of state without giving any entertainments. Cicero preferred the golden mean, and confined his boast to the fact that he gained all his magistracies at the earliest legal age ('nostro anno': *de Off.* ii. 59).

If Cicero's attack on Verres had been a damning exposure of provincial maladministration and corruption in the Courts, two

8

spheres that were at that time the monopoly of the Senate, his target had been less the *Optimates* as such than their unworthy representatives, and he soon obtained a chance to illustrate another side of the picture. He undertook, probably in 69, the defence of M. Fonteius, a former praetor who was accused of maladministration during his governorship of Gaul. Cicero's defence of his client, which was based on the alleged unreliability of any testimony from mere Gauls in contrast with that of Romans resident in the province, made a patriotic appeal to Roman prejudice. It thus gave a rosier picture of senatorial administration and upheld the *dignitas* of the Roman people. In his speech Cicero again praised such men as Aemilius Scaurus (cos. 115) and L Calpurnius Piso Frugi (cos. 133, whose *agnomen* revealed his honesty), who lived 'illis optimis temporibus, cum hominem invenire nequam neminem posses' (*pro Font.* 39). In those glorious days even a *novus homo* was accorded justice: Q. Pompeius had been acquitted on a charge of extortion because the evidence given against him even by men such as two Metelli and two Caepiones was not free from a suspicion of self-interest (§ 23).

In 67 Cicero not only was elected praetor but headed the poll; in his year of office (66) he presided over the *quaestio de repetundis*. He did not, however, confine himself to legal work; now that he had reached high office he made his first appearance in debate on public policy. In his speech to his fellow-citizens *De imperio Gnaei Pompei* (or *De lege Manilia*) he enthusiastically supported the proposal of the tribune Manilius that Pompey, who under the authority granted to him by the *Lex Gabinia* had just driven the pirates off the seas, should be entrusted with further extraordinary powers in order to defeat Mithridates the king of Pontus. Since Manilius's proposal was bitterly opposed by the extreme *Optimates*, and would be highly objectionable to Lucullus, to whose command Pompey would succeed, Cicero clearly had to walk warily if he was to avoid making too many enemies. In his speech therefore he gave high praise to Lucullus, and although he pointed out that Pompey's success against the pirates proved that *Optimates*, like Hortensius and Catulus, had been wrong in opposing Pompey's earlier command, yet at the same time he praised these men, while still emphasizing that other nobles favoured the bill. A hostile tradition (cf. Dio Cassius, xxxvi, 43, 5) might charge Cicero with playing now to the nobility, now to the people, but his speech showed a certain moderation, while pleasing many nobles, the people, and also members of the equestrian order, to which Cicero himself had belonged.

This appeal to varied interests may be a harbinger of Cicero's later desire to establish a *concordia ordinum*. At any rate, similar thoughts occur in the speech which he delivered this same year on behalf of Cluentius, the defendant in a notorious and complicated murder trial. Since Cluentius was an *eques* who had influential friends in distinguished families in many parts of Italy (e.g. Ferentinum, Teanum, Bovianum, Apulia: cf. *pro Cluent.* 197), Cicero, in defending him, gained the goodwill of a valuable part of the Equestrian Order. Further, Cicero could say that many senators, though far from all, wanted closer relations with the Knights: 'equites ordini senatorio dignitate proximos, concordia coniunctissimos esse cupiunt'. Others wanted to get the Knights into their power because of their increasing strength ('equites Romanos in potestatem suam redacturos . . . vident enim auctoritatem huius ordinis confirmari': § 152). Cicero was drawing nearer to the more moderate nobles, but he was not unmindful of the order from which he came. True, in this very speech (§ 139) he warns that in his forensic speeches he is naturally speaking as an advocate and that his real political opinions must not necessarily be sought there (these we find in his letters and other writings), yet in this point, at least, his argument probably reflects his wish.

In coming out boldly as a panegyrist of Pompey, Cicero annoyed Crassus, Pompey's colleague in the consulship of 70. Since that year Pompey had advanced to great glory, while Crassus had remained in obscurity. Even his earlier defeat of Spartacus had been overclouded by Pompey's last-minute intervention, and in this connection it was Pompey and not Crassus that Cicero praised in the *De imperio Cn. Pompei* (§ 30). Crassus and Cicero moved still further apart in the next few years while Pompey was defeating Mithridates and re-organizing the East. Fearing that Pompey might ultimately return as a second Sulla, Crassus tried to build up his political position by a series of intrigues in which he was ably abetted by Julius Caesar, who reached the aedileship in 65, the year of Crassus's censorship. In thwarting these Cicero played a considerable part. For example, when Crassus proposed what amounted to the annexation of Egypt, Cicero in a speech

De Rege Alexandrino helped to defeat the project; in this he was supporting the conservative leader Q. Catulus (who had also thwarted another scheme of his fellow-censor Crassus to gain influence in Transpadane Gaul). Thus Cicero, although a supporter of Pompey whom the *Optimates* feared, was drawing nearer to the conservatives, and this was significant since constitutionally he was free to stand for the consulship of 63. His chances of success, which for a *novus homo* would normally be negligible, were increased by the fact that one of the consular candidates was Catiline, who was alleged to be backed by Crassus's wealth and whose dubious implication in the so-called 'First Catilinarian Conspiracy' in 66/5 would increase the distrust of the *Optimates* at the thought of his possible election. They were therefore more willing to favour Cicero, despite his equestrian background, his lack of consular ancestors, his support of Pompey and some past fears that he had a *popularis* element hidden beneath his love of law and order. Thus suspicion that the noble Catiline might prove more subversive of Optimate interests than the Knight's son (fears which the latter fanned in his electioneering speech *In Toga Candida*) secured for him a sufficient swing of votes controlled by the nobility to give him victory: he and the worthless Antonius defeated Catiline. For the first time for thirty years a *novus homo* had reached the consulship. To this great achievement Cicero later looked back with justifiable pride: 'me cuncta Italia, me omnes ordines, me universa civitas non prius tabella quam voce priorem consulem declaravit' (*In Pis.* 3).

On the first day of his consulship Cicero came forward to denounce an agrarian bill which the tribune Rullus was proposing in the interest of men whom Cicero tactfully did not name; they are merely 'auctores horum consiliorum' or 'qui haec machinabantur' in his speech (*De Lege Agraria*), but whom he believed to be Crassus and Caesar. In denouncing what he considered to be a specious agrarian bill, Cicero had to be careful not to offend the people: hence he emphasized that he was 'veritate non ostentatione popularis' (*de Lege Agr*' i. 23). *Novi homines* like Cicero, men 'qui non in cunabilis, sed in campo sunt consules facti' (ii. 100), must be especially diligent in guarding the Republic. But while protecting the interests of the absent Pompey, against whom he argued the bill was directed, at the same time he championed the cause of the *Optimates* ('hunc statum rei publicae magno opere defendendum', iii. 4), and the resultant defeat of the bill was a victory for the Senate's authority.

The theme of *novus homo* came up again later in the year when Cicero defended L. Murena, one of the newly elected consuls for 62, who was prosecuted by Servius Sulpicius Rufus, an eminent jurist who had failed at the elections, and by Cato; the charge was electoral bribery. Cicero was supported by Hortensius and Crassus who joined him in Murena's defence. In his prosecution Sulpicius had held up Murena's family to contempt, while exalting his own: he was a noble, Murena was not. But Cicero was quick to point out that, although Sulpicius' family was consular, neither his father, who was *equestri loco*, nor his grandfather were well known or distinguished, whereas Murena, although lacking consular ancestors, had a father, grandfather and great-grandfather who all had held the praetorship, while the father had been granted a triumph for his campaign against Mithridates. Cicero then told Sulpicius that since they both were the sons of knights, he had always counted him 'in nostrum numerum' (§ 16), that is among the 'new men' whose talents made them worthy of the highest office. Sulpicius then had to listen to Cicero telling the Court that distinction in war or oratory rather than in civil law helped men to the consulship: 'duae sint artes igitur quae possint locare homines in amplissimo gradu dignitatis, una imperatoris, altera oratoris boni' (30; cf. 22, 23, 29). Cicero, however, conducted the defence in so witty and good-natured a way that, although he poked fun at the technical hair-splitting of the lawyer Sulpicius and at the rigid Stoic doctrines of Cato, he offended neither; indeed Sulpicius remained a life-long friend and near the end of their lives comforted Cicero on the death of his daughter in a famous letter of consolation.

Cicero's successful defence of Murena might seem light-hearted, but it was delivered in a moment of national crisis, the conspiracy of Catiline. His handling of this, and in particular his order for the execution of the nobles, P. Cornelius Lentulus (cos. 71) and C. Cornelius Cethegus, together with three other conspirators, without a trial, brought Cicero to the turning-point of his career. For having saved his country he received unprecedented honours: a thanksgiving service was held in his name, while conservative leaders, such as Catulus and Cato, called him father of his country. Clearly he was now aligned closely with the nobility of which he was now a member, while the 'popular' leaders, Crassus and Caesar, had been rebuffed: although no action was taken against them, rumours were strong that they had given Catiline some backing, even if such beliefs were unfounded at this point. Further, Cicero was greatly impressed by the way that all men of moderate opinion had rallied to him against the extremists and his hopes grew that the senatorial and equestrian orders might be reconciled. In his Fourth Oration against Catiline, he could tell the Senate that after strife with the equestrian order that had lasted many years 'this day and this case have recalled them to a cordial alliance ("ad societatem concordiamque") and have joined them to you'; 'quam si coniunctionem in consulatu confirmatam meo perpetuam in re publica tenuerimus, confirmo vobis nullum posthoc malum civile ac domesticum ad ullam rei publicae partem esse venturum'(15)

Cicero's hope to perpetuate a *concordia ordinum*, based on the *consensio Italiae*, now became his policy and ideal: it was the *optima causa*. But it could only succeed if it was not threatened by the military power of Pompey, who would soon return from the East after his victory over Mithridates. Cicero had upheld Pompey's interest in Rome during the last few years and might hope to win him over to his cause, the more so as he told him in a letter that he was willing to play Laelius to Pompey's Scipio Africanus, i.e. act as friend and adviser to the great man. But there was a fatal obstacle: as Cicero naively pointed out in his letter (*ad Fam.* v. 7), Pompey had not shown sufficient appreciation of Cicero's greatness in saving his country from Catiline. The reason for Pompey's coldness was in fact quite clear: he had hoped to return from the East to Rome in time to win the glory of having suppressed the Catilinarian conspiracy, and had been forestalled by Cicero. He had secured the help of Metellus Nepos, who entered the tribunate in December 63, but it was too late; Catiline had been thwarted. Metellus, however, harassed Cicero in various ways, and in this he received some support from Caesar (praetor in 62). Nor would Pompey have been pleased to hear that when Cicero defended Archias he gave great praise to Lucullus, who had preceded Pompey as commander against Mithridates (*pro Arch.* 21). Thus when at the end of the year Pompey landed at Brundisium, and to everyone's relief disbanded his army, his attitude to Cicero might be somewhat strained. In fact, however, he was still reported to be friendly (*ad Att.* i. 13, 3; i. 16, 11) and that despite the fact that Crassus had eulogized Cicero in the Senate in order to make Pompey jealous (*ad Att.* i. 14, 3); Cicero could also draw hope from Pompey's own speech which, although disappointing to all, was at least conciliatory and loyal to the constitution. Further, Pompey may have moved closer to Cicero when he received a rebuff from an Optimate: Cato rejected a suggestion to link the families by a marriage alliance.

Clouds, however, soon began to overshadow Cicero's bright hopes. The Clodius scandal and his subsequent acquittal despite Cicero's demolition of his alibi, not only made Clodius his bitter personal enemy but also went far to destroy any *concordia ordinum*. This was further shaken by the weakness shown by the equestrian order (by December 61 Cicero could write: 'nostros equites paene a senatu esse diiunctos', *ad Att.* i. 17, 8), and also by the foolish attitude adopted by some of the leading *Optimates* towards Pompey. While Cicero, not without success, was trying to win Pompey over to the side of the Senate, the extreme conservatives (men like Hortensius, Cato and Lucullus) were either alienating him or showing complete political indifference. With the death of Catulus in the latter part of 61 Cicero felt increasingly isolated in his struggle to maintain the 'good cause' of constitutional government: he wrote (*ad Att.* i. 20, 3) 'me hanc viam optimatem post Catuli mortem nec praesidio ullo nec comitatu tenere'. When early in 60 a tribune sponsored an agrarian bill in the interests of Pompey's veterans and the Senate opposed this, Cicero could say (*ad Att.* i. 18, 6) that there was not even the ghost of a true statesman in Rome: 'the one who could be one, my intimate friend Pompey, wraps that precious triumphal cloak of his around him in silence. Crassus never utters a word to risk his popularity. The others you know well enough, fools who seem to hope that their fish-ponds may be saved, though the country go to rack and ruin. There is one who can be said to take some pains, but, according to my view, with more constancy and honesty than judgment and ability—Cato'. In June 60 Cicero could despairingly tell Atticus (*ad Att.* ii. 1, 7), 'cum equitatus . . . senatum deseruerit, nostri autem principes digito se caelum putent attingere, si mulli barbati in piscinis sint, qui ad manum accedant, alia autem neglegant'; further, Cato would be more in place in Plato's Republic than among the dregs of Romulus's city.

Although Cicero had bought a fine house from Crassus on the fashionable Palatine Hill in 62, and might physically be moving in aristocratic circles, he was moving away from them in spirit. Nor would he have endeared himself to the older nobility either by the way he boasted of his crowning achievement in 63, or by the fact that a *novus homo* had put to death nobles without a trial, or yet by the financial difficulties in which his purchase of his new mansion had involved him (he had borrowed freely from his friends). The distaste of Lucullus and his 'fish-pond' fellow-nobles for the parvenu from Arpinum will have increased. Cicero might enjoy *ambitiosae amicitiae*, hold splendid morning levées and go down to the Forum amid a crowd of friends, but he was lonely and found genuine satisfaction only with his wife and children and in unburdening his heart to his real friend, Atticus (*ad Att.* i. 18, 1).

Of the year 61 Cicero could say, 'ille annus duo firmamenta rei publicae per me unum constituta evertit: nam et senatus auctoritatem abiecit et ordinum concordiam disiunxit' (*ad Att.* i. 18, 3). Realizing many of the causes of this collapse, he turned more to Pompey, but his rather pathetic admiration of and affection for Pompey (to whose faults he was far from blind) caused him to miscalculate the development of events which led to the political alliance of Pompey, Caesar, and Crassus, which we call the First Triumvirate. These dynasts, who were driven to co-operate largely by the folly of the *Optimates*, realized Cicero's political status and value, and therefore made an attempt to win him over. When Caesar's agent Balbus approached him, Cicero failed to realize the full significance of their intentions (*ad Att.* ii. 3, 3), but he saw clearly enough that co-operation with them would mean the betrayal of all his political ideals. He therefore boldly rejected the offer, and the triumvirate did not become a quattuorvirate. Before very long he had to pay the price for his loyalty to the constitutional cause. During 59, the year of Caesar's consulship, he gradually realized the dominating power of the triumvirs, and became increasingly disillusioned in Pompey. Soon his personal safety was threatened, when Clodius became tribune in 58 and prepared to secure Cicero's exile on the ground that he had executed the Catilinarian conspirators without a trial. His letters of this period record his constant appeals to Pompey to check Clodius and his pathetic faith in his falling idol. While Pompey went no further than to give assurances, Caesar offered Cicero a post on his staff in Gaul in order to allow him a way of escape, but once again Cicero was too honourable to compromise his principles. Thereafter the triumvirs gave Clodius his head and Cicero was hounded into exile in March 58, finally finding security at Thessalonica in the house of his friend, the quaestor Cn. Plancius.

Pompey, who was soon humiliated and even threatened by Clodius, whose gangsters ruled the streets of Rome, began to repent of his attitude to Cicero and lent support to the efforts which Cicero's friends were making to secure his recall: these included his son-in-law C. Calpurnius Piso, P. Lentulus Spinther, one of the consuls of 57, and Milo and P. Sestius among the tribunes. He could not expect much help from his Optimate associates, whom he suspected of earlier disloyalty (cf. his remarks about Hortensius in *ad Att.* iii. 9, 2; *ad Q. Fr.* i. 3, 8). After his brother Quintus had given his word that Marcus would not oppose the triumvirs, the long battle for his return was finally won and he re-entered Rome on 4th September 57.

In thanking the Senate for his return Cicero expressed his gratitude to Pompey, and soon afterwards he supported the proposal for fifteen days' thanksgiving for Caesar's Gallic victories. He also proposed a corn-commissionership for Pompey, which offended the extreme *Optimates*. He may even have begun to hope that he might weaken the Triumvirate and win over Pompey and the moderates to support the constitution. Such a hope gained temporary strength when the extremists (such as Bibulus and Curio) began to encourage Clodius in his violent attacks on Pompey in 56; for this folly they were castigated by Cicero, who reminded the Senate of the soothsayers' warning that the discord and dissension of the *Optimates* might lead to the rule of one man (*de Harus. Resp.* 50, 40). Then in his defence of P. Sestius, who was accused of *vis*, Cicero, while treating both Pompey and Caesar with respect, issued a clarion-call to all loyal moderates to rally in support of the Senate and republican constitution. In this speech (*pro Sestio*) he reveals most clearly his attitude to the nobility, together with his ideal solution for Rome's troubles. This, he argued, was to be found in an Optimate government, represented by a broadly based Senate that would resist the pressure of both Populares and those pre-eminent individuals whose struggle for *potentia* and *dignitas* might lead to autocracy. In championing the traditional claims of the Senate to be the government of Rome, Cicero aligned himself with the nobility of which he himself was now a member. Where he differed from the older nobility was on the question of the composition of the Senate. He appealed not only to the younger men who were nobles by birth to be worthy of their ancestors but also to those who could win nobility through their *ingenium* and *virtus* by following a career in which many *homines novi* had won glory (*pro Sest.* 136). If some of the older nobility were apathetic to the needs of the Republic, then these 'fish-pond' nobles must be reinforced by fresh blood: admission to the Senate should come through *industria ac virtus* (137). But Cicero looked further still. When Vatinius abusively described the *Optimates* as a 'breed' (*natio*, § 132), Cicero, by playing on the phrase *optimus quisque*, equated the *Optimates* with *optimi quique*, all good citizens. The *concordia ordinum* between the Senate and the *Equites*, which had briefly emerged in 63 B.C., was to be strengthened by a *coniunctio bonorum omnium* and the *consensus Italiae*. Thus a union of all loyal citizens who were *integri* and *sani* was to be formed, to include a widened senatorial class, Romans living in municipalities and countryside businessmen and even freedmen. These were to be the new *Optimates*, whose leaders (*defensores optimatium; principes civitatis*) would ensure 'cum dignitate otium' for the State. By this phrase Cicero meant, as recently emphasized by C. Wirszubski, internal tranquillity for the people of Rome (in place of the gangster warfare into which political life had degenerated) and political prestige and influence for the 'Best Men'. Thus a nobility of merit could replace a nobility of birth in a community from which demagogy and autocracy would be excluded.

Cicero advanced this policy in the anticipation that the Triumvirate was beginning to break down, but in this and in his consequential attempt to widen the gap between Pompey and Caesar by attacking Caesar's agrarian legislation, Cicero both misjudged the situation and forced the triumvirs to act. The result was the conference at Luca, at which the triumvirs composed their differences and secured their futures. Cicero's hopes were shattered, but he had sufficient sense of reality to recognize the facts. After an agonizing re-appraisal he could see no alternative but submission: men like Cato, who continued to oppose the triumvirs, lacked, in Cicero's assessment, a feeling for political reality. Further, they were the men who had supported Cicero's enemy Clodius and had deserted him when exile threatened. Disillusioned, Cicero wrote to Atticus (iv, 5): 'You would hardly believe the treachery of our leaders (i.e. the *Optimates*) . . . I know full well how they have taken me in, abandoned me and cast me off . . . I've done with them. Since those who have no influence ('qui nihil possunt', the *Optimates*) refuse me their affection, I may as well try to win that of those who have some influence' ('qui possunt', the triumvirs). Cicero promptly dropped his threatened attack on Caesar's legislation and composed a recantation, the notorious palinode, which was probably a letter of apology to Caesar, or less probably to Pompey (other interpretations are possible). But in addition to any private exchanges, Cicero was forced to make a public declaration of his new policy. He opposed a suggestion that Cisalpine and Transalpine Gaul should be assigned to the consuls of 55 and thus be snatched from Caesar. In his speech 'de Provinciis Consularibus' he admitted that he had disagreed with Caesar in the past (*dissensisse*), but now reconciliation was right (25); to this he added an enthusiastic panegyric on Caesar's achievements in Gaul. In another speech delivered this same year (56) in defence of Balbus, whose claim to citizenship which Pompey had granted him in Spain was being challenged, Cicero included a panegyric of Pompey. If Crassus was omitted from this paean of praise (although he shared the defence of Balbus with Pompey and Cicero), Cicero at least gained a new friend in M. Caelius whom he successfully defended on charges of sedition and poisoning; his speech *Pro Caelio* throws a lurid light on Roman society and on the nobly born Clodia in particular.

Cicero had now lost all hope of playing an independent, or indeed any appreciable role in political life. He confided to Lentulus, who as consul in 57 had urged Cicero's recall from exile: 'for what had once been my aim after I had discharged the most honourable public offices—the dignified deliverance of my opinions in the Senate, and an independent position in dealing with public affairs—that I have lost for ever, and I not more than anybody else; for we must either utterly humiliate ourselves by agreeing with a minority, or disagree with them to no purpose' (*ad Fam.* i. 8, 3). Thus in 55, the year of the second consulship of Pompey and Crassus, Cicero's old friendly feelings towards

Pompey revived (*ad Fam.* i. 8, 2). Thanks to Caesar and Pompey he also became reconciled to Crassus (whose son was 'nostri studiosissimus': *ad Q. Fr.* ii. 9, 2) after a quarrel due to Crassus's defence of Gabinius's governorship of Syria which Cicero had denounced in his *De provinciis consularibus*. The reconciliation was announced before Crassus left for Syria, and Cicero entertained him to dinner (*ad Fam.* i. 9, 20), but Cicero revealed to Atticus that he still thought Crassus a scoundrel ('O hominem nequam': *ad Att.* iv. 13, 2). Another unwelcome request from Pompey was that Cicero should defend Caninius Gallus, who as tribune in 56 had been annoying to Cicero, but Cicero got one chance to let off steam: when Piso had returned in disgrace from his governorship of Macedonia and had attacked Cicero in the Senate, Cicero launched a scurrilous reply (*In Pisonem*), in which at the same time he managed to avoid offending Caesar or Pompey.

In a well-known letter to his friend Lentulus (*ad Fam.* i. 9), Cicero explained, and excused, his political and personal relations with the triumvirs. In a letter sent to Crassus on his way to Syria, Cicero reported how he had resisted an attempt in the Senate to curtail Crassus's powers; while frankly admitting that they had quarrelled three times, Cicero now urged Crassus to accept a *coniunctio amicitiaque* which would prove mutually beneficial, and in view of this new *foedus* Cicero would do all he could to advance Crassus's interests. Under pressure from Pompey and Caesar he had to undertake some further unwelcome tasks, such as the defence of two men whom he had abused and vilified in the past, namely Vatinius and Gabinius. A by-product of the trial of Gabinius was the prosecution of Rabirius Postumus, whom Cicero defended at Caesar's request. This speech (*pro Rabirio Post.*) contains a glowing tribute to Caesar, whose greatness is shown not merely by his conquests in Gaul but no less by his help to the humble Postumus and his *incredibilis liberalitas*: 'ego enim hanc in tantis opibus, tanta fortuna liberalitatem in suos, memoriam amicitiae reliquis virtutibus omnibus antepono' (44). Indeed Cicero's friendship and admiration for Caesar finds constant expression in his letters to his brother Quintus, who was serving on Caesar's staff in Gaul and Britain (e.g. 'amor autem eius erga nos perfertur omnium nuntiis singularis'; *ad Q. Fr.* ii. 12, 5). That these feelings were genuine is shown by their repetition in letters to Atticus, who was a disinterested party (e.g. 'nos Caesari et

carissimos et iucundissimos esse' or 'suavissima coniunctio':
ad Att. iv. 15, 10; iv. 19, 2). Towards Pompey Cicero might
retain some of his old affection, but he cannot, despite what he
may say to the contrary, have relished seeing Pompey's over-
shadowing power ('unum omnia posse': *ad Att.* iv. 18, 2) nor the
rumours of possible dictatorship. One pleasant task was to defend
Plancius, who had sheltered him during his exile in Macedonia.
In the course of his speech Cicero made some interesting observations about nobility and office: he contrasted the electoral support
that Plancius derived from the country at the aedilician elections
in 55 with the neglect of canvassing by a noble but undistinguished
rival, Iuventius Laterensis, who relied, in vain, on the mere claim
of birth. Cicero pointed out that Plancius 'nonnullis rebus in-
feriorem, quam te (sc. Laterensis), generis, dico, et nominis;
superiorem aliis, municipum, vicinorum, societatum studio'
(*pro Plancio*, 30). He must have been glad to remind the nobility
whom he blamed for the present distress of the State (see e.g.
ad Fam. i. 9, 17), that their older privileges were not unchallenge-
able. But the savour had gone out of his life: 'sed vides nullam
esse rempublicam, nullum senatum, nulla iudicia, nullam in ullo
nostrum dignitatem' (*ad Q. Fr.* iii. 4, 1). Apart from some forensic
practice Cicero was being driven from public into private life:
writing and his friends now engaged most of his time.

In 53 came news of the death of Crassus and his son at the hands
of the Parthians. Cicero did not grieve overmuch at the death of
the father, but he had real affection for the son whom he now
replaced in the college of augurs, an honour which the *novus homo*
much valued. To this year also the first surviving letter of Cicero
to C. Scribonius Curio belongs: this young noble, who has been
described as a 'Roman Alcibiades', had at first been a hope of the
Optimates ('huic signa benevolentiae permulta a bonis imper-
tiuntur': *ad Att.* ii. 18, 1), but he later went over to Caesar to whom
he remained loyal until his death in Africa. He retained Cicero's
friendship, and their correspondence is interesting because it
shows the influence that the great orator exercised over men of
the younger generation. Meantime the death of Crassus, following
upon that of Julia, led to an increasing estrangement between the
two surviving triumvirs, which was emphasized by Pompey's
sole consulship in 52, a year in which Cicero failed to secure the
acquittal of Milo on the charge of murdering Clodius: Pompey's

influence, and his troops around the law-courts, were too much for Cicero. He did, however, successfully prosecute a supporter of Clodius, Munatius Bursa, whom Pompey wished to save. Then followed Cicero's governorship of Cilicia, to which he went with great reluctance. His predecessor there, Appius Claudius who was the brother of Clodius, had seriously misgoverned the province. Cicero, although still annoyed with Appius, had reached a formal reconciliation with him, and in order to please Pompey and Brutus he turned a blind eye to many of Appius's misdeeds. For his minor campaign against a threatened Parthian attack on Cilicia, Cicero was hailed by his troops as Imperator. This honour and the prospect of a Triumph later at Rome gave him immense pleasure: if military achievement combined with nobility of birth and skill in oratory marked the path to office at Rome, Cicero now had a further claim to be numbered among the *nobiles* whose ranks he had joined a dozen years earlier. Indeed his preoccupation with his hopes for a triumph often take a more prominent part in his letters of this period than his anxieties for the political scene at home.

On his journey back to Rome Cicero heard of the death of Hortensius, who but recently had sponsored his admission to the augurate. Their relations went back a long way: Cicero had first crossed swords professionally with him at the trial of P. Quinctius in 81, and then in 70 as a result of the trial of Verres he had won from him the claim to be Rome's leading orator and advocate. After his consulship in 69 Hortensius had supported the Senate in its vain attempt to deny Pompey extraordinary commands and thus he was politically as well as professionally opposed to Cicero. But the Catilinarian conspiracy threw Cicero more firmly into the senatorial camp and with the formation of the first triumvirate Hortensius retired from political life. Thus the two men could come closer together, and when Clodius's gangsters nearly murdered Hortensius because of his support for Milo, Cicero no doubt felt that the link had been further strengthened. They also often acted professionally together in these years, for instance in defending Murena, P. Sulla, Flaccus, and Sestius. But it is perhaps characteristic of Cicero's attitude to the older nobility that however cordial relations might appear he seldom felt completely at home: thus on more than one occasion he suspected (and as far as we can tell, without any justification) that Hortensius was not fully to be trusted (see, e.g., *ad Q. Fr.* i. 3, 4; *ad Att.* iii. 9; iv. 6; v. 17)· He seems, however, to have been genuinely moved by Hortensius's death (*Brutus*, 1-6).

When Cicero reached Brundisium on 24th November 50, Italy was on the brink of civil war. In Campania he talked for two hours on 10th December with Pompey, who regarded war with Caesar as 'non dubium' (*ad Att.* vii. 4, 2); a longer talk at Formiae on the 25th convinced him that Pompey did not even want peace. Although he himself longed for peace, Cicero decided that personal and political loyalties would compel him to support Pompey, now the Optimate leader, if war came. If Caesar fought and won, he would in Cicero's view (*ad Att.* vii. 7, 7) show no more clemency than Cinna in killing the nobles and no more moderation than Sulla in robbing the rich. When shortly afterwards war did come, Cicero retained this view of Caesar as a would-be tyrant as late as May 49 (cf. 'regnum' in *ad Att.* x. 8, 2), and this despite his earlier tributes to Caesar's *incredibilis liberalitas*. But although he accepted a commissionership from Pompey, Cicero showed no energy or enthusiasm in his cause: the lack of determination and foresight shown by Pompey and the nobles appalled him, and before long he could believe that the aims of both Pompey and Caesar differed very little: 'dominatio quaesita ab utroque est', and Pompey had even long been seeking 'genus illud Sullani regni' (*ad Att.* viii. 11, 2). Such thoughts tempted Cicero to think of neutrality, but older loyalties prevailed and he determined to join Pompey in Greece where he had withdrawn after Caesar had driven him from Italy. Two days after Pompey had sailed from Brundisium, Cicero wrote to Caesar (*ad Att.* ix. 11a) in a desperate attempt to mediate, or at worst to secure his own personal neutrality: 'it is many years since I chose you two men for my special respect, and to be my closest friends, as you are'. But neither this letter nor a meeting a few days later (*ad Att.* ix. 18) could move Caesar, nor could Cicero be persuaded to go to Rome. After further delays and hesitations Cicero finally sailed to Greece in June. When he reached Pompey's camp he was shocked by the lack of unity and the bloodthirsty threats of the leaders. Detained by ill-health at Dyrrhacium, he was not present at Pompey's final defeat at Pharsalus. It was a disillusioned Cicero that returned in October 48 to Brundisium, where he remained for the next eleven months, and a mood of disillusionment rather than of bitterness dictated his well-known comment to Atticus on learning of Pompey's murder: 'non possum eius casum non dolere: hominem enim integrum et castum et gravem cognovi' (*ad Att.* xi. 6, 5).

Not without reason Cicero was anxious about how Caesar would treat him when he returned in victory from Egypt and the East, but he was somewhat reassured by a letter from Caesar in August 47 ('litterae satis liberales': *ad Fam.* xiv. 23) and when he hastened to meet Caesar at Tarentum at the end of September he was received with kindness and allowed to live where he wished. He spent much time writing, mainly on oratory and philosophy, but including a panegyric on Cato at which Caesar took no offence other than to compose a counterblast. For some time Cicero had been forced to realize Caesar's great generosity to many defeated Pompeians and he himself succeeded in securing pardon for some of these exiles. When an attempt was made in the Senate to obtain pardon for M. Claudius Marcellus (consul in 51 and one of Caesar's most bitter enemies) and Caesar agreed, Cicero broke his resolve not to speak in the Senate again and delivered a speech (the *Pro Marcello*) in which he thanked Caesar and fervently urged him to restore constitutional government and internal peace; he told Sulpicius Rufus that he had been stirred to change his mind by 'Caesaris magnitudo animi et senatus officium': (*ad Fam.* iv. 4, 4). He also pleaded successfully before Caesar for Q. Ligarius in a speech (*Pro Ligario*) so eloquent that, according to Plutarch, Caesar was visibly moved. In 45 he defended Deiotarus of Galatia, who was charged with an attempt to murder Caesar after the battle of Zela. Although he shows in his letters no real appreciation of Caesar's constructive work, Cicero nevertheless was encouraged by his great clemency to begin to hope for some restoration of the Republic: he urged Varro that if Caesar wished to use them not only as architects but even as masons to build up the Republic, they should eagerly respond (*ad Fam.* ix, 2, 5; cf. iv. 4, 3). But Caesar had wider aims than those of the older Roman aristocracy, and as his behaviour became more autocratic, Cicero's hopes began to fade. However, relations remained outwardly cordial and when Caesar dined with him at Puteoli (December 45) the evening passed off pleasantly, since conversation turned on literary rather than political topics (*ad Att.* xiii. 52). But Cicero's bitterness increased and he was particularly shocked by Caesar's cavalier treatment of the consulship (*ad Fam.* vii. 30). Thus although he had no part in the conspiracy to murder Caesar, he hated what he believed Caesar stood for and after the assassination he was ready to approve the deed: he wrote later to Cassius, 'I should like you to have invited me to your banquet on the Ides of March' (*ad Fam.* xii. 4, 1). Although he played an important part in persuading the conspirators and the Caesarians to reach a compromise two days after the murder and thus avoid the risk of immediate civil war, he took little active part in politics during the next six months.

During this time he felt little confidence in the Caesarians, and less in the conspirators. Indeed he planned to spend the second part of 44 in Greece, but fearing that this would appear as desertion he turned back from Sicily. The scene was now set for the greatest period of his life. Once again he clearly saw where his duty lay and realized that he was free to speak and act once more in defence of the Republic, which he saw threatened by the despotic ambitions of Antony. In a complicated situation, which cannot be described here, he gradually forced the Senate to realize the danger to the constitution and ultimately to declare Antony a public enemy after Cicero had unmasked his autocratic aims in a series of speeches, the Philippics. But meantime Caesar's heir, Octavian, had played his cards so skilfully that he had not only outwitted Cicero and the Senate but was in a position to force Antony to come to terms with him. The result was the Second Triumvirate of Octavian, Antony, and Lepidus, and the collapse of senatorial government at Rome. The new masters cleared the decks before their final struggle with Brutus and Cassius in the East by a ruthless proscription of their political enemies in Italy. Their most famous victim was Cicero, whose refusal to admit that tyranny or anarchy were the only choices remaining to Rome led to his last stand for the Republic and to his death, which he preferred to continued life under a tyranny.

Cicero's failure may be explained in part by the fact that death had removed so many of the older *Optimates*. Appius Claudius had died before Pharsalus, Domitius Ahenobarbus had fallen in the battle, Q. Metellus Scipio and Cato, who had personified the Republican cause, committed suicide after Thapsus. In 44 Cicero might blame the *principes*: 'habemus turpissimos consulares'; 'consulares partim timidos, partim male sentientes' (*ad Fam.* xii. 4, 1; x. 28, 3). But the plain fact is that by the end of the year only seventeen consulars survived. In September 44 only three of them had dared to speak against Antony in the Senate (*ad Fam.* xii. 2, 1): these were Cicero himself, L. Calpurnius Piso, Cicero's old enemy who had become father-in-law of Caesar and censor in 50, and P. Servilius Isauricus, consul in 48. Of them Sir Ronald Syme wrote, 'in character, career, and policy the three consulars were discordant and irreconcilable'. It was Cicero's tragedy that now he possessed sufficient *auctoritas* to build up political backing among those nobles who were still ready to try to preserve the Republic, the men were lacking: the civil wars had destroyed so many of the senior statesmen who normally helped to shape and enforce policy. Earlier Cicero had to fight his way into the Optimate stronghold and then had been pulled in different directions by his personal regard for both Pompey and Caesar. As a *novus homo* he did not enjoy the full support of a faction, and he had no army at his call to help him enforce his will. Thus he lacked a broad enough basis on which to build a new society, linked in a *concordia ordinum*. Though many of the more moderate nobles recognized his worth, others never really accepted the new man and must have smiled disdainfully when they had to listen to him constantly explaining how he had saved the Republic from destruction by Catiline and how all Italy had surged forward to welcome him back from exile. If some of these men had lived long enough to witness the drive and courage of the last six months of his life, they might have held him in higher regard. But by then their aristocratic Republic was beyond recovery: they, no less than the military dynasts, had helped to kill it, and the 'new man' could not save it.

II

Honesty in Roman Politics

T. A. DOREY

As a politician Cicero's reputation has suffered most from the fact
that he was so often on the losing side. There is something in
human nature that makes it difficult for the defeated to find any
whole-hearted champions, except in the case of those who can
claim the ostentatious glory of a martyr's death. But the martyr's
path calls for certain qualities of temperament that Cicero did
not possess, and his reputation faces this additional hazard, that
although he was three times crushed and eventually destroyed by
the forces of Caesarism, yet he had not always been wholly consistent and unflinching in his opposition to Caesar.

The unsuccessful nature of his political career has brought upon
Cicero the violent attacks of such admirers of Caesar as Mommsen
and Carcopino, whose authority and eminence have given to
their verdict greater weight than is justified by the force of their
arguments. This unfavourable judgement has been reinforced by
a tendency to assess Cicero's political behaviour by what could be
expected from some ideal statesman pursuing his course in ideal
conditions, and not in the light of Cicero's own peaceable temperament and the difficult and dangerous circumstances in which
he had to act, at a time when most politicians were impelled by
motives that were utterly selfish and when the struggle for power
was being fought out with weapons increasingly naked and ruthless.

Finally, the fact that Cicero's correspondence, 'a camera with
the shutter open', exposes his whole personality so devastatingly
to our gaze, and that the personality brought before our eyes is
so unashamedly ego-centric, has tended to estrange the sympathy
of modern generations who look upon the ego-centric in an

27

unkind and unforgiving spirit, has often made us refuse to give Cicero the benefit of the doubt where the propriety of his motives are concerned, and has induced us to judge him in a harsher fashion than we should want others to judge us.

In his well-known book *Les Secrets de la correspondance de Cicéron*,[1] Jérome Carcopino puts forward the provocative theory that in the surviving Letters we have a carefully selected and edited corpus that was published by Atticus at Octavian's direction for the deliberate purpose of providing propaganda for the new régime by the systematic vilification of Cicero's character. Carcopino argues that an objective study of the Letters, as published, shows Cicero to have been a man of cowardly and venal character, devoid of any sense of loyalty or principle, who continually shifted his policies and allegiances to suit his own material advantages; the object of this defamatory presentation, Carcopino maintains, was to dispel any popular odium that Octavian may have incurred for having had Cicero put to death.

Carcopino's picture of Cicero is one that can be obtained from the Letters, but only at the cost of suppressing all the evidence that is favourable to Cicero, exaggerating whatever is prejudicial, and distorting anything that is neutral. A very good illustration of Carcopino's method of working can be obtained from his handling of the following incident. In March 45 B.C. Cicero was at Astura, and was trying to buy some park-land on the outskirts of Rome in which he could erect a shrine in memory of his daughter Tullia. A suitable property had been found, and Cicero wrote to Atticus[2] about the most convenient means of raising the purchase-price. He says that he can get 600 *sestertia* (about £5,000) from Hermogenes, and finds that he has 600 *sestertia* 'at home'—et domi video esse HS.DC.—; the balance he proposes to raise by getting credit from the vendor at interest until a debt owed to him matures, rather than sell off any of his own landed property. Now it is clear from the context that the word *domi* must mean simply 'uninvested', and will refer to Cicero's 'liquid assets'. Carcopino, however, takes the word in its most literal sense of 'in that particular house at Astura'; he says[3] that one day in 45 B.C., when, alone at Astura, Cicero was going through his drawers—*vider ses tiroirs*—and listing the contents, he reported to Atticus that he found that he had at home 600 *sestertia*. Carcopino then implies that there would be an equal amount of ready cash lying around

28

in each of Cicero's other villas. This he takes as supporting evidence for his proposition that Cicero was not merely a man of moderate wealth but was fabulously rich—and looked on no method as too base to increase his fortune.

Carcopino's arguments have already been effectively exploded by J. P. V. D. Balsdon in his reviews of the book for *Classical Review* and *Journal of Roman Studies*. It is, however, still uncertain how far Carcopino's book can be regarded as the proposition of a sober theory, and not as a brilliant, ingenious, but over-subtle *tour de force*. It is also uncertain how far the odious picture of Cicero alleged to be portrayed by the Letters coincides with Carcopino's own impression of Cicero's character. Carcopino does, however, in his concluding remarks declare that it is impossible to honour Cicero for a bravery, modesty, and foresight that he never possessed. It is true that Cicero was naturally timid; but a timid man is not necessarily a coward, and on several occasions, at the time of the Catilinarian conspiracy, in refusing to be bought off by the Triumvirs in 59 B.C., in abandoning the safety of neutrality at the start of the Civil War, and in taking up the cudgels against Antony, he chose, when faced with two possible alternatives, the course of action that was the more dangerous, and he did so deliberately. Finally, he faced death without flinching, as everyone except his detractor Asinius Pollio admits.[4] His political foresight was not noticeably more deficient than that of any of his contemporaries. Even Caesar himself, whom Carcopino so much admires, showed little evidence that he would have found any adequate solution to Rome's political malaise. On the other hand, Cicero's *concordia ordinum*, which Carcopino derides as an unholy alliance between the governing aristocracy and the business interests for the more effective plundering of the provinces, would have eased the fundamental cause of political strife at Rome during that age—the fact that there were two independent organs of government which either had to work together in some sort of harmony or else tear the State to pieces. It was also part of Cicero's policy to bring about a reconciliation between the Senate and Pompey, for he realized that the *Optimates* must accept the existence of the great military commanders, with what amounted, in fact, to private armies of their own, and must agree to work with them instead of against them. As regards Cicero's lack of modesty, there is no doubt that an incurable vanity was one of his worst faults; but if we admit this, we are admitting that his faults could not have been very gross.

In his *Life of Cicero* Plutarch says that, although Cicero's family estates were comparatively small, yet he received neither present nor fee in return for his services at the Bar. Carcopino seizes upon this statement, and goes to great lengths to prove not merely that Plutarch was wrong but that Cicero was venal and rapacious. The two points on which Carcopino bases his case are the large loan that Cicero received from P. Cornelius Sulla, the nephew of the Dictator, which was used towards the purchase of Cicero's house on the Palatine[5] and of which there is never any mention of repayment, and the celebrated *pactio provinciae* that Cicero made with his fellow-consul, C. Antonius Hybrida, in order to win him away from his support of Catiline. Carcopino argues that Cicero not only blatantly circumvented the *Lex Cincia* by receiving a non-repayable loan for defending Sulla against the charge of participation in the Catilinarian Conspiracy, but also took what was in effect a large bribe to shield a man who was obviously guilty. Whether or not Sulla was guilty is a question on which posterity will never be able to express any confident opinion, let alone a dogmatic one. But even if, for the sake of argument, Sulla was guilty of participation in the plot, nevertheless Cicero, as an ex-consul, in defending him did not act any more improperly than he did when, as consul, he defended Murena, who was obviously guilty, on a charge of contravening the very law against bribery that he himself had initiated earlier in his year of office; and although Cicero's action in defending Murena was criticized in court by Cato, one of the counsel for the prosecution, Cato's strictures found no echo either among Cicero's own contemporaries or since.

It is also a mistake to suppose that a Roman barrister acted purely gratuitously. In dealings outside their families and circle of immediate friends, few Romans ever acted gratuitously. Every action in public life was capable of having its assessed value and its price. A good service done was normally either a *beneficium*, which imposed an obligation on the recipient, or an *officium*, which discharged it. In the case of a barrister, unless he himself was discharging some pre-existing obligation (as Cicero was in defending Sestius and Milo), his defence of a client would put that client under a definite obligation that he was bound at some time or other to discharge, either by giving political support (especially at elections), by a legacy, or by some other means.[6] Cicero himself, for example, won the political support of Caelius by defending him on the charge of attempted poisoning; he hoped to get political support from Catiline at the consular elections of 64 B.C. at the time when he contemplated defending Catiline.[7] In defending the poet Archias he was putting the Optimate leader, Lucullus, as well as Archias himself, under an obligation; from Archias, he hoped for a laudatory poem, from Lucullus, political support. In defending Gabinius, he was discharging an urgent obligation to Pompey. In defending Plancius, he was repaying the latter's great kindness to him in his exile. In other cases he was defending political associates, with whom he was linked by ties of *amicitia*. But when Sulla asked Cicero to defend him, he could point to no existing obligation or tie of friendship, and as a man excluded for ever from public life as a result of his earlier condemnation for bribery, he could promise no political support. The only way he could repay Cicero for his services was by the use of his great wealth, and it is difficult to see how Cicero acted with any great impropriety in taking a loan from Sulla while Sulla was alive rather than waiting for a legacy after Sulla's death.[8]

As regards the *Lex Cincia*, the fact that it was passed as early as 204 B.C. indicates that barristers were taking fees even in the third century, and it is probable that this law, like the successive sumptuary laws, was regularly evaded. It is significant that the clamour for its re-imposition under Claudius and Nero was directed mainly against the blackmailing activities of the notorious prosecutor, P. Suillius, and a small group of similar people.[9]

The case of C. Antonius is more complex. It seems from the references in the Letters to the mysterious 'Teucris' (probably a pseudonym for Antonius himself) that the *pactio provinciae* had a number of ramifications: that Antonius withdrew his support from Catiline in return for a free choice of a province, and that, in addition, he bound himself to pay Cicero a sum of money, in return for which Cicero undertook to support his interests in the Senate and defend him if he was charged with misgovernment after his return from Macedonia.[10] This transaction Carcopino stigmatizes as a shameful bargain by which Cicero unleashed Antonius upon the unfortunate province and took for himself a

share in the plunder without taking any of the risks: Cicero is
even compared to a guilty receiver of stolen goods. But Roman
political morality consisted largely in the due performance of
obligations. It was the man of *ingratus animus*,[11] the man who
failed to discharge a debt or repay a service, who was held in
lowest repute. Towards the provincials, as such, the Romans felt
they had no obligations, except where some special fiduciary
relationship had been established, such as the hereditary *patro-
cinium* of the Fabii over the Allobroges of Southern Gaul. In any
case, it is clear that even an upright and honest governor of a
province could make a very large profit out of the allowances to
which he was legally entitled. Even Cicero, whom no one could
seriously accuse of extortion and oppression, had a balance of more
than two million sesterces to his credit after his term as governor
of Cilicia had expired, while his brother Quintus, also by repute
an honest governor, seems to have had a sizeable balance to his
credit after his term as propraetor in Asia.[12] So Cicero had good
reason for expostulation when Antonius tried to implicate him in
his illegal requisitions.[13]

On the other hand it may be argued that Cicero should have in
no circumstances accepted money from Antonius. But the payment was just one part of a complex series of agreement that all
arose out of Cicero's successful detaching of Antonius from the
side of Catiline. If Cicero carried out his side of the bargain in
full, Antonius would be considerably in his debt, and Cicero no
doubt felt that he could not rely on Antonius' future conduct
sufficiently to dispense with a cash settlement.

It is probable that money played a far bigger part in Roman
public life during the first century B.C. than is usually realized.
Many an *amicitia* was cemented by hard cash. According to
Sallust, Crassus owed his widespread influence to the gifts and
loans of money that he had made to many members of the Senate,
and even the aristocratic P. Clodius did not disdain to accept his
pay.[14] Caesar himself bought support. Apart from the obvious
cases of Curio and Aemilius Paullus, the young men given posts
on his staff in Gaul would be in his debt. Trebatius, for example,
had been a protégé of Cicero, but, having been 'enriched' by
Caesar, transferred his allegiance to him. Cicero himself received
loans from Caesar, and was at great pains to have them paid off
at the start of the Civil War in order to preserve his freedom of

action. Pompey, too, used the wealth of the East to gain himself political adherents.[15] These are the best documented examples, and they indicate that below the surface in Roman public life there were many political deals in which money played its part. But, with the Romans as with modern societies, such transactions were not talked about openly.

A more serious critic is Mommsen, who describes Cicero as a 'political trimmer', a man who 'only showed his true colours when he could do so with safety', and who was as cowardly as he was treacherous.[16] Mommsen's picture has much in common with that of Dio Cassius, who on three occasions describes Cicero as a 'turncoat' (αὐτόμολος), once in connection with his support of the *Lex Manilia*, once when, as a result of pressure from Pompey, he undertook the defence of his arch-enemy Gabinius, and once in the highly rhetorical and largely fictitious speech attributed to Fufius Calenus at the beginning of 43 B.C.[17]

Dio makes no attempt to conceal his hostility towards Cicero, and it is likely that his prejudice was partly derived from propaganda put out against Cicero after the death of Caesar by Mark Antony and his supporters; in the same way the rather lurid picture that we have of Antony owes a great deal to the storm of propaganda worked up first by Cicero and then by Octavian. But there is another significant element in Dio's account of the last twenty years of the Republic. Of all the Roman politicians who were active in that period, the only one to whom he attributes honesty and consistency and courage was Cato.[18] It is probable, therefore, that among his various sources Dio was using some of the eulogies of Cato circulated by the Stoic circle in the first century A.D., which would naturally contrast the firmness and resolution of their hero with the fickleness and inconsistency of Cicero. Propaganda apart, however, it seems from the very laboured defence of his conduct that Cicero offered in 54 B.C. in his letter to Lentulus Spinther[19] that he was at that date being openly attacked by the Optimates for changing sides.

'Idem velle atque idem nolle, ea demum firma amicitia est'[20]—'to have the same desires and the same dislikes is the strongest basis of friendship.' Cicero and the *Optimates* had a strong basis of friendship as far as the negative aspect of Sallust's quotation is concerned, for they were united in their opposition to military despotism, to unconstitutional authority, and to concentration of power in the hands of one man. But though they desired the same thing—*dignitas*—it was his own individual *dignitas* that each man desired. The aims of the leading Roman politicians of the Ciceronian age were inherently selfish, and were pursued without regard to the consequences for the rest of the community. Both Caesar and Pompey set their *dignitas* above life itself, while Cicero's Letters show that it was the main pre-occupation of Cicero himself and most of the other *Optimates*.[21] This selfishness in the political life of the period seems to be reflected in its literature, too. During the first century B.C. literature contained an increasing personal element, concentrating on the expression of the personality of the writer, and becoming more and more devoid of social and national content.[22] It was this trend that the great writers of the Augustan Age, Horace, Livy, and Virgil, were trying to counteract, acting in harmony with the official doctrine that it was the aggrandizement of the State (represented in practice by the *Princeps*) that was of supreme importance, and not the aggrandizement of the individual *nobiles*. In the last sixty years of the Republic, this emphasis on selfish agrandizement can be seen in an increasing unscrupulousness and ruthlessness in the pursuit of ambition and the preservation of *dignitas* at all costs. Apart from the vast increase in the use of bribery at elections (on one occasion this caused such an acute shortage of ready cash that the rate of interest was doubled), there was a growing tendency to resort to armed force. The examples of Sulla and Caesar are well known; Pompey and Crassus engaged in dangerous 'brinkmanship' in 71 B.C.; while even Cicero, in spite of his claim that he voluntarily withdrew into exile in order to prevent bloodshed, would probably have resisted Clodius at the risk of civil war if he thought he had any chance of success. Yet men of earlier generations, Marius and Scipio Africanus, preferred to withdraw into political obscurity rather than appeal to their victorious armies.

Dio Cassius, followed by Mommsen, says that in supporting the *Lex Manilia* in 66 B.C. Cicero deserted the nobles, whose cause he had previously supported, and went over to the side of the commons. But this whole passage in Dio, together with the following chapter about the prosecution of Manilius and Cicero's attitude towards this trial, is very tendentious and fairly reeks of propaganda. In actual fact, up to the time of the *Lex*

Manilia Cicero had taken no very prominent part in politics, and his political allegiances of this early period are not easy to determine. In the Verrines he had attacked leading members of the Optimate faction, but in the *Pro Cluentio*, in 67 B.C., he had done his best to vindicate the senatorial juries. It is doubtful how far we can base an estimate of Cicero's political position on what he says in a forensic speech; it is probable that up to the *Lex Manilia* he had not committed himself very deeply to either the *Populares* or the *Optimates*, though from what we know of his career as a whole it seems that he would have regarded as repugnant the technique used by the *Populares* to force through the *Lex Gabinia* in 67 B.C. In any case, it is wrong to regard the *Optimates* and the *Populares* as two fixed and clearly defined groups. There was a continual shifting of personnel, and one cannot conclude from the use of these two labels that there existed in Rome at that time anything like the modern political parties. In fact, these two names properly referred to two different methods of exercising political power—either through the Senate or through the Plebeian Assembly. The basic loyalty that existed in Roman political life was not loyalty to a party or a large group but to specific individuals or families.

It has been suggested that Cicero's motive in speaking on behalf of the *Lex Manilia* was to get Pompey's support for his candidature for the consulship. This motive no doubt did play some part, but there were many other equally important considerations. Cicero came from an equestrian family, and it was the *equites*, and in particular the financial and business interests, with whom he had very close connections, that acted as the main driving force behind the *Lex Gabinia* and the *Lex Manilia*. Secondly, in his first important case, the defence of Roscius Amerinus, Cicero had been engaged by the family of Metellus Balearicus, the family to which Pompey was closely connected by his marriage to Mucia. It is probable that this branch of the Metelli had assisted Cicero in the early stages of his political career, and may also have induced him to deliver his first political speech on behalf of the *Lex Manilia*.

Whatever the motives that prompted Cicero to support the *Lex Manilia*, from that time onward his chief political allegiance was to Pompey. It must be admitted that at times the allegiance seems to have been to an ideal Pompey that existed only in Cicero's own mind; it must also be admitted that at times, when the hostility of the *Optimates* drove Pompey to join forces with Caesar, the allegiance was overlaid by severe exasperation; but even at such times any move by Pompey to return to the side of constitutionalism would have gained Cicero's immediate and unqualified forgiveness for his past deviations. From the years of Pompey's absence in the East, when Cicero protected his interests against the schemes of Crassus and Caesar, to his final desperate decision to join Pompey in Greece at the start of the Civil War rather than commit any possible breach of his obligations towards him, Cicero's allegiance to Pompey never died and it was the most consistent attachment throughout the whole of his career. It may be that it was not merely a political attachment to the one man who, in Cicero's view, could give peace and security to the State, but also a psychological attachment to one whom Cicero regarded as, in a way, a father-figure. But Pompey was not a man with whom any sort of political relationship could be easily maintained for long. With his lonely pride, his dreams of isolated grandeur, he was reluctant to see any other man even as a close second, and refused to consider Cicero's early plea for a 'special relationship'.[23] However, it is certain that Cicero's main political aim in the years succeeding his consulship was to bring about an alliance between Pompey and the Senate.

Cicero's allegiance to the *Optimates* started at the time when, impelled either by the influence of Atticus or the threats of Catiline they decided that he would make a more acceptable consul than the revolutionary aristocrat. In the suppression of the Catilinarian conspiracy Cicero identified himself whole-heartedly with the *Optimates*; by putting Lentulus and the other leading conspirators to death without trial he showed that he accepted the bitterly disputed Optimate claim that the Senate, in an emergency, had the right to inflict summary execution on Roman citizens. At the same time, he was carried away by the extravagant tributes of men like Q. Lutatius Catulus[24] into believing that the *Optimates* now accepted him as their leader. This belief was completely unfounded, but it coloured his thinking during the next few years, and when, in his letters to Atticus, he talks about their changing attitude towards him, he uses language suitable to the description not merely of a political estrangement but to the desertion of a leader by his followers. From 61 B.C. onwards, Cicero's letters contained increasing complaints about how the *Optimates* have let him down, and by 59 B.C. he talks openly of their rejection of him.[25] Their behaviour in the following year, in encouraging him to offer an uncompromising resistance to the Triumvirs and then withdrawing their support after he had gone too far to draw back, was to him a complete betrayal, and their coldness towards his efforts to rehabilitate himself after his exile and their ill-concealed pleasure at the failure of his attempt to draw Pompey away from Caesar[26] consolidated this feeling of being rejected. Finally, at the start of the Civil War the savage, avaricious, and ruthless attitude of the Optimate leaders[27] filled him with such horror and disgust that for a time he was loth to follow his natural inclination to join Pompey and had no hesitation in withdrawing from the struggle after Pompey's death. From this it can be seen that during most of the decade preceding the Civil War, although Cicero felt himself from time to time to be under an obligation to individual members of the Optimate faction such as Lentulus Spinther, Sestius, and Milo, obligations which he was scrupulous about repaying, he never felt that he owed anything at all to the Optimate faction as a whole.

But it is Cicero's loyalty to his political principles that is most frequently questioned. The charge brought by people like Momsen is that, while Cicero professed to be devoted to the cause of constitutional government and the supremacy of the Senate, in actual fact he was ready and willing to sell his services to the Triumvirs and had in reality no consistent political principles except the furtherance of his own self-advantage. In this respect, Mommsen makes a point of strongly contrasting Cicero with Cato. It must be admitted that Cato was more resolute than Cicero in adhering staunchly to his political affiliations. Yet even Cato committed something of a *volte-face* when he accepted Pompey's leadership just before the Civil War although he had been personally responsible for the rejection of Pompey ten years before.[28] As Cicero himself points out, both the rejection and the acceptance were disastrous to Rome.[29] Cicero's political career is marked by certain changes of alignment, but, as has been shown, for most of his political life, Cicero had no firm attachments on which he could rely. As he himself says: 'Ego vero, quem fugiam, habeo, quem sequar, non habeo'[30]—'I have some one to run away from, but no one to follow'. The fluctuating nature of his political alignments was an inevitable result of the fluid nature of his whole political position.

However, in the face of Mommsen's charges of political dishonesty, there are certain points that should be considered: first of all, Cicero's attitude towards the Triumvirs in 60 and 59 B.C. In a letter to Atticus written in December 60,[31] he says that overtures have been made to him by Balbus to ally himself with Caesar, Pompey, and Crassus. Cicero points out to Atticus that this course would have strong material advantages, but concludes by rejecting the idea because it would be at variance with his established political principles. Similarly in April 59,[32] he tells Atticus of a report that he is to be offered an honourable mission to Alexandria. He says that this suggestion is very attractive for a number of reasons, but that he is unwilling to accept it in the circumstances because it would give the discreditable impression that he had changed his political standpoint for a bribe and had condescended to accept favours from the Triumvirs. This was at a time when the threat from Publius Clodius had clearly begun to materialize. Finally, it should be noted that, even at the end, Cicero refused all offers made by Caesar to get him away from Rome on honourable terms. Now Mommsen, when describing how the Triumvirs secured the departure from Rome of Cicero and Cato, says that Caesar feared Cato, and so could not allow him to remain in Rome, but he had no fear of Cicero, and brought exile upon him only as a well-deserved punishment for his misdeeds. This is totally untrue. Although Caesar had reason to fear that Cato might rally the *Optimates* against him as soon as he had left for Gaul, he had just as much cause to fear Cicero's influence, not merely with some sections of the *Optimates* but more particularly with the equestrian order and the country people of Italy, to whose support, both in 58 and in 49 B.C., Caesar attached great importance. Finally, those who contrast the waverng timorous Cicero with the resolute, stout-hearted Cato should remember that when Cato was offered an honourable mission to Cyprus to get him out of Rome, the kind of offer that Cicero had consistently refused, he tamely swallowed the bait.

There was another occasion when Cicero's political honesty was put to a severe test. At the beginning of the Civil War, Caesar made strenuous efforts, by letters, intermediaries, and a personal interview, to enlist Cicero's support. The two main things that

Caesar wanted him to do were to uphold the legality of the proposal that M. Lepidus, the *Praetor Urbanus*, should conduct the
consular elections at which Caesar was to be elected consul for
48 B.C., and to come to Rome to a meeting of the Senate and take
a lead in proposing steps for a reconciliation with Pompey. This
proposal for a reconciliation was very important to Caesar,
partly because he preferred, if possible, to achieve his ends
without having to fight for them and partly because of its value
as propaganda. Caesar tried to project the image of himself as a
man whose continued attempts to reach a negotiated settlement
were constantly being baulked by the uncompromising rigidity of
his opponents, and he wanted to guide the progress of the negotiations in such a way that, if they failed, the responsibility for
their failure would rest indisputably on Pompey and his advisers.
If Caesar could associate Cicero with these attempts at negotiation
he would be better able to give the impression that his offers
were genuine and that he was sincere. Apart from this, Caesar
realized that if he could not win some modicum of support from
Cicero, he could expect little co-operation from those moderate
Optimates who had not as yet joined Pompey; this in fact proved
to be the case. In these circumstances Cicero, had he chosen to
acquiesce, could have named his own price; he could have looked
forward to a triumph, a second consulship, and possibly a
censorship. However, in spite of very strong pressure from Caesar
of whose autocratic power he stood greatly in awe, and in spite
of his despair of Pompey's chances of victory, Cicero did not
waver in his refusal.

After Caesar's death and Antony's seizure of power, Cicero
withdrew for a short time into private life, but after a half-hearted
attempt to leave Italy he was drawn back into the struggle. In
the autumn of 44 B.C. he found himself faced with two possible
alternatives. Either he could abandon public life completely and
devote himself to his friends and his books—a very reasonable
course for a man of over sixty—or else he could deliberately
embark upon a struggle which would be hazardous though not,
in view of the disaffection among Antony's troops, completely
hopeless; in this struggle, however, no mercy could be expected
for the losers. Cicero's motives in choosing the latter course must
have been mixed and various. He had a personal antipathy towards
Antony, whose character was diametrically opposed to his own

and who stood for all the things that he most disliked. Since Antony had been the step-son of Catiline's right-hand man, there must have been a latent hostility between them for many years. In recent times, on two occasions Antony had, willingly or unwillingly, caused Cicero great embarrassment. First, in 49 B.C. Antony had prevented him from leaving Italy, had turned a deaf ear to all appeals, and had even gone so far as to deliberately avoid a personal interview that Cicero was seeking. Then, after Pharsalus, when Cicero returned to Italy, he had to accept Antony's patronage in order to remain in Italy at all and even so was confined for a year to the town of Brundisium. It was no doubt on Antony personally that Cicero focused all the resentment that he felt at these successive frustrations and humiliations. But his most compelling motive was the burning desire to seize at last the opportunity to replace the military autocracy of recent years by the constitutional rule of the Senate. Whatever his motives, it is to Cicero's credit that of these two alternatives he chose the more dangerous and persevered in it to the end.

As regards Cicero's conduct after the Conference of Luca, the Mommsenian view is that, having failed ignominiously in his efforts to split the Triumvirate, he had no hesitation in selling his services to the victors. Another, and more moderate criticism is that after Luca he should have accepted the failure of his political schemes and withdrawn into honourable retirement, instead of insisting on retaining some part in public affairs at the cost of his honour. But it is uncertain how far Cicero was left any free choice in the matter. It is probable that after his unsuccessful attempt to split the Triumvirate in 56 B.C., the Triumvirs were no longer content to rely on the personal assurances of Cicero and his brother but insisted on his committing himself so deeply and so thoroughly to supporting them that he would find it very difficult ever again to stir up opposition to them. Had he refused their demands, not only would his brother Quintus have been ruined but they would both have been exposed to the uncontrolled violence of Clodius. Cicero realised that whatever security he enjoyed during these years was as a result of the protection of the Triumvirs.[33] It has been suggested that[34] any attempt on Cicero's part to show real independence, as, for example, his attacks on Piso and Gabinius, resulted in his being promptly called to heel by being compelled to perform some particularly odious task, such as defending Gabinius and Vatinius. On the other hand, there is the fact that after the Civil War, when autocracy was even more firmly established, Cicero still considered himself at liberty to attack Caesar's henchmen with impunity.[35] But there is another point that indicates that Cicero was not at liberty to retire into private life after Luca. As long as any form of constitutional government was still functioning, Caesar attached great value to Cicero's services and was always very eager to obtain them. It is unlikely that Caesar, whose clemency was so effectively tempered with ruthlessness, would have let slip the opportunity to employ Cicero's personal influence and oratorical powers when he had the chance. Though he coated the pill with sugar, he insisted on it being swallowed. Had Cicero refused the loans of money and other favours that he received from Caesar during these years, he would not have found himself any more at liberty to refuse Caesar's demands.

In any case, it is wrong to judge Cicero's action in putting his services at the disposal of the Triumvirs by modern standards, rather than by the conventions of his own times. In the Ciceronian age, the main objective of a Roman Senator was not the upholding of some political principle but the maintenance of his own *dignitas*. To change sides, to join the stronger party, in order to protect or enhance one's *dignitas*, was quite in accordance with the normal and accepted code of political ethics. Cato himself was thinking of his *dignitas* when he submitted to the Triumvirs in 58 B.C. and went off to annex Cyprus, rather than stay at Rome and face violence, prosecution, and exile; he was thinking of his *dignitas* when he opposed the invalidation of Clodius's enactments, because this would involve the invalidation of his own settlement of Cyprus. Brutus and Cassius were thinking of their *dignitas* when they accepted office under Caesar after the Civil War, as did many leading Pompeians. What made many of the Optimate leaders critical of Cicero was not that his action contravened their code of behaviour but that they regarded him as a pawn, whose actions should be directed towards maintaining their *dignitas* rather than his own.

It is also said that Cicero showed insufficient gratitude to Caesar for all the favours and benefits that he received during this period. This is implicit in the charge of *amicitia violata* made by Antony in his reply to the First Philippic,[36] while in a letter of April 49 B.C.[37]

Antony reminds Cicero that he is under a greater obligation to Caesar than he is to Pompey. It is clear, however, that Cicero himself, a man who was very sensitive to the demands of obligations, did not consider himself to be under any obligation to Caesar for whatever he had received from him. This attitude was a reasonable one to adopt. The money that Cicero received from Caesar barely made up for what he had lost as a result of his exile and the destruction of his property by Caesar's henchmen. The prestige that he obtained as a source of patronage for those young men who wanted a post on Caesar's staff was no more than he would have enjoyed had the State remained free. The one tangible reward that he obtained, the Augurship, would have probably fallen to him if political affairs at Rome had been allowed to take their normal course, with perhaps the Censorship in addition. To Cicero, the favours that he received from Caesar did little to offset the immeasurable wrongs that Caesar had done to him and to the State, and were merely some slight payment of a debt that Caesar could never pay in full. Whether or not Cicero felt any personal affection towards Caesar is a matter that is disputed by the most eminent scholars, but in spite of the exaggerated praise of Caesar in the letters to Quintus (and occasionally to Atticus) and the appearance of *camaradie* in the letters to Caesar, whatever good feeling there was seems to have been of little depth.

It is interesting to compare Cicero's political honesty with that of his contemporaries. Never was there an age in the history of the Roman Republic when unscrupulous opportunism and the uninhibited pursuit of self-interest could reap a richer reward. Even if the lurid picture painted by Sallust must be regarded as somewhat exaggerated, it would still be true to say that the number of men who followed a steadfast and consistent path in politics were very few. Appius Claudius, corrupt and avaricious, switched his loyalties to suit the profit of the moment; he got help from Caesar in his candidature for the consulship,[38] and followed Pompey to Greece with the Optimate leaders in 49 B.C. He treacherously attacked Caelius Rufus after Caelius had helped to stifle the attempt made to prosecute him for misgovernment in Cilicia. Yet Appius became Augur and Censor, almost by automatic right of birth. Domitius Ahenobarbus, though a staunch Optimate, took part as consul in a corrupt bargain with his colleague, Appius, and two of the consular candidates, Memmius and Domitius Calvinus, both of whom were supporters of Caesar,[39] to procure their election in return for a promise to forge a decree enabling Appius and Ahenobarbus to proceed to their provinces without delay. Scribonius Curio the elder guided his political activities by his hatred of Caesar, and his son sold his services to Caesar for an enormous bribe. Cicero's friend, Servius Sulpicius Rufus, followed Pompey to Greece, but had already sent his son to serve under Caesar and he himself subsequently accepted from Caesar the proconsulship of Achaea.[40] Men of most distinguished families, Aemilius Paulus and C. Antonius, changed sides for a bribe. When serving as jurors, members of the Senate habitually delivered corrupt verdicts. At the trial of Clodius, in 61 B.C., the deal was clinched, in the case of some individuals, by the procuration of certain ladies.[41] At the trial of Oppianicus, in 74 B.C., the jury's votes more or less went up for auction. Q. Lutatius Catulus and C. Calpurnius Piso tried to bribe Cicero to have Caesar implicated in the Catilinarian conspiracy by the use of perjured evidence.[42] Cato himself, for all his reputation for honesty, behaved towards Cicero with unadulterated hypocrisy when he opposed the grant of a *supplicatio* to him for his campaign on Mount Amanus (while supporting a similar application on behalf of Bibulus), and then wrote to Cicero and claimed to have acted from a desire to bring him greater credit.[43] To the end of his life Cato seems to have grudged Cicero the distinction of having been made a martyr by the Triumvirs in 58 B.C. He was steadfast enough in upholding the Optimate cause, but his political short-sightedness, of which Cicero himself often complained, did more than anything else to bring about the downfall of the Republic. Those other Optimate leaders who were honest and consistent, like Marcellus and Bibulus, were usually stupid and brutal. But the majority of the Optimate faction, the men whose devotion to their fish-ponds is so hotly criticized by Cicero, were perfectly content to stand aside from the struggle as soon as their own personal ambitions had been satisfied, and let another man bear the brunt of the battle for the upholding of the privileges of their class.

The most remarkable fact about Cicero's political career is that although he never had the consistent backing of any group or party, and even when championing the *Optimates* could only count on the luke-warm support of the very people for whose interests he was fighting, yet for twenty years he played a leading part in politics. The importance that Caesar attached to winning Cicero's support gives the lie to Mommsen's picture of Cicero as as a timid, treacherous turncoat. Had Cicero, who at times did have his eyes open to the blindness and selfishness of the Optimate leaders and the vanity and unreliability of Pompey, worked out the logical consequence of this appreciation and chosen to play Laelius to Caesar's Scipio, his career would have enjoyed far richer material success. But he could never have brought himself to condone the methods that Caesar was compelled to use to achieve his ends. Cicero was a man of peace—*togatus*: he was willing to 'arm the law' against a Catiline or an Antonius, but he was out of place in a world where political power ultimately rested on the power of the sword and where those constitutional ideals that he set out to defend were in practice to be identified with the selfish interests of an exclusive clique of nobles. He was not a man to offer resistance when resistance was clearly futile; if he had to make up his mind as to which was the lesser evil of two possible courses, he often showed hesitation and irresolution; but whenever he was faced with a choice between two practicable alternatives, he usually chose the one that was the more honourable and the more dangerous.

NOTES

[1] Translated by E. O. Lorimer, *Cicero: The Secrets of his Correspondence*, (Routledge, 1951). Cf. Balsdon, *JRS*, 1950, p. 134; *CR* (N.S.), Dec. 1952, p. 178.

[2] Ad Att. xii. 25, 1.

[3] Carcopino, J., *Les Secrets de la correspondance de Cicero* (Paris, 1947), p. 93.

[4] Seneca, *Suasoria*, 6, 24.

[5] A. Gellius, xii. 12.

[6] *de Petitione Consulatus*, 5, 19-6, 21.

[7] *Ad Att.* i. 2, 1.

[8] Obligations owed to public men for help they had given were frequently discharged by legacies.

[9] Tacitus, *Annals*, xi. 5-7; xiii. 42.

[10] *Ad Att.* i. 12, 1; 13, 6; 14, 7.

[11] *Ad Att.* viii. 4, 2: nihil cognovi ingratius, in quo vitio nihil mali non inest. *Ad Att.* ix. 2a, 2: ingrati animi crimen horreo. *Ad Att.* ix. 7, 4; 19, 2.

[12] *Ad Fam.* v. 20, 9. *Ad Att.* ii. 6, fin.; 16, 4.

[13] *Ad Att.* i. 12, 2.

[14] *Ad Q. fr.* ii. 3, 4. Sallust, *Catiline*, 48, 5.

[15] *Ad Att.* i. 16, 12.

[16] Mommsen, *History of Rome*, translated by Dickson (R. Bentley, 1877), iv, pp. 169, 306.

[17] Dio Cassius, xxxvi. 43; 44; xxxix. 63; xlvi. 3.

[18] Dio Cassius, xxxvii. 22; 57.

[19] *Ad Fam.* i. 9.

[20] Sallust, *Catiline*, 20, 4.

[21] Cicero, *Philippic*, ii. 38. *Ad Fam.* i. 2, 3; 4, 2; 5a, 1; 5b, 2; 7, 2: xv. 7. *Ad Q. fr.* ii. 13, 1. Caesar, *B. C.* i. 9, 2. *Dignitas* is best rendered as 'honour', though it has some of the emotional tones of the contemporary term 'status'. Cf. C. Wirzubski, 'Cicero's *Cum Dignitate Otium*: a Reconsideration', *JRS*, 1954, p. 1.

[22] Cf. K. Quinn, *The Catullan Revolution* (Melbourne, 1959).

[23] *Ad Fam.* v. 7, 3.

[24] *In Pisonem*, 6-7.

[25] *Ad Att.* i. 18, 6; 19, 6; 20, 3; ii. 7, 4.

[26] *Ad Att.* iv, 5. *Ad Fam.* i. 9, 10.

[27] *Ad Att.* viii. 11, 4; ix. 11, 3.

[28] Plutarch, *Cato Minor*, 30.

[29] *Philippic*, ii. 24. The rejection of Pompey by the *Optimates* led to the Triumvirate; their acceptance of him as their leader in the struggle against Caesar led to the Civil War.

[30] *Ad Att.* viii. 7, 1.

[31] *Ad Att.* ii. 3, 3.

[32] *Ad Att.* ii. 5, 1.

[33] *Ad Q. fr.* ii. 14, 2.

[34] R. G. Nisbet, *Cicero, In Pisonem* (Oxford, 1961), p. xvii.

[35] *Ad Fam.* vii. 24, 1.

[36] *Philippic*, ii. 3-5.

[37] *Ad Att.* x. 8a.

[38] *Ad Q. Fr.* ii. 4, 6; 13, 3.

[39] *Ad Att.* iv. 16, 6; 15, 7. *Ad Q. Fr.* iii. 8, 3. Domitius Calvinus was one of Caesar's generals in the Civil War.

[40] *Ad Att.* ix. 19, 2; x. 14, 3.

[41] *Ad Att.* i. 16, 5.

[42] Sallust, *Catiline*, 49, 1.

[43] *Ad Fam.* xv. 5.

III

The Speeches

R. G. M. NISBET

---

qua re tibicen Antigenidas dixerit discipulo sane, frigenti ad populum, 'mihi cane et Musis'; ego huic Bruto, dicenti ut solet apud multitudinem, 'mihi cane et populo, mi Brute', dixerim. (Cicero, *Brutus*, 187)

Antigenidas the flute-player could say to a pupil who was a failure with the public 'Play for me and the Muses'. But I should rather say to our friend Brutus here, speaking as he does before large audiences, 'Play for me and the public, dear Brutus'.

THE evaluation of a classical speech is an exercise in both literary and historical judgement. Form cannot be isolated from content, any more than in history. Oratory, unlike poetry, has a practical purpose, and must not be assessed on merely aesthetic principles. It is impossible to ignore the persuasiveness of the orator's arguments, within a specific context, to a particular audience. But Cicero had no right to make the man in the forum the supreme arbiter. By publishing his speeches he appealed to a different kind of verdict. Great literature should seem impressive, and if possible make sense, to people of different ages. Cicero must play not just for the Roman public but for us.

But we too have something to contribute. We cannot hear Cicero's music until we are prepared to understand the formal prose of antiquity, *Kunstprosa* as the Germans call it. Prose could be a medium as serious, and as elaborate, as poetry; Gibbon and Macaulay were amateurs compared with the greatest ancient stylists. *Kunstprosa*, and oratory above all, was meant to be spoken and to be heard. Every device was exploited to impose a pattern on the incoherent ramblings of speech. Without rhetoric all Latin prose would look like Varro, or worse; but the Roman orators made their uncouth Italic dialect almost as flexible as Greek. Consider Cicero's tribute to that eminent reactionary, Q. Catulus (consul 78 B.C.):

> quem neque periculi tempestas neque honoris aura potuit umquam de suo cursu aut spe aut metu demovere. (*Sest.* 101)

> Neither the storms of crisis, nor the breezes of ambition, could ever divert him, either by hope or fear, from the course that he had chosen.

periculi tempestas balances *honoris aura*; by a chiastic arrangement *spe* refers to the latter, *metu* to the former. The sentence falls into corresponding phrases, with slight pauses after *tempestas, aura, umquam, cursu, demovere*. And before the stronger pauses there is a rhythmical cadence.

These cadences are fundamental for the appreciation of Cicero, so here are the facts, greatly simplified. The ends of Cicero's sentences tend to conform to a limited number of metrical patterns, *clausulae* as they are called; these patterns also occur (though less regularly) before pauses in the middle of a sentence. The following are the *clausulae* most often used by Cicero:

1. (Cretic + trochee). $-\cup--\underset{\smile}{}$ (the famous *esse videatur* is a variation of this type).
2. (Double-cretic). $-\cup--\cup\underset{\smile}{}$ ($-----\cup\underset{\smile}{}$ is also frequent).
3. (Double-trochee). $-\cup-\underset{\smile}{}$ (often preceded by $-\cup-$ or $---$).
4. (Cretic + iambus). $-\cup-\cup\underset{\smile}{}$ (less frequent than the other three).

In every case the last syllable can be either short or long. Sometimes a long syllable is resolved into two shorts. The rules for elision are the same as in verse.

These *clausulae* are illustrated below from the peroration of the *Pro Quinctio*; this is Cicero's earliest extant speech, and was written in 81 B.C., when he was twenty-five. I have indicated the ends of the cola (the major phrases) with a vertical stroke. Occasionally we find two short syllables where the basic type has a long syllable;

for instance -*ficere non posset* is a sub-class of our first type (cretic + trochee).

ab ipsō rĕpŭdĭātŭs, | ab amicis eius non sūblĕvātŭs, | ab omni magistratu agitatus ātquĕ pērtērrĭtŭs, | quem praeter te appēllĕt hăbēt nēmĭnĕm; | tibi se, tibi suas omnis opes fortunāsquĕ cōmmēndăt, | tibi committit existimationem ac spem rĕlĭcŭǣ vītǣ. multis vexatus cōntŭmēlĭīs, | plurimis iactātŭs īniūrĭīs, | non turpis ad te sēd mĭsēr cōnfŭgĭt; | e fundo ornatīssĭmo ēiēctŭs, | ignominiis omnibus āppĕtītŭs, | cum illum in paternis bonis dominarī vĭdērĕt, | ipse filiae nubili dotem confĭcĕrĕ nōn pōssĕt, | nihil alienum tamen vita superiōrĕ cōmmīsĭt. | (*Quinct*. 98)

Most of Cicero is written this way.

Even when one has learned to appreciate Cicero's style, one may be deterred by the scale of his operations. Livy said that his virtues were such that it would take a Cicero to praise them; one might almost add that it would take a Cicero to master and expound such a volume of material. His literary output was the by-product of an arduous and anxious life, composed, as he says himself, in off-moments (*Phil*. ii. 20); and the speeches are only a part of that output. Yet they are too complicated and too varied to discuss adequately in an article. It will be convenient to select nine speeches, belonging for the most part to different categories; even these must be treated summarily. One can only dip in one's bucket and see what comes up.

Cicero first made his mark in 80 B.C. by his defence of Sextus Roscius of Ameria against a charge of parricide. The speech shows to an unusual extent the qualities of pattern and proportion which counted for so much in ancient oratory. At the end of his narrative, for instance, Cicero makes an impassioned appeal to the jury.

quid primum querar, aut unde potissimum, iudices, ordiar, aut quod aut a quibus auxilium petam? deorumne immortalium, populine Romani, vestramne qui summam potestatem habetis hoc tempore fidem implorem? (§ 29)

What is to be my first indictment? Where best, gentlemen, can I make my beginning? What succour shall I summon, and from whom? Shall I invoke the protection of the immortal gods, or of the Roman people, or of you who now exercise supreme authority?

It is easy to record the rhetorical questions, and the two 'tricola' (sentences with three parallel clauses); ancient theorists even dignified the figure of speech with the title of *dubitatio*. But such pedantry explains no more about oratory than it does about poetry. Forty years earlier when C. Gracchus had made a similar appeal even his enemies had not refrained from tears (Cicero, *De Oratore* iii, 214).

> quo me miser conferam? quo vortam? in Capitoliumne? at fratris sanguine redundat. an domum? matremne ut miseram lamentantem videam et abiectam?

> Where in my misery can I betake myself? Where am I to turn? To the Capitol? But it is flowing with my brother's blood. Or home—to see my poor mother prostrate and lamenting.

So far from seeming lifeless and conventional the same rhetorical figure was used by the greatest of poets in the most intensely imagined situations. When Dido has been told that Aeneas is leaving her, she begins her agonized reproaches with the words 'quae quibus anteferam?' 'what shall I say first, what next?' (Aeneid, iv. 371). And when she has killed herself her sister Anna uses almost the same expression as Cicero: 'quid primum deserta querar?' (iv. 677).

Sometimes, it must be admitted, the rhetoric becomes too exuberant. By a quaint custom Roman parricides were tied up in a sack with a snake, a dog, and a monkey, and thrown into the sea. The topic encourages Cicero to pull out all the stops:

> etenim quid tam est commune quam spiritus vivis, terra mortuis, mare fluctuantibus, litus eiectis? ita vivunt dum possunt ut ducere animam de caelo non queant, ita moriuntur ut eorum ossa terra non tangat, ita iactantur fluctibus ut numquam adluantar, ita postremo eiciuntur ut ne ad saxa quidem mortui conquiescant. (§ 72)

> Nothing is so free as air to the living, earth to the dead, the sea to the drifting swimmer, the shore to the cast-up corpse. Yet these men live, while they can, without drawing breath from the heavens; when they die the earth does not touch their bones; they are tumbled by the waves but never washed by them; and when thrown up dead at last they cannot rest even on the rocks.

More than thirty years later Cicero recalled this effort with the condescension of the successful for their distant selves.

> quantis illa clamoribus adulescentuli diximus de supplicio parricidarum, quae nequaquam satis defervisse post aliquanto

sentire coepimus ... sunt enim omnia sicut adulescentis non tam
re et maturitate quam spe et exspectatione laudati. (*Orator*, 107)

Resounding applause greeted our own youthful observations on
the punishment of parricides; it was only rather later that one came
to realize that the froth had by no means sufficiently subsided.
The whole thing is what could be expected from a young man who
was admired not so much for any maturity of achievement as for
promise and potentiality.

He was quite right. The antitheses are too artificial: the rhetorical
form is not being used to reinforce the thought and the emotion,
but has taken control over the whole passage. Cicero is not thinking in real terms about a bizarre punishment: he is simply man-
oeuvring words.

The artificiality of such writing is sometimes summed up by the
slogan 'Asianism'. When eloquence was first exported from the
Piraeus, Cicero informs us, it took on the tastelessness and adi-
posity of the East (*Brutus*, 51; *Orator*, 25). Theorists distinguished
two sorts of Asianism, the pointed and the periodic (*Brut.* 325).
The pointed style was derived from the third century orator
Hegesias (*Orat.* 226), and ultimately from Gorgias; it was imitated
by Cicero in his *Pro Roscio Comoedo* (about 76 B.C.),[1] and had some
influence on the prose of the early Empire. The other and more
extreme variety found a champion in Cicero's great rival Hortensius. Contemporary Greek examples of this type were long
lacking; in Roman oratory as in Roman poetry we are constantly
misled by the scarcity of Hellenistic material. But towards the end
of last century a remarkable inscription was brought to notice.
At Nemrud Dagh in eastern Turkey, more than six thousand feet
high on an extinct volcano, stands the monument of Antiochus I
of Commagene, a contemporary of Cicero's. Here amid the
gigantic statues, with their toppled heads and outlandish hats,
there survives a long inscription of which a few lines will suffice[2]:

ἐπεὶ δὲ ἱεροθεσίου τοῦδε κρηπεῖδα | ἀπόρθητον χρόνου
λύμαις | οὐρανίων ἄγχιστα θρόνων καταστήσασθαι προενοήθην, |
ἐν ᾧ μακαριστὸν ἄχρι γήρως ὕπαρξαν | σῶμα μορφῆς ἐμῆς |
πρὸς οὐρανίους Διὸς Ὠρομάσδου θρόνους | θεοφιλῆ ψυχὴν
προπέμψαν | εἰς τὸν ἄπειρον αἰῶνα κοιμήσεται . . .

When I determined to establish, nigh unto the thrones celestial,
the edifice of this sacred structure, imperishable from time's defile-

ment, wherein this corporeal body, having fulfilled its life-time in felicity, and having wafted my blessed spirit to the celestial thrones of Oromasdos, may take its slumber for the aeons of eternity . . .

I have marked the pauses in this resounding period: before each pause the clausula is Ciceronian.

'Asiatic' and its opposite 'Attic' have no very precise meaning; they were simply vogue words of literary criticism.[3] Some of Cicero's contemporaries and juniors claimed to imitate the simplicity and purity of the best Attic orators. Caesar was one of these stylists, and the unadorned elegance of the 'Gallic War' shows the possibilities of the manner. Brutus was another, and when Shakespeare makes him address the crowd in dry prose, the touch is authentic. Such critics used 'Asiatic' as a term of abuse against the orotund Hortensius, and even Cicero himself. They were right in a way. By striving so persistently for rhythm and balance Cicero destroyed something of the essential savour of Latin, the quality that he himself recognized in the conversation of certain elderly ladies (*Brut.* 211), the precise choice and arrangement of words that we can still feel in Terence and Caesar and the best of Lucretius. But the Atticists pushed their case too far. For one thing their name was misleading. Cicero points out that Demosthenes had not hesitated to use the grand manner (though his opponents could have retorted that grandeur is not floridity). It is more important that the Atticists lacked variety and colour, blood and juice (*sucum et sanguinem*). Compared with Cicero, Caesar seems dull.

But pigeon-holes are an obstacle to criticism. Cicero's style did not develop in a straight line from youthful 'Asianism' to the lean and energetic sentences of the Philippics. The subject-matter counts for as much as the date. Even in the *Rosciana* the narrative and argumentation are straightforward and reasoned. The charge had been trumped up by Chrysogonus, the powerful aide of the dictator Sulla, and one should have no illusions about that régime. Cicero's attempts to win the sympathy of his audience and to isolate Chrysogonus from his master (a typical technique) are a triumph of courage and intelligence.

The peroration of the speech is particularly impressive:

> vestrum nemo est quin intellegat populum Romanum, qui quondam in hostis lenissimus existimabatur, hoc tempore

domestica crudelitate laborare. hanc tollite ex civitate, iudices, hanc pati nolite diutius in hac re publica versari; quae non modo id habet in se mali quod tot cives atrocissime sustulit, verum etiam hominibus lenissimis ademit misericordiam consuetudine incommodorum. nam cum omnibus horis aliquid atrociter fieri videmus aut audimus, etiam qui natura mitissimi sumus, adsiduitate molestiarum sensum omnem humanitatis ex animis amittimus. (§ 154)

The Roman people was once believed to show mercy to its enemies, but each of you knows that it now suffers from the barbarity of citizens. You must extirpate this evil from the nation by your verdict, and not permit it longer to prevail in the life of the republic. It is detrimental not only because it has cruelly taken from our midst so many of our compatriots, but because it has deprived the merciful of the power of pity through familiarity with trouble. When at every hour of the day we see or hear of some savage deed, even those of us who are temperamentally most lenient banish from our hearts at the repetition of unpleasantness every feeling of humanity.

There is no 'Asianism' here. One is impressed rather by Cicero's maturity and restraint, the moderation of such words as 'incommodorum' and 'molestiarum', and the quiet strength which he showed at the age of twenty-six in resisting tyranny. Cicero's main weakness is not floridity of expression but flabbiness and insincerity of thought. There is not much of these faults in the *Rosciana*.

'Quis quinque in Verrem libros exspectabit?' asks one of the characters in Tacitus's *Dialogus*; 'who could last out five books against Verres?' It is undeniable that the Verrines (70 B.C.) seem too long to the impatient reader, yet it must be remembered that the second *actio* was never delivered, and so seems verbose and unreal. The single speech of the first *actio* is very different: it gets somewhere. Oratory was commended in the ancient world, even by serious people, as the best means of creating opinion and promoting action; here for once the high claim seems to be justified. In a single morning Cicero destroyed the most magnificent of Roman viceroys and supplanted Hortensius as the leading speaker of the age. Too often elsewhere he is fighting defensive battles for indefensible causes. Here he is aggressive, successful, and right.

Cicero's energy and resource are astonishing. The ability to organize complicated material at high speed may seem irrelevant to literary critics, but no orator can do without it. The defence had hoped for the sympathy of the senatorial jury, but Cicero meets the danger with courteous threats: the whole jury system is under scrutiny, and its future will depend largely on the result of the trial. The defence hoped to postpone the hearing till the following year, when Hortensius would be consul; in a dramatic announcement Cicero declares that he will cut short his opening speech to ensure an early finish (§34). And if there is any bribery, he himself will be aedile in 69 and can rely on public opinion to support him.

> erit tum consul Hortensius cum summo imperio et potestate, ego autem aedilis, hoc est, paullo amplius quam privatus; tamen haec huius modi res est quam me acturum esse polliceor, ita populo Romano grata atque iucunda, ut ipse consul in hac causa prae me minus etiam, si fieri possit, quam privatus esse videatur. (§ 37)

> Then Hortensius will be consul with all the authority of office, while I shall be aedile, that is to say slightly more than a private citizen. Yet the action I promise to perform is of such a kind, so agreeable and welcome is it to the Roman people, that even the consul in such a cause will seem, compared with me, if such a thing is possible, less even than a private citizen.

It must have been difficult for Cicero to curtail his own eloquence, but his tactics worked perfectly, Hortensius declined to cross-examine, and Verres withdrew with the statues and vases which he had looted to the free city of Marseilles. These objets d'art aroused such intense admiration that he was murdered on Antony's orders twenty-seven years later; his one consolation was that Cicero had pre-deceased him.

The five speeches of the second *actio* may be less incisive, but they are impressive for their variety of style and subject-matter. Cicero distinguished three oratorical styles, 'tenue', 'medium', and 'grande'. The function of the thin style was to inform and explain ('docere'). Oratory is simply hot air unless it is based on a solid foundation of fact and argument. Churchill's war-time speeches were as distinguished for their rigorous argumentation as for their more memorable perorations. An oration that was eloquent throughout would be intolerable, like Pliny's *Panegyric*. The Verrines have a firmer factual basis than any other Ciceronian speech: one respects an orator who is in a position to inform us that during Verres's proconsulship farmers in the Agyrium district were reduced from 252 to 120. Unfortunately, the lucid exposition of technicalities is difficult to illustrate by extract. The critic of big books soon finds that some important qualities cannot be anthologized.

But it is perhaps in the middle style that Cicero shows his most characteristic excellence. He describes the style in the style itself (*Orat.* 21): 'isque uno tenore, ut aiunt, in dicendo fluit nihil adferens praeter facilitatem et aequabilitatem' ('his words flow with an "even tenor" bringing nothing except an easy and smoothly running style'). Echoing Cicero's words Pope finds fault with poems 'that shunning faults one quiet tenour keep' (*Essay on Criticism*, 241); but Cicero's middle style was far from being dull and negative. On the contrary, its function was to charm and entertain the hearer, and to provide relief alike from technical argumentation and high-flown rhetoric. Cicero's description of Henna is typical of the manner:

> Henna autem ubi ea quae dico gesta esse memorantur, est loco perexcelso atque edito, quo in summo est aequata agri planities et aquae perennes, tota vero ab omni aditu circumcisa atque directa est; quam circa lacus lucique sunt plurimi atque laetissimi flores omni tempore anni, locus ut ipse raptum illum virginis quem iam a pueris accepimus declarare videatur. (iv, 107)

> Now Henna, the traditional scene of the events I am describing, stands on a high and lofty elevation, on the top of which stretches a flat table-land, watered by springs that never dry, and bounded in every direction by sheer and precipitous cliffs. Round about are lakes and groves unnumbered, and flowers luxuriate at every season of the year; so that one might be forgiven for thinking that the very landscape confirms the story of our childhood, the Rape of Proserpine.

Many passages in the middle style illustrate Cicero's Hellenism and *humanitas*. He had learned this outlook on life from such men as the Scaevolae, who in turn had contacts with the cultivated milieu of Scipio Aemilianus. His own ideal orator had to be a man of liberal education, trained in the grounds of the Academy, not in the factories of the rhetoricians (*Orat.* 12). He aimed at an

Isocratean union of oratory and philosophy, yet his own blend
was more interesting than that of his long-winded exemplar. His
breadth of interest is astonishing: it is characteristic of him that
in Caesar's consulship in 59 he retired to Anzio and wrote a
treatise on geography (*ad Att.* ii, 6). Yet he has none of the
scissors-and-paste methods of the typical Roman polymath, like
Varro or Pliny. One may illustrate his cultured manner by his
account of the statues looted by Verres from the chapel of
Heius.

> erant aenea duo praeterea signa non maxima, verum eximia
> venustate, virginali habitu atque vestitu, quae manibus sublatis
> sacra quaedam more Atheniensium virginum reposita in capitibus
> sustinebant; Canephoroe ipsae vocabantur; sed earum artificem—
> quem? quemnam? recte admones, Polyclitum esse dicebant.
> (*In Verr.* iv, 5)

> There were two other bronze statues, not very big but
> exquisitely graceful, with the appearance and dress of young
> women, who with hands uplifted were holding sacred objects on
> their heads in the fashion of the girls of Athens. The statues were
> called 'The Basket-bearers', and the sculptor—who was he?—who
> do you say he was?—thank you very much—was supposed to be
> Polyclitus.

The artistic information was not very esoteric, but the charm of
the orator's treatment was civilized, and Greek, and Ciceronian.

But for Cicero it is not enough that the orator should expound
and charm; he must also be able to move the minds and bend the
wills of his hearers. Demosthenes was the greatest of orators
because he was the master of the grand style; Pericles would
never have been said to thunder and lighten if he had spoken
simply; it was the ability to sweep away an audience that Cicero
missed in the self-styled Atticists of his day. The Verrines are so
impressive because close argument is reinforced by a strong
emotional appeal. Of course the orator who attempts the grand
style too often or too soon will fail more disastrously than the less
ambitious pleader. But Cicero is a master of timing. We have
quoted his flowing description of the woods and springs of
Henna. When the audience has been sufficiently soothed he
launches a startling attack on the proconsul who had looted this
tranquil shrine:

tenuerunt enim P. Popilio P. Rupilio consulibus illum locum
servi fugitivi barbari hostes. sed neque tam servi illi dominorum
quam tu libidinum, neque tam fugitivi illi ab dominis quam tu ab
iure et ab legibus, neque tam barbari lingua et natione illi quam tu
natura et moribus, neque tam illi hostes hominibus quam tu dis
immortalibus. quae deprecatio est igitur ei reliqua qui indignitate
servos, temeritate fugitivos, scelere barbaros, crudelitate hostes
vicerit? (iv. 112)

During the consulship of Popilius and Rupilius (132 b.c.), the
area was occupied by men who were slaves, runaways, savages,
enemies. Yet they were less the slaves of their masters than you of
your vices; they were less runaways from their masters than you
from the laws and from justice; they were less savages by birth
and by language than you by character and behaviour; they were
less enemies of mankind than you of the gods in heaven. What plea
for mercy can there be from one who has surpassed slaves in de-
gradation, runaways in audacity, savages in villainy, and enemies
in ruthlessness?

The modern reader is apt to think that indignation is insincere
when expressed in such formal patterns. Yet if one accepts ancient
attitudes, the passage will do.

But the merits of the Verrines are not only stylistic. 'We have
all', says Burke,[4] 'in our early education read the Verrine Orations.
We read them not merely to instruct us, as they will do, in the
principles of eloquence, and to acquaint us with the manners,
customs, and laws of the ancient Romans, of which they are an
abundant repository; but we may read them from a much higher
motive. We may read them from a motive which the great orator
had doubtless in his view, when by publishing them he left to the
world and to the latest posterity a monument by which it might
be seen what course a great public accuser in a great public cause
ought to pursue; and, as connected with it, what course judges
ought to pursue in deciding upon such a cause.' The merits of
which Burke speaks can be seen by a comparison between Cicero
and himself. Warren Hastings may be represented as another
Verres, Sopater and Heius appear again as Nuncomar and the
Begums of Oudh, but Burke is not a Cicero either in manner or
substance. Cicero was a master of many styles: Burke was not.
People complain of Cicero's diffuseness, but Burke was much
worse, as our extract shows. Cicero understood Sicily, but Burke

knew little of India. Cicero finished in a morning, but Burke took seven years. Verres abandoned his defence, but Hastings was acquitted. Cicero's case has not been controverted, Burke's has to a large extent.

Some of Cicero's speeches dealt not with major national issues but with the vendettas of trivial clients. The *Pro Cluentio* (66 B.C.) is the outstanding example of this type. The case was unimportant compared with many another; yet the younger Pliny asserts that Cicero's longest speech (which is this one) was also his best (*Epist.* i. 20, 4). The *Pro Cluentio* is referred to by Quintilian more often than any other oration; it is quoted with evident approval by the ancient grammarians, and by Cicero himself. In more modern times Niebuhr recommended it, in the exalted company of the *De Corona*, as a speech likely to stimulate the budding classical scholar. Such testimonials deserve attention, and scrutiny.

The case was a melodramatic one: Cluentius was accused of poisoning his step-father Oppianicus. For all we know he may have been innocent, but Cicero overreached himself in his search for arguments. He alleges that Oppianicus murdered his first wife, his brother, his sister-in-law, and two of his children, as well as trying to murder Cluentius. He absurdly argues that Oppianicus was so miserable that Cluentius could have no motive for his death. One of the prosecution's strongest points was that Cluentius's own mother, Sassia, believed in his guilt. Cicero cleverly counter-attacks by representing her as an unnatural parent, but his account of her journey to Rome reads like a parody of his own clichés.

> nemo erat illorum, paene dicam, quin expiandum illum locum esse arbitraretur quacumque illa iter fecisset, nemo quin terram ipsam violari quae mater est omnium vestigiis consceleratae matris putaret. itaque nullo in oppido consistendi potestas ei fuit, nemo ex tot hospitibus inventus est qui non contagionem aspectus fugeret; nocti se potius ac solitudini quam ulli aut urbi aut hospiti committebat. (§ 193)

> There was not a man among them, I might venture to say, who did not think that the places she had passed would need to be purified, not a man who did not suppose that the very earth, that is the mother of all, was polluted by being walked upon by so villainous a mother. So in no town was she permitted to break her journey, nobody was to be found among all those innkeepers

who did not draw back from the contagion of her sight; she preferred to entrust herself to darkness and to solitude rather than to
any city or any inn.

We meet the same themes later, the senate's horror at Catiline,
Piso's furtive return from Macedonia. But Sassia did not deserve
such rodomontade.

Most of the speech has nothing to do with Cluentius's alleged
poisoning of Oppianicus. It deals with a trial of eight years before,
when Oppianicus had been convicted of trying to poison
Cluentius. This so-called *iudicium Iunianum* had become a byword
for the corruption of a senatorial jury. Junius, the trial judge, was
later convicted; several of the jury were prosecuted in the courts
or stigmatized by the censor. To attempt to change public opinion
on such an issue was an act of intellectual bravado. Yet Cicero
claims that if the jury forget what they have heard outside they
will overturn the universal verdict. Incredibly, they did.

Cicero had not simply prejudice to contend with: he himself,
both in the *Pro Caecina* and the Verrines, had commented most
unfavourably on the *iudicium Iunianum*. Worse still, he had actually
delivered a speech on behalf of Scamander, who was accused with
Oppianicus on that occasion. But now he changes direction with
slippery urbanity. He assures his audience that at the previous trial
he had had a unique opportunity for observing the nervousness
of Oppianicus, the look of worry on his face, his frequent changes
of colour (§ 54). He switches on the easy and confiding manner
which was one of his most useful skills. It would be a great mistake,
he tells the jury, to suppose that speeches in the courts are solemn
affidavits. If the brief could make its own speech nobody would
retain counsel; the orator is retained not to affirm his own beliefs
but to say what the circumstances require (§ 139). The point is
illustrated by a charming and irrelevant anecdote. The jury was
convinced that such a nice man as Cicero must be speaking the
truth this time.

Cicero uses many other sophistries[5] to deceive his audience. In
the trial of Oppianicus it seems probable that both sides bribed
a jury, and that Cluentius paid more; this is the view of the transaction that Cicero himself takes in the Verrines. Yet in the *Pro
Cluentio* (§ 64) he assumes that bribes must have been given either
by Cluentius or by Oppianicus; by demonstrating that Oppianicus
was guilty he proves, at least to the satisfaction of a Roman jury,

that Cluentius was innocent. Cicero is forced to concede that Oppianicus had been convicted by the votes of disreputable jurors, whereas honourable men had acquitted or abstained. But he can explain even this. A certain juryman called Staienus took bribes from Oppianicus and then voted against him. So the good jurymen, who had heard rumours of bribery, naturally assumed that Oppianicus was innocent. Such were Cicero's powers of persuasion that he made even this story seem plausible.

Then there is the curious figure of Fidiculanius Falcula, another juryman in the earlier trial. We meet him first in the *Pro Caecina* where his provincial name is used to provoke laughter in court:

> decimo vero loco testis exspectatus et ad extremum reservatus dixit, senator populi Romani, splendor ordinis, decus atque orna- mentum iudiciorum, exemplar antiquae religionis, Fidiculanius Falcula. (§ 28)

> Tenth to speak was a witness long awaited and reserved to the last, a senator of the Roman people, a luminary of his order, the pride and ornament of the law-courts, an exemplar of old-world honour, Fidiculanius Falcula.

But in the *Pro Cluentio* such levity would be unseemly. Cicero informs us with a straight face that C. Fidiculanius Falcula had been acquitted of corrupt practices not only once but twice (§ 103).

Cicero boasted afterwards that in the *Pro Cluentio* he had thrown dust in the eyes of the jury (Quintilian, ii. 17, 21, 'tenebras se offudisse iudicibus'). The rhetorical theorists repeat his proud claim with professional appreciation. Cicero relied above all on the sheer complication of the case, which he was not inclined to minimize. He saturated the jury with a plethora of irrelevant information, and in a court where there was no summing-up even the most clear-headed must have been confused. For ingenious misrepresentation the *Pro Cluentio* surpasses even the *De Lege Agraria*, and there is no other speech of which that can be said. Yet to make the worse argument seem the better is not the highest function of oratory. The *Pro Cluentio* is Cicero's cleverest speech, but it is not his greatest.

The Catilinarian orations (63 B.C.) seem at first sight more sig- nificant: here at last Cicero has found an important political cause worthy of his eloquence. The first of the four speeches begins dramatically: Cicero tells Catiline that his conspiracy is discovered and orders him to leave the city. For once there is no suave exordium to conciliate the audience: Cicero goes straight to the point.

> quo usque tandem abutere, Catilina, patientia nostra? quam diu etiam furor iste tuus nos eludet? quem ad finem sese effrenata iactabit audacia? nihilne te nocturnum praesidium Palati, nihil urbis vigiliae, nihil timor populi, nihil concursus bonorum omnium, nihil hic munitissimus habendi senatus locus, nihil horum ora voltusque moverunt? (§ 1)

> How long, I ask you, Catiline, do you mean to abuse our tolerance? When will you stop playing hide-and-seek with us, you madman? Will your ungovernable effrontery flaunt itself for ever? Are you impressed not at all by the all-night garrison on the Palatine, nor by the sentries throughout the city, nor by the trepidation of the people, nor by the rallying of all loyal citizens, nor by the fortification of this place where we are meeting, nor by the looks on the faces of the senators?

No passage of Cicero is better known. I have heard these words recited across the dinner-table by a friendly Spanish metallurgist, eager to bridge the gap between the two cultures, and declaimed by a German tourist, not altogether appropriately, in the senate-house of Diocletian. With austere irony Sallust assigns the familiar opening to Catiline: 'quae quo usque tandem patiemini, o fortissumi viri?' (*Cat.* 20, 9) Yet though this vigorous onslaught lives in the memory, it fails to satisfy. In this it typifies the speeches as a whole. Different reasons might be given for one's disappointment, and the problem deserves closer analysis.

Some moderns object to the Catilinarians for political reasons. Before 63 Cicero was a thrusting *novus homo*, ready to resist some abuses, and even to welcome some changes. Afterwards he was a complacent conservative, who defended the ruling oligarchy with a greater ardour and pretence of rationality than they could ever have mustered for themselves. Yet it cannot be denied that he did well in 63: Catiline's rebellion ought not to be palliated, though some people have tried. Cicero met the crisis with courage, energy, and the *vigilantia* of which he was so proud. Catiline was crushed, and a serious civil war averted. And though the execution of the conspirators was illegal, in view of the senate's vote

Cicero had no real alternative. It is difficult to be sure that at any stage he made the wrong decision.

Other readers are offended by Cicero's boastfulness, but we must judge it by the conventions of his times. If some of Hortensius's speeches had survived they might also seem arrogant. Ciceronian braggadocio may offend insular standards of good taste, but it is at least more honest than some modern techniques of self-advertisement. The pursuit of glory was sanctioned by the most rational of philosophers: 'Honour is the reward of excellence,' says Aristotle uncompromisingly, 'and it is assigned to the good.' Posthumous fame was a substitute for an illusory immortality: to live on the lips of men was the only way to defeat the pyre. Of course Cicero went too far: the Catilinarian rebellion was not in fact the most important war in the history of mankind (iii. 25). Yet he was self-distrustful and greatly provoked: by his boasts he kept up his own courage and defied his enemies.

The real objection to the speeches is not Cicero's arrogance, still less his resistance to Catiline, but an air of unreality which prevails throughout. The Catilinarians were not published till 60 B.C.; by that time Cicero was under fire for executing the prisoners, and the written speeches reflect the changed situation. The ancients adapted their speeches for publication, and everybody knows that the second Philippic and most of the Verrines were never delivered. But the rewriting goes much further than is sometimes realized.[6] In the rhetorical invective against Cicero which Dio assigns to Fufius Calenus it is alleged that the great orator had delivered none of the beautiful speeches which he afterwards published (xlvi. 7, 3). Such adaptation no doubt smoothed over many rough edges, yet if one values the content of literature as well as the form, it must have led to a loss of actuality. Cicero's speeches suggest too little of the drama of real-life situations; instead we are offered literary essays, political manifestos, apologias and libels.

Hence the theatricality of the Catilinarians. In the first speech Cicero seems too anxious to justify the expulsion of Catiline; in view of his resistance in the field, many Romans must afterwards have wondered whether it was necessary to turn him loose. There is too much irrelevant invective: when faced with a concrete and urgent problem did the Roman senate really waste time on this stuff? The *patria* in magniloquent periods addresses first Catiline and then Cicero (i. 18 and i. 27); one does not seem to be listening in on a real debate in one of the most hard-headed assemblies that the world has known. Other weaknesses of the First Catilinarian no doubt belong to the spoken speech. Cicero shows no interest in the social evils which made the rebellion possible. He describes in unnecessarily lurid terms the incendiarism of the conspirators; he admits in a letter that he lays on the paint rather thick (*ad Att*. i. 14, 3). In the peroration he makes a pretentious appeal for divine aid, but his real views on the government of the universe (as revealed in his *De Natura Deorum*) were not so simple.

The note of artificiality is particularly unwelcome in the Fourth Catilinarian, which dealt with the fate of the prisoners. A decision had to be reached by nightfall, but Cicero finds time for eloquent digressions and unseasonable *exempla*. He repeatedly alludes to the danger that might threaten himself; much of this is prompted by the changed circumstances of 60 B.C. when he had been put on the defensive. We are told by Plutarch that in the real debate Cicero failed to give a strong lead; but he might at least have stated the nature of his dilemma candidly and thoughtfully, as he does often enough in his private letters. One could forgive some loose threads if he had succeeded in recapturing the atmosphere of the occasion (as he does in the third speech in his dramatic account of the arrests). But he is betrayed alike by his rhetorical form and by the need to present himself in a good light.

The pretensions of Cicero's Catilinarians are effectively deflated by Sallust's 'Catiline'. Sallust is quite fair: he admits that the First Catilinarian was brilliant and salutary. Yet when he calls Cicero *optimus consul* the praise is maliciously faint; Cicero was very annoyed when Brutus described him in similar terms (*ad Att*. xii. 21, 1). Sallust insults Cicero the best possible way, by ignoring him; he achieves what might have seemed impossible, a *Catiline* without the consul. The speeches which he assigns to Caesar and Cato are as artificial in style and substance as Cicero's: the protagonists talk in jerky and archaic phrases; the tone of the debate is amoral and Thucydidean; there is mention of such Sallustian topics as 'avaritia' and 'luxuria'. But something is gained:

> plerique eorum qui ante me sententias dixerunt conposite atque magnifice casum rei publicae miserati sunt. quae belli saevitia esset, quae victis adciderent, enumeravere: rapi virgines, pueros; divelli liberos a parentum conplexu; matres familiarum

pati quae victoribus collibuissent; fana atque domos spoliari; caedem incendia fieri; postremo armis cadaveribus cruore atque luctu omnia compleri. sed per deos immortalis, quo illa oratio pertinuit? an uti vos infestos coniurationi faceret? scilicet quem res tanta et tam atrox non permovit, eum oratio adcendet. (Sall. *Cat.* 51, 9-10)

Most of the previous speakers have commiserated elegantly and magniloquently with the plight of the republic. They have enumerated the horrors or war, the fate of the vanquished, the assaults on girls and boys, the snatching of children from their parents' arms, the submission of married women to the conquerors' desires; churches and homes looted, fire and slaughter, everywhere arms and corpses, blood and tears. For God's sake, what was the point of such speeches? To make you resist the conspiracy? As if the man who has been left unmoved by an act so vile will be inflamed by talk.

Sallust's speeches, unlike Cicero's, are reasoned, relevant, and worthy of the Roman senate.

Cicero was exiled in 58 for his execution of the Catilinarian conspirators, and in the two years that followed his return in 57 most of his oratory was disguised autobiography. The *Pro Sestio* (56 B.C.) is the best of the whole group: it gives the most coherent account of what happened, it is remarkably varied in content, and it shows more eloquence and less hysteria than, for instance, the *De Domo* or *In Pisonem*. Cicero's exile was an intolerable wound: he felt that he had been punished for his finest achievement, and abandoned by the ruling oligarchy which he had done so much to save. But by the power of words he is able to represent his humiliation as voluntary martyrdom:

etenim si mihi in aliqua nave cum meis amicis naviganti hoc, iudices, accidisset, ut multi ex multis locis praedones classibus eam navem se oppressuros minitarentur nisi me unum sibi dedidissent, si id vectores negarent ac mecum simul interire quam me tradere hostibus mallent, iecissem ipse me potius in profundum ut ceteros conservarem quam illos mei tam cupidos non modo ad certam mortem, sed in magnum vitae discrimen adducerem. (§ 45)

If I had been sailing with my friends on a ship, and swarms of pirates had appeared on every side and threatened to sink the ship with their squadrons unless I alone were surrendered to them, if the passengers had refused and had preferred to die in my company rather than deliver me to the enemy, I should have thrown myself overboard to preserve the others sooner than bring such faithful friends, if not to certain death, at any rate into great danger of destruction.

One of the chief qualities of the *Pro Sestio* is its vividness. No historical period need be much more interesting than any other period; some areas seem exciting and some dull because of the people who have described them. Cicero has an egoist's power to communicate feeling combined with a letter-writer's eye for detail. When he goes into exile the houses and temples grieve with him (§ 53); when his enemies set out for their provinces they look like vultures in purple cloaks (§ 71 'vulturii paludati'). Best of all is the caricature of L. Piso, the father of the Calpurnia who married Julius Caesar:

> alter, o di boni, quam taeter incedebat, quam truculentus, quam terribilis aspectu. unum aliquem te ex barbatis illis, exemplum imperi veteris, imaginem antiquitatis, columen rei publicae diceres intueri. vestitus aspere nostra hac purpura plebeia ac paene fusca, capillo ita horrido ut Capua, in qua ipsa tum imaginis ornandae causa duumviratum gerebat, Seplasiam sublaturus videretur. nam quid ego de supercilio dicam, quod tum hominibus non supercilium sed pignus rei publicae videbatur? (§ 19)

> The other, heaven help us, how horrible he was as he marched along, how ferocious, how frightening to look at. You would have thought you were beholding one of the bearded ancients, a specimen of the old order, an exemplar of antiquity, a pillar of the republic. He was coarsely clad in common plebeian purple, almost black; his hair was so untidy that he seemed likely to carry off all the unguents from Capua, where in fact he was holding a magistracy at the time for the embellishment of his portrait. I say nothing of his eyebrows which in those days were considered not so much eyebrows as a guarantee of the republic.

But Cicero has more feline ways of expressing malice. At the same time that Clodius exiled Cicero he had Cato sent on an honorific mission to Cyprus. Nothing could have been more embittering: it was Cato who had insisted on the execution of the Catilinarians, and had carried the day in the senate. Now Cicero finds relief for his feelings:

> at etiam eo negotio M. Catonis splendorem maculare voluerunt, ignari quid gravitas, quid integritas, quid magnitudo animi, quid

denique virtus valeret, quae in tempestate saeva quieta est, et
lucet in tenebris, et pulsa loco manet tamen atque haeret in patria,
splendetque per sese semper neque alienis umquam sordibus ob-
solescit. (§ 60)

By that transaction they even tried to tarnish the lustre of Marcus
Cato. Little did they know the power of character, of integrity, of
largeness of spirit, and of manly virtue. In the fury of the storm it is
at peace; it shines amid the darkness; though dislodged from position it stays and clings in its true home; it is always radiant with its
own light and never sullied by another's filth.

If a nasty reader suspected something ironic in these compliments,
that would not be Cicero's fault. He goes on to ask why this
austere Stoic had yielded to Clodius:

cur igitur rogationi paruit? quasi vero ille non in alias quoque
leges, quas iniuste rogatas putaret, iam ante iurarit. non offert se
ille istis temeritatibus ut cum rei publicae nihil prosit, se civi rem
publicam privet. (§ 61)

Why then did he obey the bill? Why not, seeing that he has
sworn to obey other laws before now which he thought were
unjustly promulgated? He is not the man to sacrifice himself to the
reckless designs of his enemies, or where there is no national advantage involved to deprive the republic of a citizen such as himself.

The malice is so delicate that some readers fail to notice it.

The *Pro Sestio* is not only an apologia for the past but a mani-
festo about the future. No speech is more obviously a political
tract: such irrelevance could not have been tolerated even in a
Roman court. Vatinius had talked disparagingly about the
'natio' of *Optimates*: Cicero explains in his bland, insufferable way
that all men who are neither wicked nor mad are *Optimates*, even
if they are freedmen (§ 97). This kind of triviality impresses some
people, but Cicero is simply showing the naive complacency of
a *novus homo* who has adopted the prejudices of his new class. Of the
real issues of the time there is not a word, and it is a relief when
he returns to invective. Cicero could not or would not talk
seriously about politics in public: the most successful parts of the
Pro Sestio are not the pretentious essays of the political philosopher but the lively cut-and-thrust of the practising politician.

The *Pro Caelio*, also delivered in 56 B.C., is a less earnest speech, and Caelius is one of Cicero's most unconvincing clients. He was a brilliant attacking orator, it is true, and an amusing letter-writer; more important, in his year as aedile he proved a vigilant custodian of the city's aqueducts. But even among his own generation, he stood out for lack of sense; one might compare him with Cicero's enemy, P. Clodius, except that Clodius had political gifts. He was particularly difficult to defend because of his association with Catiline, but Cicero can cope even with this damaging fact. Catiline, he informs us, was an enigmatic blend of good and evil:

> quis clarioribus viris quodam tempore iucundior, quis turpiori-
> bus coniunctior? quis civis meliorum partium aliquando, quis
> taetrior hostis huic civitati? quis in voluptatibus inquinatior, quis
> in laboribus patientior? quis in rapacitate avarior, quis in largitione
> effusior? (§ 13)

> Nobody could be more agreeable to the eminent, when he wanted, nobody could be more intimate with the disreputable. No citizen has proved more loyal on occasion, no enemy of the republic more loathsome. Nobody could be more filthy in sensuality, or tougher in endurance, or more avaricious in rapacity, or more lavish in generosity.

Cicero goes on to confide in us that he himself had nearly been deceived. But the suave apologies of the *Pro Caelio* inspire no more trust than the crude invective of the *In Catilinam*.

Caelius's moral reputation seems to have been vulnerable, and for this reason his friendship with Catiline sounded particularly sinister. But there was an easy answer for all rumours: at the most dangerous period of his adolescence Caelius had been studying oratory with Cicero, and had never left his side. 'It is one thing to accuse, another to slander', we are told to our surprise. But one charge could not be evaded, Caelius's liaison with a Roman matron, the notorious Clodia (the Lesbia of Catullus). Cicero counter-attacks with his silkiest insults:

> si vidua libere, proterva petulanter, dives effuse, libidinosa
> meretricio more viveret, adulterum ego putarem si quis hanc
> paulo liberius salutasset? (§ 38)

> If a widowed woman lived unrestrictedly, a lively woman naughtily, a rich woman extravagantly, a lustful woman like a prostitute, there would be no reason for accusing somebody of adultery just because he had greeted her a little too familiarly.

In discussing the follies of the young Cicero assumes a note of civilized indulgence: it is often profitable to remind a jury that they are men of the world. The most estimable citizens have gone through a wild phase; nowadays even the Greeks have stopped preaching virtue (§ 40). If anybody is offended by Caelius's purple coat and rollicking companions, soon everything will simmer down with a change of age and time and circumstance (§ 77).

Cicero shows equal dexterity throughout the speech. He commiserates with the jury for working on a holiday, and reminds them of his own equestrian origin. His kindness to the youthful prosecutor must have been infuriating:

> sed istarum partium culpa est eorum qui te agere voluerunt; laus pudoris tui quod ea te invitum dicere videbamus, ingeni quod ornate politeque dixisti. (§ 8)

> The responsibility for your attitude rests with those who retained you. On the other hand it is a credit to your own sense of propriety that you seemed to be speaking with reluctance, and to your literary talent that you spoke with such elegance and elaboration.

When Cicero comes to the actual charges he follows a well-tried principle: concentrate on trivialities where your client is innocent, brush aside more serious matters where he might be guilty. Caelius had been accused of bribery at an election; Cicero finds it a perfect answer that he had prosecuted a rival on a similar charge. He was alleged to have beaten up a senator (§ 19); Cicero takes comfort in the reflection that only one senator could be found to support the prosecution. The murder of Dio, an ambassador from Egypt, is dismissed with sinister brevity: Caelius was free from any taint of suspicion, and some friends of Dio would speak up for him. But he analyses with superfluous detail the story that Caelius tried to murder Clodia, and depicts with urbane humour the alleged detection of the conspiracy in the public baths.

> quos quidem ego, iudices, testis non modo sine ullo timore sed etiam cum aliqua spe delectationis exspecto. praegestit animus iam videre primum lautos iuvenes mulieris beatae ac nobilis familiaris, deinde fortis viros ab imperatrice in insidiis atque in praesidio balnearum conlocatos. ex quibus requiram, quem ad modum latuerint aut ubi, alveusne ille an equus Troianus fuerit qui tot invictos viros muliebre bellum gerentes tulerit ac texerit. (§ 66-7)

I for my part, gentlemen, await these witnesses not only without any trepidation, but with some positive expectation of enjoyment. Already my heart yearns to see the elegant young gentlemen who are so well acquainted with a rich and fashionable lady, and the doughty warriors positioned by their commandress in the ambuscade and fastness of the baths. I shall demand of them first how and where they hid, whether it was the swimming-bath or a Trojan horse that carried and concealed so many unconquerable heroes waging a woman's war.

The strength of the *Pro Caelio* lies in its style. It is written for the most part in the 'medium genus'; avoiding for the most part technical argumentation and impassioned rhetoric, it beguiles the listener into sympathy and agreement. The poets are quoted freely, Ennius, Caecilius, and Terence; for instance, Cicero compares Clodia with Ennius's Medea 'animo aegro, amore saevo saucia' (' soul-sick and stricken with a savage love'). It is sometimes supposed that the number of such allusions in the speeches of the period has something to do with Cicero's studies at the time; but in fact he was interested in poetry throughout his life, and the quotations in the *Pro Caelio* are to be explained by its literary character. The humour of the speech is another mark of the style. Cicero himself discusses the laughable in his dialogue *De Oratore*. He points out the difficulty of analysing humour: certain Greeks who have discoursed on the subject have revealed nothing except their own 'insulsitas' (*De Or.* ii. 217). However he feels able to distinguish 'dicacitas', or epigrammatic verbal wit, from 'facetiae', the subtle humour that suffuses a whole passage (*Orat.* 87). It is this unanalysable charm that makes the *Pro Caelio* unique. Other speeches are more serious and more eloquent, but here Cicero shows a grace and lightness of touch that even the Greeks could not surpass.

The *Pro Milone* (52 B.C.) was regarded by some ancient critics as Cicero's masterpiece (Asconius, 36 KS). It is honoured with an unusual number of citations by Quintilian and the grammarians (always a useful clue to popularity, at least in the educational curriculum). It is easy to see why it was so highly regarded. No other speech was so well constructed, or at least no other preserved the formal divisions so distinctly: *exordium, praeiudicia, narratio, tractatio, pars extra causam, epilogus*. Parallels from Roman history are produced with unfailing efficiency: anthologies of improving anecdotes were available, and Cicero had all the material at his finger-tips. Many useful figures of speech were given a classic illustration. In the presence of such a store-house no ancient critic was going to ask questions about sincerity or sense.

Milo was being tried for the murder of P. Clodius on the Appian Way. Cicero recounts the incident superbly: it is not always remembered how good he was at telling a story. The *narratio* was written, according to custom, in a plain style: an unvarnished tale gives the air of truth.

> Milo autem cum in senatu fuisset eo die quoad senatus est dimissus, domum venit, calceos et vestimenta mutavit, paulisper, dum se uxor ut fit comparat, commoratus est, dein profectus id temporis cum iam Clodius, si quidem eo die Romam venturus erat, redire potuisset. obviam fit ei Clodius, expeditus, in equo, nulla raeda, nullis impedimentis, nullis Graecis comitibus, ut solebat, sine uxore, quod numquam fere. (§ 28)

> Milo was at the senate that day till the house rose; then he came home, changed out of his formal clothes, and waited a short time, as we all do, while his wife got ready; then he left at an hour when Clodius, if he had really been going to Rome that day, could have arrived in safety. Up comes Clodius, prepared for action, on horseback, with no coach, no luggage, none of his usual Greek friends, and what was almost unprecedented, without his wife.

The simple domestic scene is cleverly contrived to win our sympathy. The humorous touch about the time women take to get ready would raise a smile from the family men on the jury; as Terence had put it 'dum moliuntur dum conantur, annus est' (*H.T.* 240). Yet Cicero has a serious purpose: he is trying to put the murder a little later than it actually occurred, and so to suggest that Clodius had no reason for travelling. We are told that when he was pressed in court to give the time when Clodius was killed, he retorted 'sero'; the word can mean both 'late' and 'too late' (Quintilian, vi. 3, 49). However, in the published version of the speech one misses such spontaneous strokes of wit.

In spite of its air of candour the defence is a tissue of deceit. We have for the *Pro Milone* what we should like for all of Cicero's speeches, an independent statement of the facts. In the first century A.D. Asconius wrote a commentary which has survived;

he was a conscientious, though limited researcher, and as he had no literary pretensions he avoided some sorts of mistake. Asconius makes it clear that though the fight started by accident Clodius was ultimately killed on Milo's orders. Such information will be thought irrelevant by many critics to the merit of the speech; but if an orator aspires to write something more than a show-piece for the immediate occasion, seriousness and sincerity are surely necessary. In the long run the best way of persuading is to be right.

Yet it must be admitted that Cicero handles his bad case superbly. Brutus had advised him to claim that Clodius's death was advantageous to the republic: but Cicero was too good a lawyer to contemplate so impossible a defence, though he was ready enough to make the point incidentally. He preferred to rest his case on another of his sophistries: by proving that Milo had not intended to kill Clodius he suggests that Clodius intended to kill Milo. There are some direct falsehoods (in § 45 it is said that Clodius had no reason to travel), and some bad arguments ('why should Milo hate Clodius when he derives so much glory from opposing him?'). But when the prosecution tried to excite odium against Milo because Clodius had been killed on the road built by his most famous ancestor, Cicero neatly diverts the charge:

> proinde quasi Appius ille Caecus viam munierit non qua populus uteretur, sed ubi impune sui posteri latrocinarentur. (§ 17)

> Just as if the great Appius Caecus built his road not for the benefit of the public but so that his own descendants might become highwaymen there with impunity.

It was an essential accomplishment of an orator to make debating points like this.

Besides clever argumentation Cicero deploys emotional appeal. When Clodius's body was brought to the city it was burned in the senate-house by his faithful henchman, Sex. Cloelius[7]; Cicero can use even this incident to show his hatred for his dead enemy.

> tu P. Clodi cruentum cadaver eiecisti domo, tu in publicum abiecisti, tu spoliatum imaginibus exsequiis pompa laudatione, infelicissimis lignis semiustilatum, nocturnis canibus dilaniandum reliquisti. (§ 33)

> You flung out of doors Clodius's bloodstained corpse, you cast it away in the street; bereft of 'imagines', obsequies, funeral procession, funeral speech, and charred by ill-omened logs, you left it to be mangled by the dogs of the night.

The indignation of ancient orators was not always assumed, and Cicero's words bring out the ferocity of an Italian vendetta. However, there is less sincerity in his description of Milo's nobility of mind. Cicero claims that even if his client is convicted it will give him satisfaction to have manumitted his slaves (in fact, he did not want them to give evidence under torture). Cicero becomes particularly eloquent on religion, and invokes in the most extravagant terms the Alban groves and the chapel of the Bona Dea, near where Clodius had been killed. In the peroration he makes an impassioned appeal to the compassion of the jury: such is the firmness of Milo that he remains dry-eyed, but Cicero cannot refrain from tears. One may respect Cicero for his loyalty to disreputable supporters who have fallen on evil days, but one cannot take such speeches seriously. Humbug, however eloquent and ingenious, does not make great literature.

The *Pro Marcello* (46 B.C.) is badly named. It was not delivered in the courts but in the senate; the triumphant Caesar had agreed to recall Marcellus from exile, and Cicero expresses fulsome gratitude. Greek theorists regarded epideictic oratory as a separate category, distinct from speeches before judicial and deliberative assemblies; here the orator could indulge the most florid eloquence without involving himself in boring details or worrying about a final vote. In the Roman world funeral *laudationes* gave the speaker practice in platitudes: Julius Caesar won oratorical fame with a declamation on his aunt. Cicero's eulogies of Caesar in the *De Provinciis Consularibus* and of Pompey in the *Pro Balbo* show affinities with the genre; but his obituary of the great jurist Servius Sulpicius Rufus in the Ninth Philippic is a better speech because it has the ring of truth. Epideictic oratory naturally flourished in the imperial period when there was less demand for political speeches. One of the worst things that can be said about the *Pro Marcello* is that it pointed the way to Pliny's *Panegyric* and the *gratiarum actiones* of the fourth century.

But at least from the technical standpoint the *Pro Marcello* is one of Cicero's most perfect writings. The language is eloquent throughout, there are no loose ends, the rhythm and structure cannot be faulted. A short quotation may show something of its distinction:

> domuisti gentis immanitate barbaras, multitudine innumerabilis, locis infinitas, omni copiarum genere abundantis; ea tamen vicisti quae et naturam et condicionem ut vinci possent habebant; nulla est enim tanta vis quae non ferro et viribus debilitari frangique possit. animum vincere, iracundiam cohibere, victo temperare, adversarium nobilitate ingenio virtute praestantem non modo extollere iacentem sed etiam amplificare eius pristinam dignitatem, haec qui faciat, non ego eum cum summis viris comparo, sed simillimum deo iudico. (§ 8)

You have subdued nations barbaric in ferocity, innumerable in population, unlimited in territory, and affluent with multifarious resources; yet the things you have conquered had such a quality and nature that they permitted conquest, seeing that there is no power too strong to be weakened and cracked by violence and the steel. To subdue one's temper, to restrain one's indignation, to spare the defeated, to raise up a prostrate adversary preeminent in lineage, character, and manhood, and not merely to raise him up but actually to augment his former honour, the man who does this should not simply be compared with the greatest heroes but be considered equal to a god.

One can still perceive the eloquence of such passages; their effect must have been immensely greater when delivered by Cicero in person. An ancient orator was not simply a man of letters; he had some of the qualities of voice and delivery which would now be expected only in a tragic actor. Gesture was vehement: at the beginning of his career Cicero's lungs and neck were not strong enough for an orator's role, and during Caesar's dictatorship, when he had few opportunities for speaking, he complained that he was not getting enough exercise (*ad Fam*. ix, 18, 3). Quintilian in his eleventh book gives elaborate precepts for gesture as well as for the care of the voice. The ancients expected their leaders to look as well as talk like great men. So it is not surprising that a good orator could provoke laughter or tears at will. Plutarch tells a curious story of the *Pro Ligario*, which was delivered soon after the *Pro Marcello*. Caesar had not heard much of Cicero for a long time, so he jocularly said that it would do no harm to listen to him. Yet when Cicero spoke the dictator's face changed colour, his body trembled, and finally he dropped some of his papers

(Plut. *Cic.* 39, 7). Of all this histrionic epideixis only the words remain.

But the thesis of this paper is that eloquence is not enough: does the *Pro Marcello* have anything to say? Some readers regard the flattery of Caesar as both justifiable and spontaneous. This is absurd. Cicero had loathed Caesar at least since his own exile; more recently he had mourned the dead republic 'as a mother for her only son' (*ad Fam.* ix. 20, 3). Yet he represents the civil war simply as a struggle between rival leaders; he falsely claims that he joined the senatorial side only out of loyalty to Pompey. And when he suggests that the Pompeians would have used victory less well (§ 17), though the comment is fair, one regrets that he made it. The flattery of the *Pro Marcello* leaves a nasty taste in the mouth: already one is half-way to the Augustan age.

Some scholars who detect that the *Pro Marcello* is not an innocent encomium regard it as a salutary message for the times. Caesar's dictatorship was a disappointment, which had produced little useful legislation: perhaps Cicero was urging him to do something. Those who hold this view attach most weight to the second half of the speech, which looks forward to the future:

> omnia sunt excitanda tibi, C. Caesar, uni, quae iacere sentis belli ipsius impetu, quod necesse fuit, perculsa atque prostrata; constituenda iudicia, revocanda fides, comprimendae libidines, propaganda suboles, omnia quae dilapsa iam diffluxerunt severis legibus vincienda sunt. (§ 23)

> It is for you alone, Gaius Caesar, to build up everything which you see in ruins on the ground, shattered and laid low, as was inevitable, by the blind momentum of the conflict. Courts must be organized, credit reestablished, vice checked, the birth-rate raised, everything which has now collapsed and fallen apart must be pulled together by stringent legislation.

But Cicero was not a political thinker, and it is implausible to regard him as more radical than Caesar. He is simply flattering the dictator by urging him to do the things that he wants to do already. Several sources inform us that Caesar undertook a 'praefectura morum'; in the *Pro Marcello* Cicero promises his support with woolly generalizations.

But though the speech is neither sincere nor original, it is not contemptible either. One must realize Cicero's difficulties: frank talk would get nowhere. The vagueness of the *Pro Marcello* is carefully premeditated, and not due to any lack of acumen. Cicero is using all the politician's arts: to soften up by flattery, to switch on warmth, to find a formula so nebulous that it satisfies everybody, by pretending sympathy to manœuvre his opponent, by praising his clemency to make him merciful. Of course, he was not moved only by patriotism: like other men he had his own position to think of. Perhaps he might yet play an Aristotle to Caesar's Alexander, a Laelius to his Scipio. To those who have missed the highest prizes there are consolations in the hidden influence of an *éminence grise*. In the *Pro Marcello* Cicero is not predicting the principate, but fighting with all his old ardour and astuteness for constitutional government and his own *dignitas*.

The fourteen 'Philippics', delivered against Antony in 44-43, are generally regarded as Cicero's masterpiece. Here, even more than in the Catilinarians, he has something serious to talk about. Because of the Philippics he was thought of by later generations as the supreme champion of liberty. The second speech has been considered as the best of the series, both in ancient and modern times. Yet it was never actually delivered, and even if we had not been told, we could have guessed that it was not a speech at all but a pamphlet.

The Second Philippic begins with a reply to a speech of Antony's, and Cicero shows his usual ingenuity and wit in rebutting arguments. Antony taunted him with his services in 48 B.C., when he claimed to have saved Cicero's life. Cicero replies that this is the boast of highwaymen, to claim that they have given life to those whom they have not killed (§ 5). Antony read out Cicero's private letters to show that they had not always been enemies. Cicero puts on a fine show of indignation: letters are the conversations of absent friends, and the man who publishes them lacks humanity (§ 7). Antony complained that Cicero had shown pleasure at Clodius's murder. Cicero replies that amid such universal rejoicing he alone was not going to remain glum (§ 21). Antony alleged that Cicero had been responsible for Caesar's death. In an impressive run of rhetoric Cicero mentions each of the tyrannicides in turn, and asks whether they had needed any encouragement (26-7). Antony sneered at Cicero's defeatism in Pompey's camp. Cicero explains that he grieved because he foresaw the downfall of the republic (§ 37). Antony made fun of

Cicero's jokes on the same occasion.[8] Even here Cicero is not at a loss for an answer:

> erant quidem illa castra plena curae; verum tamen homines, quamvis in turbidis rebus sint, tamen si modo homines sunt, interdum animis relaxantur. quod autem idem maestitiam meam reprehendit, idem iocum, magno argumento est me in utroque fuisse moderatum. (39-40)

> That campaign was full of anxiety, it is true; all the same, even in the most confused situations, human beings, if they have any humanity, sometimes let their minds relax. And the fact that he blames me in the same breath for melancholy and jocularity is strong evidence that I was restrained in both.

Such passages are excellent of their kind, but by themselves they could not be regarded as the pinnacle of Roman eloquence. Still less the invective, which is all that some people remember.

The Second Philippic has never a dull moment, but its virtues are not altogether typical of the series. What gives the Philippics their unique quality is their energy. Here for once Cicero is consciously challenging Demosthenes. Comparisons between the two orators have been a common theme since antiquity. Pseudo-Longinus thought that Demosthenes was like a thunderbolt, Cicero like a steady blaze (12, 4). Quintilian says that nothing can be removed from Demosthenes or added to Cicero (x. 1, 106). In more modern times Rousseau described Demosthenes as an orator, but Cicero as an advocate. There is truth in all these judgements, yet they are not really applicable to Cicero's Philippics. Here at least is some of the true Demosthenic 'rapidity' and purposefulness.

It will be argued that in trying to restore the Republic Cicero was not showing the reasonableness which we require from our ideal orator. Yet the mere fact that he lost does not make his case absurd; he must not be judged from the point of view of thirty years later. Even the victors did not show superior foresight: they were opportunists who ran extravagant risks where they saw a hope of power. If one wants to see what Cicero was fighting against one has only to look at what followed in the century that ran from the proscriptions to Nero. The proem to the Georgics and the second ode of Horace's first book suggest alike that something was lost at Philippi. The world did not breathe such free air again till the eighteenth century.

At least in the peroration the second Philippic deserves all the praise it has been given:

> respice, quaeso, aliquando rem publicam, M. Antoni, quibus ortus sis, non quibuscum vivas considera. mecum, ut voles: redi cum re publica in gratiam. sed de te tu videris; ego de me ipse profitebor. defendi rem publicam adulescens, non deseram senex; contempsi Catilinae gladios, non pertimescam tuos. quin etiam corpus libenter obtulerim, si repraesentari morte mea libertas civitatis potest, ut aliquando dolor populi Romani pariat quod iam diu parturit. etenim si abhinc annos prope viginti hoc ipso in templo negavi posse mortem immaturam esse consulari, quanto verius nunc negabo seni. mihi vero, patres conscripti, iam etiam optanda mors est, perfuncto rebus eis quas adeptus sum quasque gessi. duo modo haec opto, unum ut moriens populum Romanum liberum relinquam—hoc mihi maius ab dis immortalibus dari nihil potest—; alterum ut ita cuique eveniat ut de re publica quisque mereatur. (118-19)

Remember the republic for once, Mark Antony; think of your ancestors, not of your associates. With me as you like, but make peace with the republic. But that is for you; I shall speak for myself. I fought for the republic when I was young, and in my old age I shall not desert her. I scorned Catiline's daggers, and I shall not be afraid of yours. Rather I should willingly interpose my body if by my death the liberty of the nation can be realized, and the agony of the Roman people bring its long travail to fulfilment. Nearly twenty years ago in this self-same temple I said that death could not be untimely for a consular; how then now for an old man? Why, for me, gentlemen, death is actually desirable now that I have seen all the things which I have attained and accomplished. I have only two wishes, first that at my death I may leave the Roman people free, the greatest boon which the immortal gods can grant me; secondly that each citizen may prosper as each deserves well of the republic.

In this short passage the *res publica* is mentioned four times. The idea was soon to become less popular.

Cicero was the greatest prose stylist who has ever lived, with the single exception of Plato. He had supreme intellectual gifts, especially for a public man. He devoted his vast energies to mastering the science of persuasion. He moved at the summit in an age when orators could do something. Yet most of his speeches fail to satisfy. Though both eloquent and serious, he was seldom both at once. He championed unworthy causes for short-term results in front of audiences that he despised. He turned on spurious emotion so often that it is difficult to know when he is being sincere. He used his outstanding talents to frustrate rather than to promote action. Except at the beginning and the end of his career, the moral authority of a Demosthenes or a Lincoln or a Churchill eluded him.

Yet it would be ungrateful to end with criticism. When we are tempted to disparage we should look at other ages when Cicero seemed the outstanding representative of a lost and superior civilization. In the middle of the twelfth century Wibald, abbot of Corvey on the Weser, made a collection of Cicero's writings; he wrote to the abbot of Hildesheim; 'nec . . . pati possumus quod illud nobile ingenium, illa splendida inventa, illa tanta rerum et verborum ornamenta oblivione depereant'.[9] The frontispiece of his manuscript shows three saints, Vitus, Stephen, and Justin, a cleric with the manuscript, and Cicero in the insignia of a consul. And when Poggio in the early fifteenth century recovered seven lost Ciceronian speeches he wrote a triumphant colophon on his autograph manuscript:

> has septem M. Tullii orationes, quae antea culpa temporum apud Italos deperditae erant, Poggius Florentinus, perquisitis plurimis Galliae Germaniaeque summo cum studio ac diligentia biblyothecis, cum latentes comperisset in squalore et sordibus in lucem solus extulit, ac in pristinam dignitatem decoremque restituens Latinis musis dicavit.

After all, very few ages can produce a Cicero. He may have been too devious sometimes, but at least he had a free and open mind. 'Rare is the felicity of the times,' says Tacitus, 'when you can think what you like and speak what you think.'[10]

NOTES

[1] See F. Klingner, 'Ciceros Rede für den Schauspieler Roscius', *Sitzungsb. der bayer. Akad.*, Phil.-hist. Kl., 1953, Heft 4.

[2] K. Humann and O. Puchstein, *Reisen in Kleinasien und Nordsyrien* (Berlin, 1890); E. Norden, *Die antike Kunstprosa*, 2nd edition (Leipzig and Berlin, 1909), i. 141-5.

[3] See R. G. Austin's note on Quintilian, xii. 10, 6 (Oxford, 1948).

[4] Impeachment of Warren Hastings, Esq., Speech in Reply, Ninth Day.

[5] See the edition of P. Boyancé (Budé: Paris, 1953).

[6] See Schanz-Hosius, *Röm. Literaturgeschichte* (Munich, 1914-1935), i. 453; J. Humbert, *Les Plaidoyers écrits et les plaidoiries réelles de Cicéron* (Paris, 1925).

[7] This man's name was Sex. Cloelius, not Sex. Clodius (as is generally supposed): see D. R. Shackleton Bailey, *CQ* (N.S.), x (1960), 41-2.

[8] When Pompey asked reproachfully 'Where is your son-in-law?', Cicero retorted, 'With your father-in-law' (Macrobius, *Sat.* ii. 3, 8).

[9] For this and the following quotation see my edition of *In Pisonem* (Oxford, 1961), xxiii-xxv. The picture is reproduced by A. Boeckler in *Westfälische Studien . . . Alois Bömer gewidmet* (Leipzig, 1928), p. 144.

[10] *Hist.* i. 1: 'rara temporum felicitate, ubi sentire quae velis et quae sentias dicere licet'. This quotation significantly appears on the title-page of Hume's *Treatise of Human Nature*.

IV

'Non Hominis Nomen, Sed Eloquentiae'

M. L. CLARKE

'AND SO it was not without justification that Cicero was said by his contemporaries to exercise sovereignty at the bar, while in subsequent ages the name of Cicero has come to be regarded as the name not of a man but of eloquence itself.' So wrote Quintilian.[1] Yet for more than a century after Cicero's death orators and writers generally showed no great desire to follow in his footsteps; indeed they reacted rather strongly against him. Even in his own day he was criticized by the self-styled Atticists, who thought him turgid and long-winded and cultivated an unadorned simplicity; and shortly after his death, encouraged by the rise of declamation in the rhetorical schools, a new style developed, neither Ciceronian nor Attic, characterized mainly by a striving after epigrammatic point. Cestius, one of the most popular of the Augustan declaimers, was bitterly hostile to Cicero, and his pupils, so it was said, would have preferred him to Cicero, 'if they were not afraid of being stoned'.[2] One of Cestius's contemporaries, Cassius Severus, a practising advocate rather than a rhetorician, deliberately abandoned the Ciceronian style of pleading; he was the first, according to a speaker in Tacitus's Dialogue, to despise the orderly arrangement of subject-matter, to take no account of moderation or restraint in the use of words, to brawl rather than fight.[3] In the middle of the first century after Christ the popular style was that of Seneca, with his short sentences and his epigrammatic brilliance. Seneca had no use for Cicero; convinced of his own merits as a stylist and unwilling to allow any rival influences, he discouraged his pupil Nero from reading the older orators.[4] Tacitus in his Dialogue puts into the

81

mouth of Aper the views of the modernist who rejects the older tradition of oratory. Aper argues that taste has changed with the times; audiences would no longer tolerate the style of Cicero and his contemporaries, but looked for something more brilliant; striking epigrammatic phrases and poetic colouring were now required of the orator.[5] To this we may add the testimony of Quintilian, according to whom popular opinion condemned Cicero as *durus atque ineruditus*.[6]

Oratory then had turned its back on Cicero. It is likely enough that he was not even widely read. Cestius's pupils, so it was said, read only those Ciceronian speeches to which Cestius had composed replies,[7] and this may well be no exaggeration. The reading of prose writers had small place in the Roman educational system. The *grammaticus* confined himself to poets, and the rhetorician concentrated on rhetorical theory and declamation. Quintilian tried to introduce the reading of oratorical and historical texts with selected pupils, but the experiment was a failure; students preferred to model themselves on their teachers rather than on the great masters of the past.[8] One suspects that only the unusually studious, unless they were professional rhetoricians, achieved the extensive reading advocated by Quintilian in his tenth book, and that not a few orators went straight from the schools to the courts with a very slight acquaintance with Cicero's works.[9]

Yet Cicero was not without his admirers even in this period of reaction against him. It is recorded that Livy, in a letter addressed to his son, laid down that one should read first Cicero and Demosthenes and then such writers as were closest to them.[10] The advice was presumably given to an aspiring orator, and does not necessarily reflect the experience of a historian. But it would not have been given if Livy had not studied and admired Cicero and learnt something from him. He wrote, probably early in life, dialogues and philosophical works, for which Cicero would be the obvious model,[11] and if his historical work shows obvious differences of language and style from Cicero, it is at least Ciceronian by contrast with the then fashionable Sallustian brevity.[12] Some years after Livy we find the elder Pliny moved to unwonted eloquence in praise of Cicero, whom he hails as *facundiae Latiarumque litterarum parens*,[13] and Aper in Tacitus's Dialogue is balanced by Messala the admirer of 'the ancients', that is of Cicero and his contemporaries. Quintilian, who regarded it as his mission to combat what he considered the debased style of his day, had an unbounded admiration for Cicero, and was even prepared to call him perfect, using the word in the ordinary sense.[14] 'Let us look to him,' he writes 'and set him before us as a model, and let a strong admiration for Cicero be the proof of progress.'[15] This does not mean, however, that he advocates the exclusive imitation of Cicero, or of anyone else. Indeed he expressly advises against taking him as sole model, and condemns the superficial imitators who think that they have succeeded in reproducing the Ciceronian style if only their periods are sufficiently long and end with an *esse uideatur*.[16] Throughout his chapter on imitation he is as much concerned to point out its dangers as its uses, and he ends by expressing the hope that the large number of excellent models available will result in something even better being produced in the future.[17] His own practice confirms that he was no great believer in imitation. What his speeches were like we do not know, but in the *Institutio*, where some Ciceronian imitation would have been not inappropriate, his style is very much his own.

Quintilian's pupil, the younger Pliny, shared his master's admiration for Cicero, and in some degree took him as a model. When Regulus, intending to slight Pliny, said of a certain Satrius Rufus that he did not attempt to rival Cicero but was content with the eloquence of his own age, Pliny took this as a compliment. He admitted that he tried to rival Cicero; he thought it stupid not to choose the best models for imitation.[18] But Cicero was not his only model. 'I have tried,' he says of one of his speeches, 'to imitate Demosthenes who has always been your favourite and Calvus who has lately become mine. . . . I have not however avoided the ornaments of Cicero.'[19] In another speech he tried to imitate Demosthenes's *Meidias*, and yet another, he says, was regarded as the *Ctesiphon* of his speeches.[20] The only speech of his that has survived, the *Panegyricus*, shows some Ciceronian features, though the language is that of Pliny's own day. Cicero had laid down that the oratory of praise demanded a rhythmical style, and Pliny faithfully reproduces Cicero's favourite *clausulae*.[21] Perhaps he imitates Cicero's faults rather than his virtues; a hostile critic might well apply to the *Panegyricus* the words the Atticists used of Cicero, 'too bombastic, Asiatic, redundant and excessively repetitive'.[22]

But, paradoxical though it may seem, it is Pliny's contemporary Tacitus, a writer of much greater force and originality, who provides the best example from this period of the literary influence of Cicero. When he decided to use the dialogue form for a discussion of oratory his natural model was Cicero. Like Cicero in *De Oratore* he set his dialogue in the past, recording the views of the distinguished orators of his youth; and a number of reminiscences both of *De Oratore* and of other works of Cicero show the influence exercised on him by the creator of the Roman dialogue.[23] And, what is surprising in view of the distinctive and noticeably unciceronian style of his other works, he writes here in a fairly close approximation to the style of Cicero. Yet for all its Ciceronian character the Dialogue is thoroughly original. The treatment of the theme is independent and uninfluenced by Cicero's authority, and from the literary point of view the work, with its firm characterization and its clear presentation of contrasting views, might be considered an improvement on the Ciceronian dialogues.

After Quintilian, Cicero's reputation as the great master of Latin oratory was reasonably secure. Gellius exclaims indignantly against the sacrilegious madness of those who criticize him[24]; to Fronto he is 'a man of outstanding eloquence' and 'the chief mouthpiece of the Roman tongue'.[25] Fronto does not however admire him without some reservations; while acknowledging his beauty and grandeur of style he criticizes him for not choosing his vocabulary with sufficient care and for using few unexpected words 'such as are not hunted out except with study and care and watchfulness and an extensive familiarity with old poems'.[26] For Cicero's letters, however, he expresses unreserved admiration. His pupil Marcus Aurelius asked to be sent extracts from the letters in order to improve his style, and Fronto replied that they deserved to be read in their entirety, 'for nothing could be more perfect'.[27] One of Fronto's followers, Julius Titianus, published imaginary letters attributed to famous women, in which he attempted, though with no great success, to imitate the style of Cicero.[28] The imitation of Cicero's letters is something new. When the younger Pliny recommended letter-writing as an aid to style[29] he did not suggest using Cicero as a model, and his own letters, in spite of his occasional adaptation of Ciceronian themes, do not show any noticeable stylistic imitation.[30]

Though Cicero was no longer depreciated and generally speaking maintained his reputation as a great orator and stylist until the end of the ancient world,[31] this does not mean that he was widely imitated. Latin prose writing of later antiquity tended to declamatory exaggeration and florid exuberance. A revived classicism was not to be expected of a rhetorician practising the oratory of display in declamation and panegyric, or of a Christian preacher transferring to the pulpit the manner of the declamation hall. But if Cicero as an orator was more admired than followed, Cicero as a philosopher was both read and to some extent imitated.

His philosophical works had had little influence in the two centuries or so after his death, when Stoicism was the dominant philosophy at Rome. The Stoics of the Empire were primarily moralists and preachers, and they had little of Cicero's interest in intellectual problems or of his delight in discussion and debate. But with the spread of Christianity among the educated classes of the Roman world there was a revival of interest in Cicero's philosophical works. Christianity aroused a new interest in old problems, and provided a stimulus to discussion and controversy. And what better form of propaganda to the intellectual was there than the dialogue, in which the enquiring pagan could be shown giving way to the irresistible arguments of the champion of Christianity? This was at any rate the method followed by Minucius Felix in his *Octavius*, and the obvious model for such a dialogue was Cicero. So we are not surprised to find the *Octavius* opening with words which are evidently inspired by the beginning of *De Oratore: cogitanti mihi et cum animo meo Octaui boni fidelissimi contubernalis memoriam recensenti*. . . . Minucius draws on Cicero for many of his arguments, and his urbane and liberal spirit recalls that of Cicero. He does not however attempt a close stylistic imitation; his style has been described as a fusion of two entirely different styles, the Ciceronian and the Senecan.[32]

The most Ciceronian of the Latin Christian writers is undoubtedly Lactantius. He himself expresses the wish to attain to a style of writing if not exactly that of Cicero, at any rate approximating to it, and no writer is more profuse in expressions of admiration for Cicero's eloquence[33]; Jerome called him 'a kind of river of Ciceronian eloquence',[34] and at the Renaissance Gianfrancesco Pico della Mirandola gave him the title of the Christian Cicero.[35] Though he did not use the method of exposition in dialogue the influence of Cicero's philosophical works on him was strong. One can see this, for example, in his work on the Wrath of God, where he begins with a reminiscence of the opening of the *Paradoxa*, and after the conclusion of his argument remarks: 'It remains for me to follow Cicero in ending with a peroration. As he did when discoursing on death in the *Tusculans*, so I . . .'.[36] But more remarkable than such superficial resemblances is the generally Ciceronian manner of writing, the orderly arrangement, the forceful argumentation and the stately periods. Lactantius was a rhetorician by profession, but his was not the declamatory rhetoric of later antiquity, but the more sober and dignified manner of earlier days. If he used the Ciceronian style in those declamations, practice in which, he claimed, enabled him to argue the cause of truth with greater copiousness and facility,[37] he must have been something of an exception among the rhetoricians of his day. But he was perhaps by temperament more of a student and a scholar than a rhetorician. He was well versed in classical thought and had a taste for philosophical disputation; he would hardly have been as successful as he was in reproducing Cicero's style if he had not felt a considerable degree of sympathy with the matter as well as the manner of his philosophical works.

More original than Lactantius, and therefore perhaps less classical and less Ciceronian, was St. Augustine. He had a good knowledge of Cicero's philosophical works and a particular admiration for the *Hortensius*, which influenced him so strongly in his youth; and his admission that when he first read the Scriptures he was offended by their lack of *Tulliana dignitas* shows that he had some appreciation of Ciceronian style.[38] We might therefore expect to find Ciceronian influence in the philosophical dialogues which he wrote when he gave up his chair of rhetoric and retired to Cassiciacum. But in fact such influence is not strong. It is true that he follows Cicero in beginning with dedicatory prefaces before proceeding to the actual dialogues, but unlike Cicero, who makes his characters for the most part expound their views in long speeches, he uses, though not consistently, the dialectic, or Socratic, method; nor is his style noticeably Ciceronian. If these dialogues are, as they purport to be, records of actual conversations taken down by a shorthand writer, this would sufficiently explain their character; even if there is a strong element of fiction in them, they convey an impression of impromptu discussion rather than of arranged debate. 'There is no better way,' says Augustine in the *Soliloquia* (where he conducts a discussion with himself), 'of arriving at the truth than by question and answer.'[39] He adopted the dialogue form not only because it was the traditional method of philosophical exposition, but also because it was the natural way of expressing his own search for truth.

Jerome's famous dream, in which he heard the accusing words 'Ciceronianus es, non Christianus'[40] is an indication of the hold which Cicero and all that he represented still had on men's minds in the later fourth century. It also indicates the strength of the opposition presented to the old culture by the new religion. Augustine, familiar though he was with classical culture, moved away from it as he advanced in years and became more firmly committed to Christianity. He rejected the ideals of the rhetorical schools in which he had been brought up and condemned the vanity of the cult of words and the deceits of the art of persuasion. Christians, he laid down in *De Doctrina Christina*, might go to the pagan authorities for useful learning, but only in order to contribute to the interpretation of the Scriptures; the usefulness of secular studies was small compared with that of sacred learning. Thus when St. Ambrose adapted Cicero's *De Officiis* and Augustine himself took over ideas from Cicero's rhetorical writings in the fourth book of *De Doctrina Christiana* they were not so much contributing to the future influence of Cicero as superseding him, or attempting to do so. Similarly when Augustine, again in *De Doctrina Christiana*, illustrated the various styles of writing by quotations from the Scriptures and from works of Ambrose and Cyprian, he was showing that there was now a new literature which made recourse to the old stylistic models unnecessary. Cicero was no longer wanted. If the views of the more rigorous churchmen had been consistently carried into effect, his works might have been completely forgotten. As it was, they receded into the background, a process helped by the general decay of culture resulting from the barbarian invasions.

In his well-known book *Cicero im Wandel der Jahrhunderte* Zielinski dismissed the Middle Ages, the period from St. Augustine to Petrarch, in a few pages as offering nothing relevant to his theme. He did rather less than justice to the Middle Ages. Cicero's influence in this period was small, whether on thought or on style, but he was not forgotten. He was a recognized authority on rhetoric, and some at any rate of his works, in addition to his rhetorical treatises, were read. We find isolated examples of medieval men of learning, like the humanists of the early Renaissance, seeking out manuscripts of Cicero and reading them with appreciation. One such was Lupus of Ferrières in the ninth century. His letters show him writing to ask for a copy of *De Oratore*, a work which he himself transcribed, and acquiring a copy of the Letters to compare with his own.[41] He complains of the decay of learning and the difficulties in the way of the student, and describes how he was dissatisfied with the writings of his day 'because they departed from the dignity of Cicero and the rest, which the great Christian fathers imitated'.[42] The passage shows a consciousness of the superiority of classical Latin over that of Lupus's day. It does not however suggest that he had much feeling for the distinctive qualities of Cicero's style; Cicero to him was the typical representative of a tradition which had continued into the Christian period.

In the later tenth century Gerbert of Aurillac (Pope Silvester II), another keen collector of manuscripts, described himself as 'a diligent follower of the precepts of Cicero',[43] refers to him as *Romanae eloquentiae parens*[44] and shows an acquaintance with his works, notably the speeches.[45] An *o tempora o mores* in one letter and a *quousque tandem* in another[46] testify to his knowledge of the *Catilines*, and even apart from such tags his Latin is not without a certain Ciceronian flavour.[47]

At the beginning of the twelfth century there was a revival of literary studies in the school of Chartres, under Bernard of Chartres and his successors. The pupils of this school were taught grammar and rhetoric on classical lines, and made to practise composition in prose and verse and to imitate the poets and orators, whose beauties Bernard expounded.[48] 'Orators' suggests Cicero; yet there is little sign of a cult of Ciceronian latinity springing from the school of Chartres. John of Salisbury, its most distinguished product, though he is accounted one of the best of medieval Latin writers and had a good knowledge of the classical authors, including Cicero, can hardly be described as Ciceronian in style.[49] Some degree of Ciceronian imitation can be found in a work of another twelfth-century writer, unconnected with Chartres, Ailred, abbot of Rievaulx. He tells how he read *De Amicitia* as a boy and was impressed by both its sentiments and its style; when however he grew up and entered the monastic life he was dissatisfied with Cicero's work and decided to write 'On Spiritual Friendship'. We are reminded of Ambrose's attempt to recast Cicero in *De Officiis Ministrorum*, but more of Cicero's spirit survives in Ailred's work than in Ambrose's. It may seem a far cry from the circle of Scipio and Laelius to a Cistercian house in medieval Yorkshire, but the theme of friendship brings the two societies together. Like Cicero, Ailred uses the dialogue form; he adopts many of Cicero's sentiments and not a few of his words,[50] and his Latin style, though it would not have satisfied a Renaissance humanist, is not altogether unworthy of his model.

The man who really rediscovered Cicero, however, was Petrarch. Even in boyhood, before he could understand him, he was charmed by the sound of his language.[51] Later in life he read all that he could of Cicero, including the letters to Atticus, which he found in 1345. At first he was dismayed by the picture of Cicero given in the letters, so different from the wise philosophic teacher he had imagined, but he soon recovered his feelings of admiration, and addressed Cicero as the father of Roman eloquence, an object of gratitude to all who cared for Latin style; 'for from your springs we water our meadows, we frankly acknowledge ourselves to be guided by your leadership, assisted by your support, illuminated by your light'.[52] He admired Cicero not only as a stylist, but also as a teacher of practical morality, one who, unlike the Aristotelians of his day, moved the reader and inspired him with a love of virtue.[53] But for all his admiration Petrarch did not attempt to imitate Cicero.[54] He was a Ciceronian in the sense of being an admirer of Cicero, but he had no wish to model his writing on that of Cicero or of anyone else.[55] His Latin, though clear and easy to read, is by classical standards, and by the standards of later humanism, incorrect and inelegant.[56]

It was not until the fifteenth century that any real advance was made in the direction of Ciceronianism.[57] Leonardo Bruni, papal secretary from 1405 to 1415, regarded himself as the restorer of the Latin language, and was praised by Cortesi as the man who first introduced a rhythmical style in place of the old inelegant manner of writing;[58] his younger contemporary Poggio claimed Cicero as his model in style. The same period saw the beginning of a new humanist education, based on the study of the classics, with Cicero as the main model for Latin writing. Barzizza, appointed professor of rhetoric at Padua in 1407, expounded Cicero's letters, *De Oratore*, *De Senectute*, and *De Amicitia*, and encouraged the imitation of his style; his work was continued by his pupil Vittorino da Feltre, who began to teach at Mantua in 1423. Guarino Veronese, who taught successively at Florence, Venice, Verona, and Ferrara between 1410 and 1460, began his teaching with Cicero's letters, maintaining that Cicero's style should be drunk in by the young like mother's milk. None of the men of this period however wrote a strictly Ciceronian style; unclassical words and phrases still remained even in the Latin of scholars. The work of Valla, author of the influential *Elegantiae Linguae Latinae* (1471) brought about a more accurate sense of Latin style and idiom. Valla was no Ciceronian—indeed he preferred Quintilian to Cicero—but he was a keen and discriminating student of language and did much to spread a knowledge of classical Latinity.

The flourishing period of Italian Ciceronianism was in the late fifteenth and early sixteenth centuries. Cicero was now the accepted model for orations, letter-writing and philosophical dialogue. Imitation of Cicero, however, had its critics. Politian disclaimed any desire to be an 'ape' of Cicero. Mere imitators, he said, writing to the Ciceronian Cortesi, were like parrots or magpies; their writings lacked life. ' "You do not express Cicero," someone says. 'Well, I am not Cicero; I express myself, so I think.' You should, he goes on, read Cicero and other good writers; when you have read them thoroughly, then write on your own. 'Then, according to the saying, you should swim without a cork, and be your own adviser, laying aside that over-gloomy and worried anxiety to reproduce Cicero only.'[59] Cortesi in reply claims that one must have some model; that model should be the best available, and the best is Cicero. He denies being a strict Ciceronian; he wishes to follow Cicero not like an ape, but as a son follows his father, retaining his own personality; at the same time he would rather be an ape of Cicero than a pupil or son of others.[60] Cortesi showed what he could do in the way of Ciceronian imitation in his dialogue *De Hominibus Doctis*, written about 1490 but first published in 1734. This might be described as a mixture of *De Legibus* and the *Brutus*. As Cicero had laid the scene of *De*

Legibus Book II on an island in the river Fibrenus, so Cortesi makes his dialogue take place on an island in the lake of Bolseno, and as Cicero in the *Brutus* described himself and two friends discoursing on the history of Roman oratory, so Cortesi depicts himself conversing with two friends on the history of humanism from Petrarch onwards.

The argument between Politian and Cortesi was continued by Gianfrancesco Pico della Mirandola and Pietro Bembo, papal secretary and later Cardinal. Pico in a short treatise on imitation (1512) maintained that one should imitate all good authors and not one only. Bembo replied that different styles do not mix well together and that if one tries to imitate all one succeeds in imitating none; we should take one author as model and strive to equal, indeed to surpass him. Cicero is the best model, and with his varied style and matter is well suited to all subjects.[61] Bembo, whose practice agreed with his theory, had an apt pupil in Longolius, a Fleming by birth who came to Rome and thereafter devoted all his talents to the imitation of Cicero. On Bembo's advice he made Cicero his sole model; he studied him for five years and resolved to use no word not found in his writings.[62] He published letters and orations in the style of Cicero; his Latin was elegant, but his matter trivial and unsuited to Ciceronian eloquence. According to Erasmus his letters lacked the 'simplicity and grace of unaffected language' found in Cicero, and his works were more admired than read.[63]

Italy of the early sixteenth century, the period when the cult of Cicero was most flourishing, produced the best known adaptation of Cicero in the vernacular, Castiglione's *Il Cortegiano*, which though an independent work and not a mere imitation, contains many reminiscences of Cicero and is evidently inspired by *De Oratore*.[64] As Thomas Hoby, Castiglione's English translator, put it:

> Cicero an excellent Oratour, in three bookes of an Oratour unto his brother, fashioneth such a one as never was, nor yet is like to be: Castilio, an excellent Courtier, in three bookes of a Courtier unto his deare friend, fashioneth such a one as is hard to find, and perhaps unpossible. Cicero bringeth in to dispute of an Oratour, Crassus, Scevola, Antonius, Cotta, Sulpitius, Catullus, and Cesar his brother, the noblest and chiefest Oratours in those daies. Castilio, to reason of a Courtier, the Lord Octavian

Fregoso, Sir Frideric his brother, the Lord Julian de Medecis, the Lord Cesar Gonzaga, the L. Frances comaria Delle Rovere, Count Lewis of Canossa, the Lord Gaspar Pallavisin, Bembo, Bibiena, and other most excellent Courtiers. . . . Both Cicero and Castilio professe, they folow not any certaine appointed order of precepts or rules, as is used in the instruction of youth, but call to rehearsall, matters debated in their times too and fro in the disputation of most eloquent men and excellent wittes in every worthy qualitie, the one company in the olde time assembled in Tusculane, and the other of late yeares in the new Pallace of Urbin.[65]

The cult of Cicero, as we have seen, had its critics even in Italy, but the most effective attack on it came from the north, in Erasmus's *Ciceronianus* (1528). Erasmus as a boy had preferred Seneca to Cicero, and it was not until he was twenty years old that he could bear to read Cicero for long.[66] As he grew older he came to admire him more, but he never attempted to imitate him; he preferred, he said, a style that was solider, conciser, more vigorous, less adorned and more manly.[67] His own Latin was correct, fluent and vigorous, but it was not Ciceronian. It was the Latin of a modern man of letters, well read in the classical authors, drawing his vocabulary from the whole of antiquity, but expressing his own thoughts and creating his own style.

In his *Ciceronianus* he reduces to absurdity the position of the extreme Ciceronian in the person of Nosoponus (believed at the time to be based on Longolius), who has been reading nothing but Cicero for seven years, has made an index of all his words, phrases and rhythms, and will use no form not found in his works, although, as Erasmus points out, many of his works do not survive, some attributed to him are spurious and in some the text is corrupt.[68] He mocks the superficial imitator who collects phrases and formulae, and thinks himself a Cicero if he begins with a *quanquam, etsi, animadverti, cum* or *si*. Even supposing one can represent Cicero as accurately as a consummate painter:

> where is Cicero's soul, where his copious and happy powers of invention, where his skill in arrangement, his devising of propositions, his judgment in handling arguments, his power in arousing emotion, his charm in giving pleasure, his memory so ready and so happy, his wide knowledge, where finally is that mind which still breathes in his writings, that genius which brings a peculiar and secret energy?[69]

One of the virtues of oratory, according to Cicero himself, is appropriateness, and what was appropriate in Cicero's day was not appropriate in Erasmus's. And this brings Erasmus to the argument to which he gives particular emphasis, that Ciceronianism is incompatible with Christianity. Not that he considered Cicero to be in any way anti-Christian; indeed he regarded him as one who would have been a Christian if he had lived later. But he objected to a classicism which abandoned the language of Christianity and used, or might use, such terms as Jupiter Optimus Maximus for God the Father, Apollo or Aesculapius for the Son, Diana for the Virgin Mary, and so on. 'We do not dare,' he writes, 'to profess paganism. We hide behind the name of Ciceronian.'[70]

Erasmus's view is that to express Cicero thoroughly and completely means to be unable to express oneself and is therefore undesirable. One can however be like Cicero in following his methods of acquiring eloquence and emulating his wide learning. The true Ciceronian will write clearly, fully, vigorously and in a manner appropriate to his subject and his age, and the result may be quite different from Cicero. There is a place for imitation, and Cicero should be one of the chief writers studied by the young, but the model should be emulated rather than followed, and imitation should never involve departing from one's own bent.

Erasmus's *Ciceronianus* soon provoked reactions. They came from France, which since the sack of Rome in 1527 regarded itself as the home of true eloquence.[71] In 1531 J. C. Scaliger published an oration on behalf of Cicero, and this was followed in 1535 by Dolet's *De Ciceroniana Imitatione adversus Erasmum*, and by a second oration by Scaliger in the next year. Both writers were mainly concerned to defend Cicero and attack Erasmus, and Scaliger did this with considerable violence. Erasmus declined to answer these attacks.

When the resentment aroused by Erasmus's wit had died down, a compromise was reached in what may be called a modified Ciceronianism. Ramus, better known for his innovations in logic, contributed to the debate in a *Ciceronianus* published in 1557. His theme is that the true Ciceronian should follow not only Cicero's language but also his learning and his virtues. He should like Cicero study philosophy and read Greek, and like him should be a patriot and a good man. Ramus regards the period from Terence to Cicero as the best period of Latin, but would not impose his views on others. Much that is Ciceronian can be derived from writers other than Cicero; Cicero himself had held that all good authors should be imitated. A rather stricter Ciceronianism was represented by Sturm, of Strassburg. Only the best, he held, should be imitated, and Cicero is the best; but he is not the only model, and one cannot imitate him properly without a knowledge of Demosthenes, whom he himself followed.[72] Imitate Cicero, but as he himself imitated the Greeks, is the formula of Sturm and his followers. As his English admirer Roger Ascham put it, 'I approve strongly of the imitation of Cicero. But by this I mean first in order and in importance the imitation which Cicero practised in following the Greeks. . . . For if a man is not only careful but also well versed in learning, observes with prudent judgment the footprints in which he treads, attains to or advances beyond those steps taken by Cicero himself in following the Greeks and knowingly observes in what places and by what art he emerges generally equal and often superior to the Greeks, he will arrive safely and by the right road to the imitation of Cicero himself.'[73] An even freer version of Ciceronianism was that of Gabriel Harvey, fellow of Pembroke College, Cambridge, who describes in his *Ciceronianus* (1577) how he had been converted from strict Ciceronianism of the school of Bembo. He had started by imitating Ciceronian openings such as *cogitanti mihi saepenumero* and Ciceronian clausulae such as *esse videatur*, but after reading Ramus, Sturm and others had decided that one should imitate not so much Cicero's style as his matter and his qualities of intellect and character.[74]

Meanwhile strict Ciceronianism was by no means dead in Italy, and the publication of Nizolius's *Lexicon Ciceronianum* in 1535 provided its adherents with a touchstone of correct Latinity. They were attacked by Muretus in an oration delivered at Rome in 1572. 'Today if a man has simply learnt the common precepts of rhetoric and studied Cicero's writings so far as to be able with the aid of Nizolius's Lexicon to write an oration or letter whose individual words, structure and arrangement smack of Cicero, he at once claims the title of an eloquent man, with the hearty agreement of those who can imagine nothing more lofty and sublime.'[75] In the course of his lectures Muretus used deliberately to introduce Ciceronian words omitted by Nizolius. The Ciceronians in the audience would indicate their disapproval, until they discovered that the words in question were those of Cicero, when they hastily changed from condemnation to praise.[76] Muretus's own practice was to base his Latin as far as possible on that of Terence, Cicero, and Caesar, but to use post-Ciceronian words, even down to Sidonius, where appropriate; like Erasmus he condemns the practice of substituting classical for christian terms.[77]

By the end of the sixteenth century Ciceronianism was in retreat. A new Latin style, more Senecan than Ciceronian, was popularized by Lipsius (1547-1606). He had once been a Ciceronian, but he came round to the view that all ancient writers could be followed and had a special liking for the style of the Empire. The student, he held, should begin with Cicero, then proceed to Quintilian, Curtius, Velleius, Livy, and Caesar; as an adult he would go on to Sallust, Seneca, and Tacitus.[78] He himself cultivated an extreme brevity, which in the hands of some of his followers degenerated into obscurity and affectation. The following quotation will illustrate both his views on style and his own non-Ciceronian indeed anti-Ciceronian, way of writing: 'Ciceronem amo. olim etiam imitatus sum: alius mihi sensus nunc viro. Asianae dapes non ad meum gustum, Atticae magis.'[79]

The seventeenth century was on the whole a period in which Ciceronianism was in eclipse. The Jesuit François Vavasseur in an oration delivered in 1636 spoke of the 'old style', the Ciceronian, as a thing of the past, and attacked the corrupt style of his day in words borrowed from Quintilian's attack on Seneca.[80] Facciolati in his edition of Nizolius's Lexicon, published in 1734, wrote of the spread of barbarism (*per causam libere cogitandi et loquendi*) which had led to the decline of literature and the neglect of Cicero, and with him of Nizolius, in the preceding hundred or so years.[81] In England the Ciceronian tradition was perhaps never very strong. Men learned to write Latin, at any rate in the early stages, more from phrase books and manuals of rhetoric than by imitation of particular authors, and the Latin of the phrase books was not strictly Ciceronian. Erasmus's *Copia*, which was prescribed in so many grammar schools of the Tudor period, drew on a great variety of Latin authors, and a perusal of some of the books in use in the seventeenth century suggests that schoolboys were by no means restricted to the Latin of Cicero. Thomas Drax, it is true, described his *Calliepeia* (1631) as 'a rich storehouse of proper choyce and elegant Latin words and phrases collected (for the most part) out of Tullie's works', but Hugh Lloyd's *Phrases Elegantiores* (1654) were drawn 'from Caesar's Commentaries, Cicero and others' and the *Phrases Latinae* of Hugh Robinson (tenth edition, 1684) were simply 'gathered out of the best authors'. Farnaby's *Phrases Oratoriae Elegantiores* (tenth edition 1664) offered its users a by no means Ciceronian vocabulary, including words from Plautus and the elder Pliny, and John Clarke's *Phraseologia Puerilis* (1638), following the tradition of Latin conversation books such as Erasmus's *Colloquies*, provided a very diverse vocabulary for everyday use, including Latin phrases for playing 'stoole ball', bowls, cards, and chess. William Walker in *Idiomatologia Anglo-Latina* (1670) drew on Plautus, Terence, and others in addition to Cicero and Caesar.

The influence of Ascham did not succeed in establishing a firm tradition of Ciceronianism in the English universities. Bacon, writing in 1623, after describing how Ascham and Nicholas Carr 'almost deified' Cicero and Demosthenes and allured 'all young men that were studious into that delicate and polished kind of learning', went on to say that another style, characterized by pointed words and short sentences had now come into vogue.[82] At about the same time Archbishop Abbot found that the prevailing style at Oxford was 'an affected brevity rather than the old Ciceronian oratory'.[83] Equally unciceronian was the luxuriant style, deriving from later antiquity, which was in favour in the middle of the seventeenth century. Milton attacked the clergy of his day for 'preferring the gay rankness of Apuleius, Arnobius or any modern fustianist, before the native Latinisms of Cicero'.[84] A favourable specimen of this style is provided by Isaac Barrow's Cambridge orations, copious, eloquent and witty, but recalling Apuleius rather than Cicero. In the speech which he delivered as praelector in humanity at Trinity College, where he might have been expected to hold up Cicero as the model of eloquence, he dismisses him as lacking in matter and meaning while overflowing with a copious stream of words.[85]

As the vernacular languages increased in importance and Latin declined, the problem of who should provide the model for Latin writing ceased to arouse the same interest as it had in the flourishing period of humanism. What had once engaged the attention of the educated public now became a matter of teaching technique;

and the less Latin was required in a modern context the easier it was to insist on a classical standard. Today the teaching of Latin prose composition, in this country at any rate, is generally based on the principle that one should take as one's standard the Latin of the 'best' or 'classical' period, the Latin that is of Cicero and Caesar; for Sallust and others of the same period are only to be used 'with caution'. At the same time it is recognized that there is a place for the imitation of particular authors and styles, even of a 'silver age' writer like Tacitus, where the subject suggests it and where it can be done with sufficient skill to be convincing.[86] In the orations and formal letters of the ancient universities Ciceronianism generally speaking prevails. As the former public orator of Oxford puts it, 'in structure and rhythm and often in diction Oxford orations follow the Ciceronian model, but not slavishly'.[87]

The persistence of the Ciceronian standard to the present day suggests that the Ciceronianism of the Renaissance should not be too readily dismissed as a pedantic aberration justly laughed out of court by Erasmus. It is sometimes said that the Ciceronians killed Latin by making it too difficult, that by going back to classical models and cultivating the elegances of an essentially literary style they made the language one for scholars rather than for everyday use. If there is anything in this charge it applies also to non-Ciceronian humanists like Erasmus, who were no less opposed to 'barbarous' Latin than the Ciceronians. Erasmian Latin cannot have been any easier to acquire than Ciceronian; the mastery of the *Copia* was no less exacting than the mastery of Nizolius's *Lexicon*. There was general agreement that there should be a return to classical Latin; the question was whether classical Latin should be narrowed down to a particular age or author. From the practical point of view there was much to be said for establishing a standard Latinity based on a single model, or a single period. As Melanchthon put it in 1519, 'Since at this time our Latin has to be learnt entirely from books, it is easy to see the necessity of imitation, to enable us to acquire a fixed form of speech which can be understood everywhere and in all ages. . . . So then we must choose a particular period, that in which the authors used the most correct and pure language.'[88] The ancients themselves, including their best educational authority Quintilian, pointed to the late Republic as the best period and to Cicero as the best model. Melanchthon's words suggest that the movement for restoring classical Latinity was as much the result of the rise of the vernaculars as its cause. That it accelerated the decline of Latin would be hard to prove; that it weakened its position by making it too difficult seems to be disproved by the vast output of humanist Latin writing, which suggests that so far from imposing a burden, the establishment of classical standards released creative energies and gave new life to the language.

Limitations of space, and, even more, of the writer's knowledge, preclude a full treatment of the influence of Cicero on the literatures of modern Europe; all that will be attempted here is some consideration of his influence on English literature. In the period from the sixteenth to the end of the eighteenth century, when most English writers were educated in the classics and learnt the art of writing by composition in Latin, one would certainly expect English prose to show Latin influence, and in particular the influence of the most admired of Latin prose writers. But English is different in structure and rhythm from Latin, and even those who cultivated an elegant Ciceronianism in Latin would not necessarily use the same style in English.[89] There were other Latin influences besides Cicero; Seneca was the natural model for the essayist, and the Christian fathers exercised a strong influence on preachers and religious writers. Moreover since the days when Cheke proclaimed that Demosthenes was the orator best fitted to make an Englishman a good speaker in parliament or pulpit,[90] Latin was not the only ancient literature which might help to form a writer's style. It is hard to distinguish a specifically Ciceronian from a generally classical manner of writing. We find too that certain turns of speech tend to recur in writing of the same type whatever the language. When the oratory of Abraham Lincoln or Winston Churchill, men known to have had little classical learning, recalls that of Cicero, we may ascribe the resemblance to classical influence mediated through other English writers; but it may also be that the orator of whatever age and language tends to use the same methods. It would be hard to substantiate the statement that 'English prose goes straight back to Cicero'.[91] The fact that one recent writer describes Milton as 'a convinced Ciceronian' while another classes him as non-Ciceronian[92] suggests that some caution should be exercised in making such assertions.

It would however be not unreasonable to see Ciceronian

influence in Hooker, a product of the humanist foundation of Corpus Christi College, Oxford, whose lengthy periods betray their Latin models, and perhaps in some of the more copious and rhythmical writers of the seventeenth century, though we should remember that such a style does not necessarily derive from Cicero.[93] The Restoration period brought a cult of the plain style, of what in Cicero's day would have been called Atticism. This is the period of Dryden's easy, natural prose, when in pulpit oratory the 'metaphysical' style of Donne and Andrewes gave place to the straightforward simplicity of Tillotson, and the Royal Society resolved 'to reject all the Amplifications, Digressions and Swellings of Style' and 'exacted from all their Members a close, naked, natural way of Speaking'.[94] Swift may be counted among the representatives of this movement. He has been classed as a Ciceronian,[95] but he himself would hardly have endorsed the description. He regarded Cicero as inferior to Demosthenes, and in advising a young clergyman on the art of preaching warned against any attempt at imitating the Ciceronian appeal to the emotions.[96] He is essentially Attic in style, and it was not until later in the eighteenth century, with Johnson, Burke, and Gibbon, that an ampler and more Ciceronian style came into favour.

England under the Georges, with its aristocratic society and parliamentary institutions, the England of scholarly statesmen like the Pitts, Burke, and Fox, of letter writers such as Horace Walpole, has much about it that recalls the Rome of Cicero, both in its life and in its literature. Middleton's *Life of Cicero* and the translations of the speeches by Guthrie and of the letters by Melmoth, all of which appeared about the middle of the eighteenth century, are evidence of an increased interest in Cicero. Hitherto he had been known to the general public mainly as the writer of *De Officiis* and the works on old age and on friendship; now it was possible to become acquainted with him as man and politician. We should however beware of exaggerating the extent to which his works were known at first hand. He had only a minor place in school reading; even more than in previous centuries the English grammar school of the eighteenth century concentrated on Latin and Greek poetry, and in the Eton curriculum no complete work of Cicero was included.[97] A thorough study of him would be undertaken only by those with a zeal for learning or a deliberate intention of training themselves as orators.

For the future advocate or parliamentarian classical oratory provided the obvious model. Lord Mansfield when at Oxford paid particular attention to Cicero's speeches, some of which he translated into English and back again into Latin.[98] Chatham, writing to his nephew Thomas Pitt, recommended the study of Cicero and Demosthenes. 'Arm yourself with all the variety of manner, copiousness and beauty of diction, nobleness and magnificence of ideas, of the Roman consul; and render the powers of eloquence complete by the irresistible torrent of vehement argumentation, the close and forcible reasoning, and the depth and fortitude of mind, of the Grecian statesman.'[99] William Pitt the younger was advised by his father to acquire readiness of speech by translating orally, particularly from Latin and Greek, and he faithfully carried out this programme while studying at Cambridge with his private tutor. It does not appear that Cicero had any pre-eminence in his reading; his favourite occupation was to compare opposite speeches on the same subject drawn from the historians Livy, Thucydides, and Sallust.[100] But he was clearly well acquainted with Cicero. In speaking on the peace negotiations with Napoleon in 1800 he remembered what Cicero had said of peace with Antony. 'As a sincere lover of peace I will not sacrifice it by grasping at the shadow when the reality is not substantially within my reach. cur igitur pacem nolo? quia infida est, quia periculosa, quia esse non potest.'[101] The very inaccuracy of the quotation shows his familiarity with the Philippics.

With regard to the influence of Cicero on Burke, contemporaries give different opinions. According to Sir Philip Francis, Cicero was 'the model on which he laboured to form his own character, in eloquence, in policy, in ethics and philosophy'.[102] On the other hand Dr. Johnson expressed the view that Burke had not read much of Cicero, and that he was like neither Cicero nor Demosthenes nor any one else.[103] It can at any rate be said that Burke knew one series of speeches by Cicero. His impeachment of Warren Hastings irresistibly recalls Cicero's prosecution of Verres, and he himself was conscious of the similarity. 'We have all', he says in one of the speeches against Hastings:

> in our early education, read the Verrine orations. We may read them, not merely to instruct us, as they will do, in the principles of eloquence, and to acquaint us with the manners, customs and laws of the ancient Romans. . . . We may read them from a motive which

the great author had doubtless in his view, when by publishing them he left to the world, and to the latest posterity a monument, by which it might be seen what course a great public accuser, in a great public cause, ought to pursue.... In these orations you will find almost every instance of rapacity and peculation which we charge upon Mr. Hastings.[104]

We should not take too seriously Burke's assertion that all his hearers had read the *Verrines*,[105] but that he himself had read them cannot be doubted. As neither they nor any speeches of Cicero were included in the course of reading prescribed at Trinity College Dublin when Burke was a student,[106] he must have read them on his own as part of his preparation for a career as lawyer and parliamentarian. And as there was then no English translation of the *Verrines* available (Guthrie's *Orations of Cicero* did not include them), he presumably read them in the original. But whatever the extent of Burke's knowledge of Cicero, the two orators had much in common. As Johnson put it, 'Burke has great knowledge, great fluency and great promptness of ideas, so that he can speak with great illustration on any subject which comes before him.'[107] Cicero would have recognized him as one who fulfilled his own ideal of the *doctus orator*.

The stately periods of Gibbon no doubt owe something to Cicero, whom he had studied assiduously as a young man.

I read, with application and pleasure, *all* the epistles, *all* the orations, and the most important treatises of rhetoric and philosophy; and as I read, I applauded the observation of Quintilian, that every student may judge of his own proficiency, by the satisfaction which he receives from the Roman orator. I tasted the beauties of language, I breathed the spirit of freedom, and I imbibed from his precepts and examples the public and private sense of a man.[108]

But Gibbon has also recorded how in order to acquire an English style (his first writing was in French) he read Swift and Addison, and his Scottish predecessor in history writing, Robertson. 'The perfect composition, the nervous language, the well-turned periods of Dr. Robertson, inflamed me to the ambitious hope that I might one day tread in his footsteps.'[109] Cicero was not the only master of a periodic style, nor was he the obvious model for a historian. On the other hand, to quote Gibbon himself, 'Cicero's

Epistles may in particular afford the models of every form of correspondence'.[110] When he entertained Fox in Lausanne, Gibbon remembered how Cicero had entertained a less agreeable guest. 'Our conversation', he wrote to Lord Sheffield:

> never flagged a moment; and he seemed thoroughly pleased with the place and with his company. We had little politics; though he gave me, in a few words, such a character of Pitt, as one great man should give of another his rival: much of books, from my own, on which he flattered me very pleasantly, to Homer and the *Arabian Nights*.

σπουδαῖον οὐδὲν in sermone; φιλολογὰ multa. Quid quaeris? delectatus est et libenter fuit.[111]

Cicero was not on the whole regarded with much favour in the nineteenth century, and it would be idle to look for Ciceronian influences in most of the writers of this period. But surprising though it may be, perhaps the only English writer who, by his own admission, modelled himself on Cicero and on Cicero only belongs to this age. 'As to patterns for imitation,' wrote Cardinal Newman, 'the only master of style I have ever had (which is strange considering the difference of the languages) is Cicero. I think I owe a great deal to him, and as far as I know to no one else.'[112] And in a Dublin lecture on literature he was at pains to defend Cicero against charges of pretentiousness and artificiality.

> His copious, majestic, musical flow of language, even if sometimes beyond what the subject-matter demands, is never out of keeping with the occasion or with the speaker. It is the expression of lofty sentiments in lofty sentences, the 'mens magna in corpore magno.' . . . As the exploits of Scipio or Pompey are the expression of this greatness in deed, so the language of Cicero is the expression of it in word. And, as the acts of the Roman ruler or soldier represent to us, in a manner special to themselves, the characteristic magnanimity of the lords of the earth, so do the speeches or treatises of her accomplished orator bring it home to our imaginations as no other writing could do. Neither Livy, nor Tacitus, nor Terence, nor Seneca, nor Pliny, nor Quintilian, is an adequate spokesman for the Imperial City. They write Latin; Cicero writes Roman.[113]

Much of Newman's writing may seem to the modern reader remote from Cicero, but where the matter recalls his Roman

model his style also recalls him. When he discourses on the gentleman and the educated man, the nineteenth-century counterpart
of the Ciceronian *humanus*, his sentences take on a Ciceronian
ring. The passage on university education in his Dublin lectures is
perhaps as good an example as one could wish for of the Ciceronian style, or one of Cicero's styles, in English.

It is the education which gives a man a clear conscious view of
his own opinions and judgements, a truth in developing them, an
eloquence in expressing them, and a force in urging them. It
teaches him to see things as they are, to go right to the point, to disentangle a skein of thought, to detect what is sophistical, and to dis-
card what is irrelevant. It prepares him to fill any post with credit,
and to master any subject with facility. It shows him how to accom-
modate himself to others, how to throw himself into their state
of mind, how to bring before them his own, how to influence
them, how to come to an understanding with them, how to bear
with them. He is at home in any society, he has common ground
with every class; he knows when to speak and when to be silent;
he is able to converse, he is able to listen; he can ask a question per-
tinently, and gain a lesson seasonably, when he has nothing to
impart himself; he is ever ready, yet never in the way; he is a pleasant companion, and a comrade you can depend upon; he knows
when to be serious and when to trifle, and he has a sure tact which
enables him to trifle with gracefulness and to be serious with effect.
He has the repose of a mind which lives in itself, while it lives
in the world, and which has resources for its happiness at home
when it cannot go abroad. He has a gift which serves him in
public, and supports him in retirement, without which good
fortune is but vulgar, and with which failure and disappointment
have a charm.[114]

NOTES

[1] Quintilian, x. 1, 112.
[2] Seneca, *Suas.* vii. 12, *Contr.* iii. pref. 15.
[3] Tacitus, *Dial.* 26, 5.
[4] Suetonius, *Nero*, 52.
[5] Tacitus, *Dial.* 20.
[6] Quintilian, viii. pref. 26.
[7] Seneca, *Contr.* iii. pref. 15.
[8] Quintilian, ii. 5, 1-17.

[9] Note that Fronto had scarcely touched any of the ancient authors at the age of twenty-two. Fronto, p. 23, Naber (Leipzig, 1867).

[10] Quintilian, x. 1, 39. Cf. ii. 5, 20.

[11] Seneca, *Epp.* c. 9. P. G. Walsh, *Livy, his Historical Aims and Methods* (Cambridge, 1961), p. 205, suggests that Livy's experience in writing Ciceronian dialogues was of service to him for the descriptions in his history of conferences and discussions.

[12] For the popularity of Sallust's style see Seneca, *Epp.* cxiv. 17.

[13] Pliny, *N.H.* vii. 117.

[14] Quintilian, xii. 1, 19. No orator had yet attained perfection in the strictest sense of the word.

[15] Quintilian, x. 1, 112.

[16] Quintilian, x. 2, 17-18, 25-26.

[17] *id.* 28.

[18] Pliny, *Epp.* i. 5, 11-13. Cf. iv. 8, 4.

[19] *id.* i. 2, 2-4.

[20] *id.* vii. 30, 5. vi. 33, 11.

[21] Cicero, *Orator* 210. See Durry's edition of the *Panegyricus* (Paris, 1938), pp. 40-72, for Pliny's language and style.

[22] Quintilian, xii. 10, 12.

[23] For details of these reminiscences see Gudeman's edition of the *Dialogue* (Boston, 1914), pp. lxxxvii-xciv.

[24] Gellius, xvii, 1.

[25] Fronto, pp. 184, 125, Naber.

[26] Fronto, p. 63, Naber.

[27] Fronto, p. 107, Naber.

[28] Sidonius, *Epp.* i. 1, 2.

[29] Pliny, *Epp.* vii. 9, 8.

[30] Epp. viii. 24, was no doubt suggested by *ad Q. Fr.* i. 1, ix. 1, perhaps by *ad Fam.* vii. 1.

[31] cuius linguam fere omnes mirantur, pectus non ita. Augustine, *Confessions*, iii. iv, 7.

[32] Minucius Felix, ed. Adelaide D. Simpson (New York, 1938), p. 23.

[33] Lactantius, *Div. Inst.* iii. 1. For his references to and quotations from Cicero see the index of Brandt's edition, *C.S.E.L.*, 1890-95. vol. 27. Cf. R. Pichon, *Lactance* (Paris, 1901), p. 247.

[34] Jerome, *Epp.* lviii. 10.

[35] Quoted *C.S.E.L.*, vol. 19, p. xi.

[36] Lactantius, *De Ira Dei*, 22, 1.

[37] *Div. Inst.* i. 1, 10.

[38] Augustine, *Conf.* iii. v, 9.

[39] Augustine, *Soliloquia*, ii. vii, 14.

[40] Jerome, *Epp.* xxii. 30.

[41] Lupus of Ferrières, Correspondence, ed. L. Levillain (Paris, 1927), i. p. 8, ii. p. 4. For Lupus's autograph MS. of *De Oratore* see C. H. Beeson, *Lupus of Ferrières as Scribe and Critic* (Cambridge, Mass., 1930).

[42] Correspondence, i. pp. 4-6.

[43] Gerbert, *Epp.* clviii (Havet's edition, Paris, 1889).

[44] *id.* 86. The phrase is probably a reminiscence of Macrobius's *Romanae facundiae parentes*, used of Virgil and Cicero (*Comm. Somn. Scip.* ii. v, 7), rather than of Pliny's *facundiae Latiarumque litterarum parens* quoted above.

[45] See Gerbert, *Epp.* ix and lxxxvi.

[46] *id.* xi and cv.

[47] Norden, *Die Antike Kunstprosa*, ii. p. 707.

[48] John of Salisbury, *Metalogicus*, i. 24.

[49] For John's knowledge of the classics see the introduction to Webb's edition of the *Policraticus* (Oxford, 1909). Add to his list of classical reminiscences that of Seneca, *Contr.* 1, pref. 6, in *Policraticus*, ii. p. xxii, where John writes: ille in quo Latinitas nostra solo invenit quicquid insolenti Greciae eleganter opponit aut praefert, Ciceronem loquor, Romani auctorem eloquii.

[50] See especially the praises of friendship at the beginning of Ailred's second book (Migne, *Patrologia*, vol. 195, p. 671).

[51] Petrarch, *Epp. Sen.* xv. 1.

[52] Petrarch, *Epp. Fam.* xxiv. 4.

[53] Petrarch, *De sua . . . ignorantia* (Petrarch, *Prose* (Milan-Naples, 1955), p. 724), *Invectiva contra eum qui maledixit Italiae* (*id.* p. 800).

[54] *Epp. Sen.* xv. 1.

[55] *De Sua . . . Ignorantia* (*Prose*, p. 790).

[56] Huius sermo nec est Latinus et aliquanto horridior. Cortesi, *De Hominibus Doctis Dialogus* (Florence 1734), p. 7; est ubi desideres in eo linguae Latinae peritiam et tota dictio resipit saeculi prioris horrorem. Erasmus, *Opera* (1703-6) i. 1008.

[57] In what follows I am indebted to Sabbadini, *Storia dei Ciceronianismo*; Sandys, *History of Classical Scolarship*, *Harvard Lectures on the Revival of Learning*; Norden, *Die Antike Kunstprosa*; Izora Scott, *Controversies over the the Imitation of Cicero.*

[58] Cortesi, *de Hominibus Doctis*, p. 10.

[59] Politian, *Epp.* viii. 16. Cf. i. 1, where he defends his varied style.

[60] *id.* viii, 17.

[61] Pico's treatise and Bembo's reply in Bembo, *Opere* (Venice 1729), vol. iv. Cf. the report of Bembo's views in Casa's life of him: cum nonnulli a Cicerone discedere suique plane esse vellent, cum aliter atque ille dicere studerent, quoniam is perfectus absolutusque esset, deterius dicere cogebantur. *Vitae Selectorum aliquot Virorum*, London, 1681, p. 141.

[62] Longolius, *Epp.* v. 3; *Vita Longolii* (attributed to Cardinal Pole) in *Vitae Selectorum aliquot Virorum*, pp. 242-9.

[63] Erasmus, *Opera*, i. 1016.

[64] The opening sentence, however, is a translation of the opening of the *Orator*.

[65] Castiglione, *The Book of the Courtier*, Everyman edition (London, 1956), p.3.

[66] Erasmus, *Epp.* (ed. Allen), v. p. 340.

[67] *id.* vii. p. 194.

[68] Thus we find the elegant Ciceronian Cardinal Bembo using *multissimis.* This form was then read in *ad Att.* xi. 2, 1, where the true reading is *multis meis.*

[69] Erasmus, *Opera*, i. 989.

[70] *id.* 999; cf. 998, 1026, *Epp.* (ed. Allen) vii. p. 194.

[71] See J. C. Scaliger, *Epistolae Aliquot* (Toulouse, 1620), *Epp.* iii and iv.

[72] Sturm, preface to *Ciceronis Orationes* (Strassburg, 1564); *De Imitatione Oratoria* (Strassburg, 1574), i. p. iv, ii, p. ii.

[73] *Works of Roger Ascham*, ed. Giles, 1864-65, ii. p. 180.

[74] Harvey's *Ciceronianus* has been edited and translated in University of Nebraska Studies, November 1945.

[75] Muretus, Oratio XXI, *Opera* (Leyden, 1789), p. 169.

[76] Muretus, Variae Lectiones XV, 1, *op. cit.* pp. 343-4.

[77] *id.*, p. 346.

[78] Lipsius, *Institutio Epistolica* XI, *Opera* (Antwerp, 1637), ii. p. 538.

[79] Lipsius, *Epistularum Centuriae* II, *Misc.* X, *Opera*, ii. p. 75.

[80] *Oratio pro vetere genere dicendi* in Francisci Vavassoris Opera Omnia, 1709.

[81] Nizolius, *Lexicon Ciceronianum*, ed. 1820, iii. p. v.

[82] *De Augmentis Scientiarum*, *Works*, ed. Ellis and Spedding, 1858, i. p. 452. The remarks abour Ascham and Carr are found in the earlier version written in English; those about the new style were added in the Latin version.

[83] *Register of the Visitors of the University of Oxford, 1647-8*, ed. Montagu Burrows, Camden Society Publications, 1881, p. xcvii.

[84] Milton, *Works*, Columbia edition, iii. p. 347.

[85] Barrow, *Works*, 1852, iii. p. 325.

[86] Hardie, *Latin Prose Composition* (London, 1908), pp. 1-2; T. F. Higham in *Some Oxford Compositions* (Oxford, 1949), p. xxvii. Cf. Krebs-Schmalz, *Antibarbarus der lateinische Sprache* (Basle, 1905), i. pp. 4-5, 'vorsichtiger zu gebrauchen und nachzuahmen sind *Sallustius, A. Hirtius, Cornelius, Nepos, M. Terentius Varro*'. Higham defines 'standard Latin' as the elements common to Cicero, Caesar, Nepos, Sallust, and Livy. According to Krebs-Schmalz Livy is 'nur mit grosser Vorsicht nachzuahmen'. *op. cit.*, p. 6.

[87] T. F. Higham, *Orationes Oxonienses Selectae* (Oxford, 1960), p. iv.

[88] *Corpus Reformatorum*, xiii. p. 493.

[89] Samuel Collins, an elegant Latinist, devoted to Cicero and to modern Ciceronians such as Bembo and Longolius, cultivated a plain English style. W. F. Mitchell, *English Pulpit Oratory from Andrewes to Tillotson* (London, 1932), pp. 101-2.

[90] Thomas Wilson, Dedicatory Epistle prefixed to translation of Demosthenes *Olynthiacs*, quoted in Arber's edition of Ascham's *Scholemaster* (London, 1927), p. 7.

[91] M. Grant, *Roman Literature* (Cambridge, 1954), p. 7.

[92] *id.*, p. 48; G. Highet, *The Classical Tradition* (Oxford, 1959), p. 325.

[93] The sermons of Barrow, the reading of which the elder Pitt recommended to his son, were based on St. Chrysostom. Mitchell, *op. cit.*, p. 327.

[94] Sprat, *History of the Royal Society* (London, 1722), pp. 24-5.

[95] By Highet, *Classical Tradition*, p. 327.

[96] Swift, *Letter to a Young Gentleman lately enter'd into Holy Orders*.

[97] M. L. Clarke, *Classical Education in Britain* (Cambridge, 1959), p. 51.

[98] *D.N.B. s.v.* William Murray.

[99] *Correspondence of William Pitt, Earl of Chatham* (London, 1838), i. p. 152.

[100] Stanhope, *Life of Pitt* (London, 1879), i. pp. 7, 15.

[101] William Pitt, *Orations on the French War*, Everyman Library (1906), p. 337. Cicero, *Phil.* iii. 9. Cicero wrote *quia turpis est, quia periculosa.*

[102] P. Francis, *Letter Missive to Lord Holland* (London, 1816), p. 17. Francis, however, goes on to say that Burke acted on a principle of general imitation only.

[103] Boswell's *Life of Johnson*, ed. Hill and Powell (Oxford, 1934-50), v. pp. 213-4

[104] Burke's *Works* (London, 1884-85), viii, p. 407. See H. V. Canter in *Classical Journal*, ix (1913-14), p. 199 f., for resemblances between the Verrines and Burke's speeches against Hastings.

[105] 'Many of the members of this House,' said Gladstone, when quoting Lucretius in the House of Commons, 'will recollect the majestic and noble lines. . . .' On which Morley comments: 'But few perhaps recollected their Lucretius or had ever read him.' Morley, *Life of Gladstone* (London, 1903), iii. pp. 19-20.

[106] Stubbs, *History of the University of Dublin from 1541 to 1800* (Dublin, 1889), pp. 199-200.

[107] See note 103.

[108] Gibbon, *Autobiography*, World's Classics edition (1907), p. 69.

[109] *id.*, p. 95.

[110] *id.*, p. 69.

[111] Letter to Sheffield, 4th Oct. 1788. Cicero, *ad Att.* xiii. 52, 2. The resemblance between the passages was pointed out by G. M. Young, *Gibbon* (London, 1952), p. 161. In general, however, I do not find Gibbon's letters particularly like Cicero's.

[112] J. H. Newman, *Letters and Correspondence*, ed. Anne Mozley (London, 1891), ii. p. 477.

[113] J. H. Newman, *The Idea of a University* (London 1931), p. 145.

[114] *id.* p. 101.

V

The Poems

G. B. TOWNEND

CICERO the orator, Cicero the statesman, Cicero the philosopher, Cicero the letter-writer: all these we accept as at least familiar ideas. Cicero the poet is less familiar, and, at first sight, somehow paradoxical. Yet in his own day there was evidently nothing strange about it. In the earlier period of Latin literature, from about the middle of the third century B.C. to the end of the second, poetry seems indeed to have belonged more or less to men who were virtual professionals. But by the time when Cicero was reaching manhood, men of the highest rank were beginning to try their hand at the writing of verse no less than of other forms of literature. Julius Caesar was only the first of the supreme rulers of Rome to experiment in a variety of styles. He was followed, with no very striking success, by Augustus, by Tiberius, by the short-lived Germanicus (a good number of whose lines have, exceptionally, survived), by Nero, Nerva, and Hadrian. At the beginning of the second century after Christ, the younger Pliny, justifying his own indulgence in the writing of frivolous epigrams (*Epp.* v. 3, 5-6), looks back over a long list of distinguished citizens from Sulla to Seneca who composed *versiculi*, as an elegant and harmless entertainment. More positive approval might be given to those who attempted the ambitious and serious forms of epic and tragedy, with their moral content and their power to inspire patriotic and philosophical zeal in the young Roman. And as soon as this recognition was given to poetry among the wealthier citizens, it threatened almost to rival rhetoric as a useful exercise for the aspiring young statesman. It had great advantages over the formal study of speechmaking, where the subject-matter was necessarily restricted. As Accius, the tragic and epic poet of the late second century B.C., explained: 'In poetry I can say what I like: in the courts my opponents dictate themes which do not suit me at all' (Quintilian, v. 13, 43). The attraction of verse was to draw many gifted young men away from oratory, in which they had shown considerable proficiency. Ovid, Lucan, and Juvenal are examples of success achieved in this way, however much redundant rhetoric they carried over into their verses. Silius Italicus, the ex-consul who devoted his later years under the Flavian emperors to the composition of a lengthy poem on the Punic Wars, falls into the category of those who wrote 'with greater diligence than inspiration' (Pliny, *Epp*. iii. 7, 5), and might as well have written in prose, had not Livy rendered that a hopeless task. A glance at some of the rhetorical school-exercises preserved by the elder Seneca (e.g. *Suasoriae*, iii. 1) shows what a small step it was from the fanciful conceits of imperial Latin oratory to the versified paradoxes of an Ovid or a Lucan. It is alarming to imagine how many hopeful young Romans chose the seemingly easier path of poetry in the pursuit of fame as a poet.

But this phenomenon belongs only to the closing years of the Republic and the ensuing period of the Empire. After the death of Lucilius the satirist in 103 B.C. there seems to have been a virtual vacuum in Roman poetry; although Accius, born in 170 B.C., survived long enough to converse with the young Cicero in the early eighties. We have a few odd lines of the Homeric translations of Matius and Ninnius, and of the short poems of Laevius, together with the bare names of other poets now lost entirely—none, in any case, capable of impressing following generations with their importance. In the fifties a new era was to begin with two of Rome's greatest poets, Lucretius and Catullus, the latter the best of the numerous school of *poetae novi*, whose merit was generally recognized. But for the young Cicero, in the middle eighties, well aware of the achievements of the Greek poets and anxious to make Rome rival Greece in every respect, the challenge must have been unavoidable. He accepted it as he accepted the challenge to provide Rome with speeches to rival Demosthenes, with philosophical dialogues to rival Plato, or at least to act as a substitute for him—and as he did not accept the challenge, seriously contemplated in *de Legibus* i. 5,[1] to write history to rival Thucydides—a challenge which he was to leave to Sallust. Besides exhibiting a considerable love of poetry in the quotations which occur throughout his works, Cicero explicitly tells us a good deal of the value he attached to it. In particular, his speech in defence of Archias, a very minor Greek versifier, contains an elaborate justification of his client's calling. Pleasure is perhaps the main fruit of poetry: but, in terms which the practical Roman might better appreciate, it also improved one's prose style, rendering speeches in the forum or the assembly more attractive to the hearer; it gave instruction, alluring the reader with beauties of language which prose could not rival; it gave encouragement to virtue, civic and military; and, not least important, it led a man to the goal of glory, the end and aspiration of so much Roman activity. Just how Cicero hoped to gain glory by his poetry, he was to show in more than one way—and how inadequate this was as a source of inspiration.

Of his youthful works we know very little.[2] A few lines are quoted by late Roman grammarians, who perhaps knew only odd excerpts from the poems; and half a dozen titles have survived, some quite uncertain in meaning. The 'Halcyons', of which we have two verses quoted by Nonius, sounds like an Alexandrian-type epyllion, like the *Ciris* in the Virgilian Appendix; likewise the *Glaucus Pontius* (the sea-god), in the rather unusual trochaic metre, and the 'Mourning Thalia' (if the name has been correctly restored from the manuscripts of Servius), in elegiacs. The 'Uxorious Man' may be satirical, possibly a dramatic mime; the 'Nile' may be no more than a confusion of the name of the better-attested work *Limon* or 'Meadow', a miscellany, of which the surviving four lines are a criticism of the comic poet Terence. Probably none of these survived in full after the author's death (except the *Glaucus*, known to Plutarch a century and a half later)[3]; it is certain that copies were never widely circulated. Cicero himself refers to none of them in his own prose works, and evidently chose to suppress them when Catullus and other younger men effectively surpassed them. Yet on these minor works presumably rested Cicero's early reputation, attested by Plutarch (*Cicero*, 2, 4), that he was 'the best poet in Rome as well as the best orator'. At this time (perhaps about 80 B.C., when the speech *pro Roscio Amerino* firmly established Cicero's position at the bar) this might not mean much. It was certainly encouraging to him to try greater things.

During this period, before Cicero's entry into active political life, is probably to be placed the work on which his poetical reputation must chiefly depend: the *Aratea*, a translation of a didactic poem in Greek hexameters, the *Phaenomena*, composed by Aratus at Alexandria in about 275 B.C. on the basis of an earlier prose treatise on astronomy. Cicero's was only the first translation into Latin of a considerable number, whether because of the general interest in the topic at Rome throughout the classical period or because later writers were attracted by the thought of improving on the great Cicero in a field where emulation was really possible. Next after Cicero came P. Terentius Varro Atacinus, who also translated that other Alexandrine poem, the *Argonautica* of Apollonius Rhodius, probably during the later years of Cicero's life; then Tiberius's heir Germanicus, of whose version nearly 700 lines have come down to us; the emperor Gordian I (158-238), who is alleged to have attempted to improve on all Cicero's early works including the *Aratea* (*Script. Hist. Aug.*, *Gord.* 7, 1); and the prolific poet Avienus, of the fourth century, whose translation is extant in nearly 1900 lines. But of his original version Cicero was clearly proud. He quotes it extensively in his prose works, and it is likewise quoted by Priscian and the other grammarians; and, uniquely among Cicero's poetical output, it was preserved as an independent work during the Dark Ages, 469 lines surviving in two manuscripts of the ninth and tenth centuries; so that Aratus was accessible to the Middle Ages at a time when Homer was unknown. With the fragments, we now have about 600 lines in all, as against 732 of the Greek original—though the correspondence is not exactly line by line. Cicero's translation can thus be fairly judged beside the original. It is free, certainly (as are the other surviving translations): sometimes he omits what fails to interest him, sometimes he expands matter which seems obscure; and he is guilty of an occasional misinterpretation of the Greek, which he might have avoided at a later period. Inevitably the limitations of the original determine his success. 'Aratus's subject-matter', as Quintilian justly observes, 'lacks movement, seeing that it contains no variety, no feeling, no characters, no speeches' (a great deficiency from the point of view of an orator of the Silver Age). 'Nevertheless he satisfies the purpose to which he considered himself equal.' The Greek is on the whole clear and elegant, and it has survived while Eudoxus, his prose source, has not; although Cicero himself (*de Rep.* i. 22) acknowledges that Aratus did not always understand the astronomy involved. Cicero could fairly claim to have matched his model, and could hardly expect to do more. His ability as a versifier we shall consider below. His language, despite the small suitability of the subject to oratorical treatment, is lucid and effective. If there were more interest today in the texts of Roman astronomy, Cicero's translation would earn more readers. But, as little was lost in the change from Greek to Latin, so an English translation can be entirely adequate to reproduce most of the effect of the Latin version.

There is a suggestion, however, advanced especially by Malcovati (p. 248), that Cicero has added 'a human note'. To some extent, an addition of an element of this sort appears to characterize the finest Roman poetry in comparison with Greek, and especially Lucretius and Virgil's Georgics, the closest parallels to the *Aratea*. Thus Malcovati's statement is important if it is true. And it is certainly true to a noticeable extent of the last section of the *Aratea*, known sometimes as the *Prognostica* or 'Weather-Signs', of which a number of odd passages have survived in quotations, none longer than six lines. This part of the poem appears to date from about 60 B.C., as is suggested by a reference in the first letter to Atticus (i. 1, 1), written in June of that year. Moreover, there is a clue which may be very revealing of Cicero's growing poetical gifts. Isidore, the eighth-century Spanish bishop, quotes from Cicero a translation of Aratus 948, describing what may be a nightingale, a tree-frog or some other creature, the single line (xii. 3. 37):

> et matutinos exercet acredula cantus.

In Cicero's *de Divinatione*, written about 45 B.C., his brother Quintus is made to quote from the *Aratea* no less than four lines, translating and expanding the same original:

> saepe etiam pertriste canit de pectore carmen
> et matutinis acredula vocibus instat,
> vocibus instat et assiduas iacit ore querelas,
> cum primum gelidos rores aurora remittit.

Unless it is to be supposed that Isidore, or some earlier grammarian whom he is copying, has quoted from memory and compressed the four lines into one (or that the line he gives comes

from one of the less well-known versions of the *Aratea*, such as
that of Germanicus), there is here a significant indication of two
versions of the *Prognostica*, the latter being presumably a revision
made by Cicero after an interval of fifteen years or more. This view
is argued plausibly by A. S. Pease,[4] and finds confirmation in the
stylistic arguments of Traglia (pp. 25-38), although precisely the
same considerations lead Büchner to the opposite view (1237-
1238), both on general grounds and (1265) for reasons of style.
If the arguments from style are ignored, as subjective and
based on inadequate material, the theory of two versions certainly
provides the best explanation at once of the letter to Atticus and of
Isidore's odd verse.

What follows from this hypothesis is of no small interest.
The five passages from the revised *Prognostica* are very much freer
translations than most of the earlier *Aratea*; and there is much to
be said for Malcovati's view (p. 249) that Cicero has here enriched
the rather dry texture of Aratus with elements of personal observation,[5] drawn possibly from his early years at Arpinum. At the
same time, there is an added intensity in more than one of the
extracts. This is especially clear in the repetition of 'vocibus
instat'[6] in the passage quoted above—a trick which was to become
almost commonplace in Augustan verse, but which with Cicero
is still fresh and effective.[7] Likewise in the fifth fragment, which
translates Aratus 214-215, of which a literal translation would be:

> Or rather the unhappy tribes, prey of watersnakes, the fathers
> of tadpoles, shout right from the water.

Cicero omits the rather frigid phrases 'prey of watersnakes' and
'father of tadpoles',[8] and expands in his own manner:

> vos quoque signa videtis, aquai dulcis alumnae,
> cum clamore paratis inanis fundere voces,
> absurdoque sono fontis et stagna cietis.

The frogs are addressed directly, by a common rhetorical trick;
and Malcovati claims (p. 249) with reason that the sound and
rhythm of the lines reproduce to some extent the insistent croaking
of the frogs. The passage as a whole seems to contain precisely
that element of sympathy which Aratus lacks. It is legitimate to
wonder whether this element appeared for the first time in the
second draft of this passage, as it did in the case of the *acredula*:

whether, that is, the more mature Cicero realized that he could put more of himself and of his ability to handle emotive language into what had, in his original treatment of it, been as dry and unimaginative as the extant astronomical section of the *Aratea*.

There is a further interest in the surviving extracts of the *Prognostica*, dealing with the indications of stormy weather to be drawn from waves (fr. 3), coots (fr. 4), crows (fr. 6), and cattle (fr. 7). These weather-signs are all employed by Virgil in the passage of the first Georgic which is based largely on the *Prognostica* of Aratus.[9] Virgil, of course, is not presenting simply a translation, in the sense that ties Cicero, even at his freest, to the order and pattern of the original; and he has another advantage, that of having the work of Cicero before him, as well as the Greek text. This is clear especially from lines 361-364, where he describes the behaviour of three sea-birds before the storm: the *mergus* (gull), *fulica* (coot),[10] and *ardea* (heron). Aratus (913 ff.) had described the heron, petrel, duck, and gull. The coot appears for the first time in Cicero (fr. 4), in the alternative form *fulix*. We cannot be certain, from the isolated nature of the fragment, that the other birds were not also mentioned; but a comparison of Cicero's Latin with the Greek text shows that the coot has actually taken the place of Aratus's heron (a distinctive enough bird) by deliberate substitution on Cicero's part. Virgil, respecting Aratus's observation sufficiently to restore the heron to the list, has also recognized the appositeness of Cicero's inclusion of the coot, and has combined both in a passage which inevitably surpasses either of the models.

In the following section of the first Georgic Virgil's technique was still more complex. For his lines 375-377, 379-380, 387, he had at his disposal the second Latin translation of the *Prognostica*, not necessarily covering the whole poem, by P. Varro Atacinus. His version of Aratus 942-945, 954-957, is quoted by Servius, in his commentary on the passage in Virgil—unfortunately omitting, as Virgil did, the lines discussed above concerning the frog and the *acredula*. By good fortune, however, Varro's seven lines contain his version of the description of the ox, or heifer, also translated by Cicero. This corresponds to Aratus 954-955, which goes as follows:

> And already before water from the sky oxen, gazing up to heaven, have snuffed the air.

I give the Latin versions in chronological order, together with that of the much later translation by Avienus (that of Germanicus is lost for this section):

CICERO. mollipedesque boves spectantes lumina *caeli*
naribus umiferum duxere ex aere sucum.

VARRO. et bos *suspiciens caelum*—mirabile visu—
naribus aerium *patulis* decerpsit odorem.

VIRGIL.   aut bucula *caelum*
suspiciens patulis captavit *naribus* auras.

AVIENUS. imber erit, latis cum bucula *naribus* auras
concipit.

Here Virgil, as in the other lines covered by Servius's note, has copied Varro so closely as to depart almost entirely from Cicero's version; and there is no doubt that Varro, in emphasizing the spreading nostrils of the beast, and perhaps in making it singular and so individual, has introduced that poetic element which characterizes the Georgics in comparison with Aratus. Yet Cicero was the first to introduce the idea of 'nostrils'; and his *mollipedes*, based on nothing in Aratus, is an attempt at the same sort of effect. This time, however, the compound adjective, modelled on the Homeric formations in Ennius's poems, is less successful,[11] as is the similar adjective *umiferum*. He can at least claim to have pointed the way, and provided two of the less striking words, for his more poetical successors. It is a great misfortune that we have not the whole of Cicero's and of Varro's versions of this passage, so that we could better observe the gradual transformation of the Latin into living poetry. It would appear from what we have that Varro generally made a decisive advance in the movement initiated by Cicero, and that Virgil brought the process to its climax.

The comparison of these few lines shows, however inadequately, the nature of Cicero's task as the first translator and as the first to attempt to give life to the static elegance of Aratus—a task almost as onerous as that of the unhappy Avienus, bringing up the rear and seeking to cover the same ground as his illustrious forerunners.[12] Cicero, moreover, like Avienus and perhaps like Varro, was bound to reproduce more or less what he found in Aratus, without the free play for ideas which Virgil could enjoy. Yet the *Prognostica* at least allowed him the opportunity for certain

effects, in which he seems to anticipate Virgil: the increased rich-
ness of the texture, the restrained rhetorical devices, the feeling
towards onomatopoeia, the insertion of observations from his
own experience. Little of this had been possible in the astronomical part of the work, although even there the beginnings of the
process have been divined by some critics.

There is no doubt that Cicero regarded the *Aratea* as a whole as
a creation of which he might be proud. He speaks of it as 'Aratea
mea', in a way which he does not of his other translations. These
indeed fall into a very different category. In his philosophical
works, written in the last years of his life, Cicero had occasion to
quote extensively from the Greek poets, from Homer onwards, to
illustrate his arguments. Since the conventions of formal Latin
prose excluded the quotation of more than single words of Greek,
he was obliged, by no means reluctantly,[13] to provide his own
renderings. But in these circumstances he clearly aimed at a lesser
degree of originality than even in the first version of the *Aratea*.
There is a certain elaboration, due apparently to the sheer
impossibility of reproducing the masterly economy of the Greek.
The verses, whether hexameters or tragic iambics, are thoroughly
competent, with a reasonable degree of movement and variation,
and constantly have an impressive weight which seems inherent
in the Latin language. But they are to be judged solely as translations, and rather as translations of the type normally found in
the Loeb classics than those of Dryden or Pope. Cicero was never
tempted to produce a translation of even one whole book of
Homer, to be read for its own sake, nor of a whole tragedy; and
he would not have thought of having his iambics delivered on the
stage, as Ennius's versions of the Attic dramatists had been. It
should be noticed that there is no dialogue in the extracts from
tragedy, only long speeches from Aeschylus and Sophocles and
famous *dicta*, especially from Euripides. In particular, where it
was legitimate to hope to add poetic life to Aratus, it was never
conceivable that Cicero should improve on the great masters in
this respect. As a result, the translations neither stand out from the
prose contexts in which they are set, nor do they hold up the
flow of the argument, so well adapted are they to their purpose.

If the *Aratea* provided Cicero with an immediate reputation as
a master of versification, it was not surprising that he should
seek to improve upon this by composing a major original work:

at the same time, one which would directly add to his political *gloria* by handing down to posterity an inspired account of the statesman's achievements in the criticial year 63, when Cicero the consul overthrew the conspiracy of Catiline. The three books *de Consulatu*, written in 60 B.C., seem to have been an innovation, as an autobiographical poem combining apologia (such as earlier public men had sometimes written in prose) with many traditional elements of panegyric. The manner was to a great extent that of literary epic, despite the difference of subject; and in many ways the poem anticipates such laudatory pieces as Claudian was to write about his patrons at the beginning of the fifth century[14]— with the distinction that Cicero was his own panegyrist. A work of this sort had little chance of becoming popular; and the atmosphere was particularly unpropitious at a moment when the good will gained in 63 had largely been dissipated, when Cicero had just refused to lend his support to the triumvirate of Caesar, Crassus, and Pompey, the last of whom he was liable to offend whenever he reiterated his claim to the title of saviour of the Republic—and when plans for his exile from Rome were perhaps already being prepared. If Cicero hoped that the poem would in itself secure the favour of the public, or even of the intellectuals, and restore his declining popularity, he was disappointed. It seems to have been regarded only as pompous and arrogant, and as saying nothing that the author had not already said to satiety in public speeches.

Criticism (which is the only reaction it appears to have produced) soon concentrated on two notorious verses. The former

cedant arma togae, concedat laurea laudi,

looked like a taunt openly directed at Pompey, the acknowledged military champion of Rome. The point seems to have been given additional bite by the critics' substitution of *linguae* for *laudi*[15]; and both Piso and Mark Antony, bitter enemies of Cicero, used the line to belabour him with, provoking him into pained retorts (*In Pisonem*, 74; *Philippic*, ii. 20; also *De Officiis*, i. 77). The other line,

o fortunatam natam me consule Romam,

inevitably invited criticism by its excessive assonance as well as by its pomposity (Quintilian, ix. 4, 41; Juvenal, 10, 122). Both verses were picked on for mockery in the pamphlet, *Invectiva in*

Ciceronem, attributed on very slender grounds to the historian Sallust, together with the episodes of the poet's introduction by Jupiter to the council of the gods and his instruction in the arts by Minerva—lapses from taste which Quintilian (xi. 1, 24) says his enemies never ceased to reproach him with. Yet 'cedant arma' is an effective line (hence much of its value in attacks on its author), and in context may have been relatively inoffensive. It is referred to with positive approval in a letter from Cassius (*ad Fam*. xiii. 13, 1), in the *Laus Pisonis* (36) of the time of Nero, and by the elder Pliny (*Nat. Hist*. vii. 117). 'O fortunatam', which is less easy to defend, may not even be the line that Cicero wrote. Walter Allen[16] has argued with some plausibility that *natam*, which yields questionable sense, quite apart from the jingle,[17] originally had no place in the line[18]; and that the pronoun was originally not *me* but *te*, the words being set in the mouth of one of the deities of the epic apparatus,[19] in some such form as

o fortunatam, Tulli, te consule Romam.

The embellishments would be easy enough for some such mocker as the pseudo-Sallust, and the emended form would soon oust the original, as so often happens with popular tags. The suggestion cannot be accepted without reserve, but is at least supported by the variant *linguae* for *laudi* in the other unlucky line. Whatever the truth, these are the Ciceronian verses which every Roman knew, and which set the tone for common opinion concerning his poetry as a whole. Apart from them, the grammarians preserved two or three further verses, of little interest in themselves. As a whole, the *De Consulatu* seems to have sunk from public notice almost at once.

Luckily we are saved from having to judge Cicero entirely on his two worst lines by his own pride in certain favourite passages. In a letter to Atticus (ii. 3, 4) he quotes, with some enthusiasm, three lines from a speech put into the mouth of the muse Calliope, prophesying future glory; and in *De Divinatione* (i. 17) 72 consecutive lines from a speech of Urania, informing the poet of the omens preceding the crisis of 63. We may fairly take this passage as representing the best that Cicero could write, since he himself selects it for commendation. It is unquestionably competent, with some rolling phrases worthy of Cicero the orator; but the faults are too apparent. There is a lack of vividness, so that nothing stands out as a living image; the level is monotonous, deficient in light and shade, and neither vocabulary nor phrasing is sufficiently varied. To realize how unreadable the passage ultimately is, the reader cannot do better than refer to the third speech *In Catilinam* (18-22), where Cicero expounds, for the first time and before an audience whose emotions he was deeply concerned to arouse, much the same list of portents as occupies the second half of the verse passage. In prose and with the popular assembly listening, Cicero gives the topic immediate life. His words are chosen from the fulness of his experience as a speaker, and the structure and rhythm of the paragraph actually contribute to the sense, instead of detracting from it as they do in Urania's address. Ewbank (p. 34) compares the verses to the weaker parts of Lucan. Worse than that, they resemble a Lucan without point (if that can be conceived), who not only lacked material but had not even the rhetorical ingenuity to give the appearance of meaning by sheer cleverness. Perhaps the root of the trouble here was not so much that Cicero was no poet as that he had nothing to say: that his thoughts were turned backwards to matter which he had already given utterance to all too often, so that the dominant flavour of the hymn to the glories of 63 is of stale ideas expressed in stale words.

Cicero was evidently unconscious of this weakness. At all events, some five or six years later he composed three further books of the same sort, entitled *De Temporibus*, on the theme of his exile in 58 and his triumphant recall after a year. There can have been little in these books, apart from the mythological apparatus, that had not been treated to excess in the speeches which Cicero delivered on numerous occasions on his return. At best the equal of *De Consulatu*, it has left not a vestige to posterity, unless the famous episodes concerning Jupiter and Minerva belonged to this, and not to the earlier poem. No greater fortune has attended the poems written in praise of Caesar (a panegyric which would lack even the sincerity which inspired Cicero's praises of himself), and on the subject of Britain, of which he knew nothing but what his brother could report. His letters reveal some lack of confidence in both projects; and if they were ever completed, they can hardly have been put into circulation. The attempt during these years to become a sort of poet laureate to the triumvirs was perhaps Cicero's least successful venture in the realm of literature.

The one remaining major work might be expected to have

avoided all the dangers of subject-matter incurred variously by the *Aratea*, the autobiographical poems and the panegyrics. This was the *Marius*, a semi-historical poem on Cicero's great fellow-townsman. The subject was rich enough, if the vicissitudes of a man who succeeded as a soldier and failed disastrously as a states-man could be adapted to the requirements of such a work; and at the same time it gave enough occasion, though not too much, for Cicero to feel involved in the fortunes of the first citizen of Arpinum to attain the consulate. Unfortunately our understanding of the *Marius* must depend on the date which we attribute to it. About this there is no certainty. It has been placed in Cicero's youth, when Marius was, for a short time, a dominant and respec-table public figure; in the seventies, after the death of Sulla, when Marius's faction, the *populares*, recovered some of its former position and when Cicero himself was rather inclined to follow the popular line against the great aristocrats in the senate; in the sixties, presumably in an attempt to restore Marius's reputation as a great patriot and to reconcile his followers to the optimate faction in Cicero's longed-for *concordia ordinum*; or in the late fifties or early forties, when to praise Marius was to praise Caesar, his nephew by marriage. This last consideration might be a strong argument for the late date; and it is supported by the fact that Cicero refers extensively to the *Marius* in two of his late philosophical works, the *De Legibus* (46-44) and the *De Divinatione* (44). Against this is the complete lack of reference to such a project in any of the letters written during this period[20]; and it might have been difficult for Cicero to avoid presenting an un-fortunate parallel between Marius's deplorable return from exile and his own—though an ingenious contrast might have been effective. In favour of a date in the sixties is the verse quoted in a letter to Atticus in 59 B.C. (*ad Att.* ii. 15, 3),

in montes patrios et ad incunabula nostra.

There is no certainty that the verse is by Cicero at all; and even if it is, it could belong to the *De Consulatu*, where it is placed by Morel in his edition of the fragments (no. 19). So far as the sense is concerned, a context in the *Marius*, with reference to Arpinum, would fit in excellently; and we have so few of Cicero's letters from the whole of the sixties that the lack of reference to the poem is not surprising. One other clue, a quotation in *De Legibus* from an epigram by Scaevola on the undying glory of the poem, has caused much debate on the identity of the Scaevola in question. None of the arguments is cogent enough to do more than support a conclusion reached on other grounds. Most critics agree that the style of the *Marius* is mature, but their evidence is thin.[21] Traglia, on the other hand, would place it among the early works, precisely on stylistic grounds (p. 41). It is impossible to estimate how far the quality of the fragments depends on the nature of the subject, rather than on the date of composition.

The fragments are scanty enough. A single verse, from the narrative part of the poem, is quoted by Isidore (xix. 1, 20):

tunc se fluctigero tradit mandatque paroni.

The same verse can be deciphered with difficulty on the pavement of a building in North Africa, attached to a picture of the vessel known as *paro* (*I.L.S.* 9456). It was evidently the sort of verse preserved by grammarians after the work itself had perished, precisely because it was one of the few contexts where a rare word occurred. It tells us little of the method used in relating Marius's adventures: only that Cicero was still using epic compound adjectives, and did not object to otiose synonyms. Likewise, the Venerable Bede was somehow aware (*de Orth.* vii. 292 K) that the *Marius* contained the word *torques* as a feminine noun—another reference preserved, we presume, by some earlier grammarian. Otherwise we must rely on the thirteen lines describing the omen of the eagle and snake, quoted with evident pride in *De Divinatione*, i. 106, with one other line quoted in *De Legibus*, i. 1, 1, from the same immediate context.

hic Iovis altisoni subito pinnata satelles
arboris e trunco, serpentis saucia morsu,
subrigit ipsa feris transfigens unguibus anguem
semianimum et varia graviter cervice micantem.
quem se intorquentem lanians rostroque cruentans
iam satiata animos, iam duros ulta dolores
abicit ecflantem et laceratum adfligit in unda
seque obitu a solis nitidos convertit ad ortus.
haec ubi praepetibus pinnis lapsuque volantem
conspexit Marius, divini numinis augur,
faustaque signa suae laudis reditusque notavit,
partibus intonuit caeli pater ipse sinistris.
sic aquilae clarum firmavit Iuppiter omen.

It is perhaps unlucky that here we are nearly back in the field of translation, since the omen is based on a famous passage of Homer (Iliad, xii. 200-229)—a passage, incidentally, which was also exploited by Virgil in Aeneid, xi. 751-756 and xii. 247, though this time without any reference to Cicero's version. Not surprisingly, Cicero has modelled his treatment largely on Ennius, as the master of Roman epic. Despite its dependence on models, it compares well with another portent of snake and birds given in *De Div.* ii. 63, an actual translation from Iliad, ii. 299-330; and has an element of action and vividness which places it well above the extant passage of *De Consulatu*. Cicero's reputation might well rest on this fragment, and critics are inclined to concentrate on it, while discounting the other works on account of their subject-matter. Thus Ewbank (p. 35) calls it 'a vigorous piece of work', not unjustly. Malcovati goes further: it attains 'Augustan perfection' (p. 266); it is the work of an accomplished artist, comparable with Homer's or Virgil's treatment of the same material; it is vigorous, lively, dramatic (p. 270). Traglia (p. 41) is more cautious, pointing out the clumsiness of structure, and especially the excess of present participles. It seems clear that, despite its considerable merit, the passage does not establish itself immediately on a simple reading, but requires to have its good points brought out by argument. It is open to conjecture whether the less derivative passages of the poem would have earned more or less approval.[22] The evidence of *De Consulatu* is not encouraging.

Ultimately it must be recognized, as Cicero himself did in moments of depression, simply that he lacked inspiration. He was well aware that this was a condition of real poetry, sometimes using the Greek word 'enthusiasm', in its proper sense of possession by a divinity, or referring less elaborately to 'quickening of spirit' or 'a firing of the spirit and as it were a breath of frenzy'— states which he describes in language mainly derived from Plato, and which he surely never experienced for himself. He continually distinguishes the two sides of the poet's activity, inspiration and technique, and seems never clearly to have perceived that his considerable mastery of the latter did not in any way ensure the former. His famous judgement of Lucretius[23] is very significant in this connection: 'Many brilliant passages of genius, yet much technique'. Even here he was only accepting the opinion of his

brother Quintus. One wonders how far he really recognized the
poetic genius of Lucretius, and how much it meant to him. No
other indication is to be found in the letters or in other passages of
literary criticism that he had so much as looked at the *De Rerum
Natura*, far less that he had responded to a quality that Latin
poetry had not known since Ennius. It is only fair to add that such
recognition of true creative quality was not common in Roman
criticism, which tended to concentrate either on the subject-
matter (especially its moral content) or on the use of recognized
verbal devices to obtain effects. The strong condemnations of
Cicero's own poetry which we find in the elder Seneca (*Contro-
versiae*, iii, praef.), in Martial (ii. 89, 3), in Tacitus (*Dialogus*, 21, 6),
and in Juvenal (10, 122), are probably based on the general reputation of a few unhappy lines rather than on any sensitive reading of
the poems as a whole.

Cicero's importance as a poet, then, is to be sought, if anywhere,
in the part he played in the development of Latin poetical technique. An estimate of his achievement in this field is made the more
difficult by our relative ignorance of what was written by other
poets before Cicero. We can form a fair impression of the hexameters of Ennius, at the beginning of the second century B.C.
We have Cicero's two younger contemporaries, Lucretius and
Catullus, the latter represented by a single poem in hexameters,
'The Marriage of Peleus and Thetis' (64), in some 400 verses;
some poems of similar extent from the next decade or so, attributed on uncertain evidence to the young Virgil; and the complete
works of Virgil himself, which exhibit certain changes of technique from the Eclogues, beginning in the late forties, to the
Aeneid in the twenties. For the rest, we have a few odd lines from
such writers as Accius, which indicate only how much heroic and
didactic verse from the crucial formative period has been lost to
us—the satiric hexameters of Lucilius, which might even in their
fragmentary form help to bridge the gap between Ennius and
Cicero, are written in accordance with entirely different conventions, as may be seen from a comparison between the two Augustans, Virgil and Horace.

But at least we are able to observe Cicero as a stage in a significant process of change. A number of specific features may be
dealt with in turn. Firstly, in Ennius the natural preponderance
in Latin of long syllables often produces lines in which all four

of the first four feet are spondees (that is, consist of two long syllables); while a considerable proportion have a spondee even in the normally dactylic fifth foot. Secondly, Ennius has hardly developed the regular application of the caesura-rule, whereby in the later poets a break between words in the middle of a foot, usually the third, prevents the monotonous identity of word and foot exemplified in the monstrous line attributed to Ennius by Macrobius:

spársīs / hástīs / lóngīs / cámpūs / spléndĕt ĕt / hórrĕ̄t

(*Scipio*, fr. 6W). This line also illustrates a third point: whatever was the force of the metrical ictus on the first syllable of each foot, and whatever the nature of the normal Latin word-accent, there is no doubt that the classical poets aimed at placing a word-accent on the first syllable of both the last feet of the line, while at the same time they avoided the complete coincidence of accent and ictus in the previous four feet, as in the line quoted. Ennius has hardly begun to feel the desirability of this. The ends of his lines especially reveal this, as he continually closes them with words of four, five or more syllables or with a monosyllable, any of which will spoil the coincidence of the close. The Augustan poets were to aim more and more at ending in a word of two or three syllables, which makes coincidence almost inevitable. On the other hand, Ennius often has coincidence in three or four of the first four feet: for example (Ann. 40W),

córdĕ că/péssĕrĕ; / sémĭtă / núllă pĕ̆/dēm stăbĭ/lítăt.

Here the vital fifth foot is without a word-accent on its opening syllable, and there is virtually no caesura at all. Finally, Ennius shows little refinement in the elision of final vowels or syllables ending in the weak Latin -m before an initial word in the next word, even monosyllables being elided freely.

Now in all these respects a complete revolution has taken place by the time the hexameter reaches its perfection in Virgil; although many of his lines deliberately echo Ennius for archaic effects, as in the famous

únūs / quī nò/bīs cūnc/tándō / rēstĭtŭ/ĭs rĕ̆m (*Aen.* vi 846)

with the four first feet spondaic and the ending monosyllabic. It is a complex matter to define Cicero's precise position in the development from Ennius to Virgil; and the problem becomes much more difficult when both Lucretius and Catullus are brought into the comparison. Statistics are really essential, with unusual hazards attending both their collection and their use, in a field concerned with such fragile matters as the sounds of verse. Detailed studies of Cicero's practice in various respects have been made,[24] as they have for the other poets; but the basis of the resulting statistics is seldom strictly comparable, as different scholars bring different preconceptions to the assessment. One of the few really revealing tables is to be found in Bailey's *Lucretius* (vol. i. p. 115), giving a comparison of the figures for spondaic and other unusual endings in Lucretius, Ennius, Cicero's *Aratea* and Virgil —Catullus unfortunately is not included. Certain conclusions are clear. Lucretius has markedly less of these endings than Ennius (except that the frequent use of such words as *mātĕrĭāī* and *prīncĭpĭōrŭm* in his books on atomic structure makes his proportion of pentasyllables higher than Ennius's); but Cicero has consistently about a quarter of Lucretius's proportion for each type of ending, and Virgil very many less examples again (except for the spondaic fifth foot, in which he tends deliberately to echo Ennius). The same thing seems to be true of the regularization of the caesura and of the lightening of the line by the increased number of dactyls. Ewbank (pp. 46-8) gives some enlightening figures for the favourite patterns of dactyl and spondee in the first four feet, showing a general anticipation in Cicero of Virgil's normal practice. Altogether Cicero, even in his earliest work, stands relatively close to Virgil. Lucretius, writing appreciably later, demonstrates the dangers of assuming that verse-technique advances in a straight line from one poet to another. Either because he chose to affect the archaic tone of Ennius (as his vocabulary often shows) or because he regarded contemporary refinements as effete, he is scarcely influenced by the advances already achieved by Cicero, if not before. Catullus, again, occupies a special position as a member of a school of deliberate innovators who copied the Greek Alexandrines in respect particularly of the spondaic fifth foot, 27 examples of which occur in the 391 verses of 'Peleus and Thetis', several of them involving the long names of Greek mythology which the Alexandrines had loved to introduce in the same way.

One rather superficial feature of technique perhaps illustrates the complex relationship between the poets. The early poets, Ennius and the comic playwrights alike, had regularly dropped the weak final -s after a short vowel, so as to allow the syllable to remain short before a consonant at the beginning of the next word. In the *Aratea*, but nowhere else in the extant fragments, Cicero does this seven times, as in

> sunt inter partis gelidas Aquiloni' locatae. (97)

Bailey's figures (*op. cit.* p. 124) show that Ennius had about 12 times as high an incidence of this practice. Lucretius, writing about twenty years after the *Aratea* were completed (there are no examples from the more nearly contemporary *Prognostica*), has about half as many as Cicero. After this there are no examples at all, except the single instance in the very last line of the collection of Catullus' poems, in an unusually rough epigram:

> at fixus nostris tu dabi' supplicium. (116, 8)[25]

It was certainly no part of the epic technique of the *poetae novi*. Cicero himself, writing in 46 B.C., comments (*Orator*, 161) that it used to be considered cultured to drop the -s in conversation, and so in verse, a practice which the new poets now avoid; and it sounds rather countrified.[26] Despite the small number of the fragments, it seems reasonable to conclude that in the later works he gave up this licence, thus following for once the school of Catullus. Lucretius had evidently no objection to sounding countrified or archaic, whichever impression we are to suppose the practice would give in the fifties, yet even he has a smaller proportion than Cicero's early verse. It is noticeable that we have here an illustration of a change in Cicero's taste during his poetical career; and the same thing appears in the extent to which his later works contain a marked reduction in other irregularities. As Ewbank's analysis shows (pp. 60 ff.), there are no examples later than the *Aratea* of spondaic fifth[27] or of lines ending in words of one, four, or five syllables. To observe a difference in technique between the early and late works of a poet is not to prove that the innovations are all the poet's own—an illuminating parallel can be drawn with the change in metrical technique in Propertius, where Tibullus and Ovid both point the way to the refinements of Book IV. But such evidence as there is supports the conclusion that Cicero's ear for the cadences and rhythms of words was largely responsible for some at least of these advances which the Augustans were to appropriate to their own use. Büchner, in a detailed study of the fragments of the lost poets (*loc. cit.* 1260-1266), concludes that the credit must go to Cicero himself. Traglia (pp. 159-233) gives a less statistical appreciation, and makes bolder claims on rather less objective evidence. In the absence of further epic fragments from the early first century, no greater certainty is possible.

There is still greater uncertainty over the question of vocabulary and phrase-making. Ennius had undoubtedly taken the decisive step in forming a distinctive poetic vocabulary (or perhaps two, for epic and tragedy respectively), and provided models of the way in which words could be organized within the limitations of the hexameter. Cicero certainly derives some phrases from Ennius; many others may reasonably be taken as his own creation. Now when we find a large number of phrases in Lucretius employed in just the same way as they are in Cicero, it is a fair inference that Lucretius has read his older contemporary and copied him, whether consciously or not; and this is the more likely when one considers the tradition in Lucretius's scanty biographies, that Cicero in some way corrected the *De Rerum Natura*, and the fact that the *Aratea* were an obvious model for the author of a didactic work concerned largely with cosmology.[28] H. A. J. Munro, in his edition of Lucretius (on v. 619, and vol. ii. p. 3), drew attention to some of the more important of these echoes; and Merrill gives a comprehensive list of apparently every instance of words used in similar ways by the two writers.[29] Some of these are certainly so trivial that they can safely be regarded as fortuitous, or as dependent on the natural limitations on the place certain Latin words can occupy in dactylic verse; but to regard Lucretius as entirely independent of Cicero is surely unreasonable. Such a view can only be upheld by means of another hypothesis, propounded especially by E. Norden[30]: that almost every verbal similarity shared by Cicero and Lucretius, or by Cicero and Virgil, or by all three, must be derived from an original in Ennius, even when the supposed Ennian archetype is lost. Great though Ennius' influence certainly was on the following two centuries of Latin verse, such an extreme position is very difficult to defend. If nothing else, it completely rules out the contribution of such poets as Accius and Hostius, which is even more impossible to calculate, in the dearth of fragments of their works. In fact, unless it could be shown that neither Lucretius nor Virgil had ever read any of Cicero's poetical works, it is perverse to deny him a share in the creation of the vocabulary of his successors. There is every external probability that Lucretius did read the *Aratea*, and sometimes the similarities of language are so closely involved in similarities of subject-matter as to indicate deliberate imitation. This is true especially of *Arat*. 284 ff., compared with Lucretius v. 680-695, as shown by Büchner (1242-1245, 1265-1266) and Traglia (pp. 259 ff.). Here Lucretius has manifestly referred to Cicero to see what he had to say on the subject of equinoxes, which he is himself discussing. Ennius cannot possibly have been a common model for this. And if the imitation of Cicero is certain here, the argument against imitation elsewhere in less striking respect collapses completely.[31]

In Virgil there are certainly less traces of imitation; and with a poet so widely read and so receptive of linguistic usages of all sorts, Cicero's own contribution could hardly be as great as it was in Lucretius. We have seen, however, that Cicero's words had their influence on the weather-signs in Georgic i, together with Aratus's original Greek and with Varro's later translation (influence, that is, for their exact verbal content, not merely for the subject-matter); and another clear and revealing echo is in Georgic, iii. 78,

> audet et ignoto sese committere ponti,

Somehow recalling Cicero's

> hoc cave te in pontum studeas committere mense. (*Arat*. 62)

It is an oblique echo, of which Virgil may hardly have been aware; but the use of the reflexive *committere* in the same position of the line shows how the idea of Virgil's *ponti* (to a bridge) has been suggested by Cicero's *in pontum* (to the sea). There are many examples of the same sort of indirect borrowing of phrases in Virgil, especially from Lucretius.[32] In the Eclogues there seem to be some less distinctive echoes from Cicero; in the Aeneid virtually nothing. Virgil was unlikely once more to turn to the didactic *Aratea* for that work, either on account of the subject matter or of the general level of language. Nor would he find many phrases from Cicero lingering in his mind, as did so many evocative expressions of the *De Rerum Natura*. There is no indication at all that Virgil ever read the *Marius* or *De Consulatu*; but it is quite impossible to say, on the basis of our limited knowledge of those poems.

Consequently it is difficult to estimate the importance of Cicero's contribution to the poetical vocabulary of his successors, as it is to decide how far he, as distinct from his immediate predecessors and his contemporaries, was responsible for the gradual formulation of laws for the dactylic hexameter which took place during the first century B.C. The indications are all in favour of granting him a large part in both processes, in which his authority as a prose writer will not have been insignificant. Indeed, this is probably the aspect of Cicero's genius on which criticism should concentrate: his supreme mastery of the manipulation of words on many levels, from the driest legal arguments to the richest emotive language of his great perorations, from the informal and elliptical letters to Atticus to the imaginative descriptions in the philosophical works. These last provide examples of what can fairly be judged the truest poetical language of which Cicero was ever capable. Traglia (pp. 112 ff.) quotes and analyses a passage from the *De Natura Deorum*, ii. 98, showing how Cicero could exploit the fullest resources of epic and lyrical language to convey the loftiest ideas of his imagination. This command of language could achieve almost every effect for him, and it was responsible for such success as he won in the field of poetry. But somehow or other the effort of adapting his words from the free rhythms of prose to the fixed patterns of metre seems to have taken away their force and colour. And this is probably the simplest reason for his failure: that, for all his absorption of the metrical conventions and linguistic devices of Ennius and other Latin poets, Cicero remained the master of prose, always adapting purely prosaic levels of thought to the external shape of didactic or panegyric verse. He could improve the traditional patterns, whether of metre or of language: he left it to the true poets to make these patterns serve the purposes of creative expression.

Only in one respect have we observed the beginnings of true poetic expression in Cicero: in those fragments of the *Prognostica* in which his own vision was briefly allowed to force its way through the restrictions of the translator, and to produce lines which we can recognize as belonging to the same world as some of the finest of Lucretius and Virgil. Whether Cicero was actually responsible for suggesting to Lucretius the idea of expressing his cosmology in verse, and of quickening his arguments with flashes of personal observation; whether he even suggested to Virgil the beginnings of the whole process of making animal creation the microcosm of human behaviour, which forms such a vital link between the Georgics and the Aeneid—these are questions which we could not venture to answer without much greater knowledge of Cicero's complete works and of his relationship to Lucretius, and even with that knowledge the answer would still be presumptuous. Briefly it may suffice to suggest that Cicero's importance in the field of poetry, as in that of philosophy, was not for his original contribution so much as for his ability to interpret, to indicate the ways in which the peculiar achievements of the Greek spirit might be adapted to the requirements of the Latin West.

In the end, the loss of most of the poetical works can hardly be regretted, except in so far as they would satisfy our curiosity. With only the limited fragments that have come down to us, we can safely forget about Cicero's claims to be a poet, as we have forgotten the claims of Caesar and Brutus: men who, as Tacitus remarks, 'wrote verse not better than Cicero, but more fortunately, because fewer people are aware that they did so' (*Dialogus*, 21, 6). For Cicero, poetry served the purpose only of glory: to win him yet more laurels in the world of literature and to present to posterity a picture of the great statesman which he falsely hoped would prevail even when his speeches failed to speak for him. Such motives could never succeed in producing works which would contain the essence of the writer. Where Lucretius was driven to write by his deep hatred of the empty superstitions of Italian religion and by his ever-present dread of death, and Virgil by the compelling need to reconcile the contradictions of human existence and of the cruelties of necessity, Cicero's driving-force was his vanity. We can sympathize with this side of his character here, as we do when we encounter it in his letters. But sympathy must not mislead us into believing him to have been a poet, for more than a few short moments of his life.

NOTES

[1] Atticus, one of the speakers in the dialogue, is made to say: 'People have long been expecting, or demanding, a historical work from you. For they think that if you tackled it we might come to rival Greece in this form of literature as well. . . . Therefore attempt it, I beg you'. Cicero might well have imagined a similar invitation for him to dignify Latin poetry with his contribution.

[2] Cicero's poetical works are most easily accessible in the following editions:

> E. Baehrens, *Poetae Latini Minores* (Leipzig, 1879), vol. i. 1-28 (Aratea only).
>
> C. F. W. Müller, *Ciceronis Opera* (Leipzig, 1898) vol. iv. iii, 350-404.
>
> W. Morel, *Fragmenta Poetarum Latinorum* (Leipzig, 1927), 66-78 (excluding Aratea).
>
> W. W. Ewbank, *The Poems of Cicero* (London, 1933), with introduction and commentary.
>
> V. Buescu, *Les Aratea* (Bucharest/Paris, 1941).
>
> A. Traglia, *Ciceronis Poetica Fragmenta* (Rome, 1950).

Discussions of the works of particular interest are as follows:

> K. Büchner in Pauly-Wissowa VII. A. 1. (1939), 1238-1267.
>
> E. Malcovati, *Cicerone e la Poesia* (Pavia, 1943).
>
> A. Traglia, *La Lingua di Cicerone Poeta* (Bari, 1950).
>
> B. Farrington, *Primum Graius Homo* (Cambridge, 1927).

Reference to these books in text and footnotes will be given by the author's name only.

[3] The *Glaucus* may well have been in Greek. The Greek biographer mentions none of the other works, and no Latin writer mentions this.

[4] 'Were there two versions of Cicero's *Prognostica?*', *Cl. Phil.* xii (1917), 302-304.

[5] See E. E. Sykes, *Lucretius* (Cambridge, 1936), 13-14, on the lack of human reference in Aratus, which Lucretius in his own poem avoided through metaphors, even at the cost of inconsistency with his basic scheme of a mechanistic universe.

[6] Lucretius, v. 298-299, has an apparent echo of this very epanalepsis in 'ignibus instant, instant . . .', of a constant stream of light. The purely scientific context excludes the more intense repetition of both words. For other examples, one involving two words, see C. Bailey, *Lucretii de Rerum Natura* (Oxford, 1947), i. 156.

[7] See Traglia, 232-233, for a sensitive appreciation of this fragment.

[8] In fact, he could hardly have translated the latter, for Latin has no word for tadpole. *Pace* Lewis and Short, *ranunculus*, used by Cicero in this passage of *de Div.* i. 15 in prose comment on his passage of verse, and in *ad. Fam.* vii. 18, 3 with facetious reference to the inhabitants of the Pomptine marshes, is plainly a creature capable of croaking. Pliny, *N.H.* ix. 159, is obliged to use the same Greek word that Aratus has here: 'minimas carnes nigras, quas gyrinos vocant'.

[9] Farrington, 30-32, gives an interesting comparison of the two Latin poets with the Greek original. The whole of this work should be studied for an illustration of the problems faced by Latin writers in translating from the Greek, and of their varying standards of accuracy, whether in verse or in prose.

[10] Though it may rather be a cormorant (T. F. Royds, *Beasts, Birds and Bees of Virgil* (Oxford, 1914), 38-39).

[11] Even if, as Ewbank asserts (p. 225), it means 'slow-footed'.

[12] It is noticeable how Avienus retains only those features from Virgil which were not themselves borrowed from Varro: viz. the original Virgilian contributions *bucula* and *auras*.

[13] Plutarch, *Cicero*, 40, 3, refers to Cicero's composition of verse, in his retirement under Caesar's dictatorship, for amusement (παίζων) and with great fluency, to the extent of 500 verses in a night. No work of this length, or anything like it, can be identified as written at this period. Perhaps an argument for a late dating of the *Marius*?

[14] Did Cicero even provide the first example of the mythological panegyric? His credit for it would not be considerable.

[15] Both variants are found in the MSS.: *laudi* is attested for Cicero's own speech *In Pisonem* 74 (where see Nisbet's note) and in most MSS. of *de Officiis* i. 77; *linguae* in the later quotations. Baehrens judged that Cicero substituted *laudi* for his own original *linguae*. He could have done the opposite, to avoid the excessive assonance of *laurea laudi*. Traglia (231-232) argues strongly for *laudi* as Cicero's, *linguae* as parody.

[16] 'O fortunatam natam. . .', in *TAPA* lxxxvii (1956), 130 ff., following G. Pascoli in *Epos*[5] (1938), 68 ff.

[17] Not necessarily displeasing to Cicero. Traglia (230) regards the repetition as deliberate.

[18] It is not found in some of the best MSS. of the first known quotation, in Pseudo-Sallust 5, nor of the reply in Pseudo-Cicero 7. Other MSS. could well have been emended to accord with the familiar line of Juvenal.

[19] At all events the poem was not written in the first person. The phrase *te consule* is certainly used in this way by Virgil in *Ecl.* 4, 11; and Horace appears to echo the line as a whole in *Epp.* ii. 1, 256, 'et formidatam Parthis te principe Romam' (cf. M. T. Tatham, 'An echo of Cicero in Horace', *CR.* xxxix (1925), 71).

[20] It is difficult to see how the topic could have suffered from the sort of censorship of the correspondence which J. Carcopino supposes to have been responsible for so many large gaps in the series of letters, in the interests of Caesar's heir Octavian (*Secrets de la Correspondance de Ciceron* (Paris, 1947), 436 ff.).

[21] See the general discussion of all the arguments in Büchner, 1254-1255.

[22] Unless they were composed 500 lines at a sitting (cf. n. 13).

[23] 'Lucreti poemata, ut scribis, ita sunt: multis luminibus ingenii, multae tamen artis' (*ad Q. Fratrem*, ii. 10, 3). The antithesis has seemed odd to many scholars, who have arbitrarily inserted a *non* before one or other element. But the distinction is familiar in Roman literary criticism, as most clearly in Quint. x. 1, 40, on the early Latin poets.

[24] T. Peck, 'Cicero's Hexameters', *TAPA* xxviii (1897), 60-70; W. A. Merrill, 'The Metrical Technique of Lucretius and Cicero', *Calif. Publ. in Cl. Phil.* vii (1924), 293-306; Büchner, 1260-1266; Ewbank, 40-71.

[25] This is also the only example in any poet of this period of the licence applied to a verbal ending.

[26] Almost 'provincial', as we might say. The contrast of *urbanus* (in the sense of 'cultured, refined') and *rusticus* appears to depend largely on habits of pronunciation and vocabulary which prevailed in country districts where Sabine or similar dialects were spoken before Latin became dominant.

[27] This feature, common in earlier hexameters, is the subject of a joke in *ad Att.* vii. 2, 1, where Cicero presents the *poetae novi* with a line of this type which he has just composed. The spondaic fifth foot is a marked feature of Catullus 64. Elsewhere Cicero has only one example, *Orionis* (*Phaen.* 3), which occurs in the same way in the pseudo-Virgilian *Ciris* 535, in *Aen.* iii. 517, and in Hor. *Od.* i. 28, 21, perhaps all copied from some earlier model.

[28] Bailey, *op. cit.* 146-152, discusses the development by Cicero of alliteration and assonance, and says: 'It is not improbable that it was Cicero's example which suggested to him (Lucretius) the lines of his own use of these ornaments.' We simply cannot tell who else may have experimented in the same direction before Cicero.

[29] Merrill remarkably concluded, in the face of his own collection of the evidence ('Lucretius and Cicero's Verse', *Calif. Publ. in Cl. Phil.* v (1921), 144, ff.), that Lucretius was in no way influenced by Cicero; even that he had never read the *Aratea*, nor Cicero the *de Rerum Natura*. This view has hardly convinced anyone, except Spaeth, in 'Cicero, Model for Lucretius?', *Cl. J.* xlii (1946-7), 105-106, a palinode (which he does not acknowledge to be such) to a more conventional paper (*ib.* xxvi (1930-1), 502-505). The case for Lucretius's dependence on Cicero is argued convincingly by W. B. Sedgwick, 'Lucretius and Cicero's verse', *CR* xxxvii (1923), 115-116, and by Traglia, 'Sulla Formazione spirituale di Lucrezio' (Rome, 1948), 90 ff.

[30] *Aeneis Buch VI*[3] (Leipzig/Berlin, 1926), 309 ff.

[31] Lucretius may also have read and imitated the *de Consulatu* (Büchner, 1249-1250, Malcovati, 259-260); but the imitations might possibly be the other way round. In any case, the alleged borrowings from this work are hardly cogent.

[32] E.g. the echo of Lucr. v. 267, 'radiisque retexens aetherius sol', in *Aen.* iv. 119, v. 65 (both of the sun), 'radiisque retexerit orbem', the verb in these passages being derived from *retego* (uncover), but recalling Lucretius' *retexo* (unweave). For a discussion, see W. F. J. Knight, *Roman Vergil* (London, 1953), 89.

VI

Cicero the Philosopher

A. E. DOUGLAS

WE have more first-hand information about the composition of Cicero's philosophical works than about any other ancient writings of comparable scale and importance. Not only do Cicero's letters provide much vivid detail about his plans, methods, and progress and the actual processes of publication: it was also his habit to provide each work, and often each book of a work, with a preface which served both as a dedication and as an explanation and, if necessary, justification of his scope and purpose. Particularly valuable for the present survey is the preface to the second book of *De Divinatione*, of which the text is given as an appendix to this chapter. In it Cicero, after repeating earlier expositions of his aims and methods, looked back at what he had achieved in both the periods of his mature life which he had devoted to theoretical or reflective writing. He looked back, that is, as far as *De Oratore* and *De Re Publica* of 55-52 B.C. He also mentioned the projected *De Fato*, but among works now extant, *De Amicitia* and *De Officiis* were evidently not yet contemplated, and they are absent from the list.[1] Noting the need for these additions, we turn to consider the information given in this preface.

At its beginning and again at its end (§§ 1, 6-7), Cicero indicates that he had been led to write these works through his determination 'to help his fellow-citizens' and 'never to stop seeking the good of the community'. In the latter passage he states that he was deliberately seeking relief from the political troubles of the time and an outlet for his energy at this time of enforced political inactivity. We know from the letters that he read and wrote feverishly at this time also in an attempt to console and relieve his mind after the shock of his daughter's death. But though he alludes to it in general terms in another preface (*Nat. D.* i. 9) he does not dwell on this personal sorrow and motive: he encourages us to see primarily in his philosophical writings a continuation by other means, as it were, of his political and public career. To agree with this assessment is not by any means to say, as some have suggested, that Cicero's philosophical works are *merely* a reflection of his political and personal disappointments in the two periods of his life when they were written. It is, however, to say—and the fact is important for the understanding both of the works and of their long influence on European thought—that, some parts of the *Academica* and the *De Fato* excepted (and these as we shall see have the least to offer for the understanding of Cicero's own outlook), these works do not attempt, and therefore should not be expected, to make the same kind of appeal as, for instance, the epistemological and metaphysical speculations that were fashionable in the last century, and are what many people still suppose philosophy to be primarily about. These writings deal with the kind of philosophy which concerns man as a political and social being. We shall repeatedly see that their value depends not on their speculative quality—they have little—nor their originality—for the later group of works at least Cicero claimed none, conceiving his task to be the presentation of the relevant parts of Greek thought to Roman readers—but on the fact that they explore the particular issues and arguments that seemed important, and propose an ordering of personal and social living that commended itself to a man of great personal sensitivity and much experience of affairs.

Hence it has always been as practical guides to the good life that Cicero's philosophical works have had their main influence, except in special circumstances, as when early Christian writers availed themselves of the information he gives on Roman religion. But here something must be said about the prevalent view that the Roman writer and his Hellenistic sources were sharply distinguished from their great precursors of Classical Greece, Plato and Aristotle, by an exclusive concentration on ethics and the practical life, and were self-evidently much the worse for it. The answer is twofold: first the alleged distinction did not exist; secondly, even if it did, the conclusion is based on a presumption about the inferior status of ethics as a branch of philosophy which is not axiomatic. But first the facts.

The Hellenistic Greeks and Cicero devoted much attention to theory of knowledge and theology, and the Stoics, though not Cicero, were deeply concerned with problems of logic. But it is much more to the point that the philosophy of Plato and Aristotle is much less dominated by metaphysics than is conventionally supposed. The historical origins of the illusion about this are easy to trace. The thirteenth century needed Aristotle's metaphysics for theological reasons, and the nineteenth century was another age of lively metaphysical speculation which concentrated on those aspects of Plato and Aristotle which were more relevant to its own interests. But Aristotle was interested in everything, while Plato's metaphysics arises from his concern about the problem he had inherited from Socrates, the problem of establishing a rational basis for morality; indeed his abiding appeal lies surely not in the details of his teaching, so often manifestly wrong-headed, but in the way that everything springs from a consuming concern for goodness. Hence Cicero's claim (*Acad. post.* 3) 'philosophiam veterem illam *a Socrate ortam* Latinis litteris inlustrare'—and by this he explains that he means (*a*) a sceptical method of enquiry, and (*b*) emphasis on *ethics*—is not ill-founded, even though his actual sources were of Hellenistic date and largely ethical in content. The truth is that the almost obsessive quest for the *beata vita*, the good life for the human being, and the concern for the place therein of *virtus*, moral goodness, which is the leading thread in Cicero's ethical writings, is not the result of a peculiar cast of the Hellenistic mind nor of the Roman 'instinct for the practical'. It is Plato's question (see *Rep.* i. fin. and ii. init.; the whole of the rest of that work is an attempt to answer it).

There is of course a difference, but not where it is customarily looked for. The Hellenistic contribution, apart from much acute detailed clarification of the issues, was to sever the unusually close ties between individual and society which reflect in classical Greek thinking the realities of life in the classical Greek *polis*, but do not have universal application. If, as has often been observed, the break-up of the classical system of internally close-knit independent 'city-states' left the individual often bewildered and rudderless, at the same time it conferred certain new responsibilities and forms of ethical status. The frontiers are wider—and more like our own. For man confronts the universe not as a citizen but as an individual. The emphasis moves away from the problems of 'wronging' and 'being wronged' so prominent in Plato[2] to the problem of facing pain, bereavement, and death. Significantly, the notion of 'free will' becomes for the first time a problem.

Nor did Roman 'practicality' distort philosophy from its true end. The Roman came as a pupil, as a self-confessed cultural and intellectual inferior of the Greek. But the pupil by his demands may shape his instructors' thought, and both in the Scipionic Circle and in Cicero himself such a shaping, which is not a distortion, is taking place. Thus it was a modified Stoicism, stripped of its more extreme and paradoxical tenets, which appealed most to the Roman outlook. If philosophy were or could be mere ratiocination in the void, such abandonment of intellectual rigour would properly be found shocking. But to philosophy, as to anything else, a man brings his experience, and the enlightened Roman was within his rights in requiring of his Greek teachers a philosophy which made sense of his own and his country's experience. The kind of philosophy which is mere intellectual skylarking he evaluated as it deserved, as no fit pursuit for grown and responsible men.[3] Much of what follows will illustrate and expand these points, as we return to more particular considerations, and apply in detail the points which have just been made in general terms.

How did Cicero in detail approach the task of presenting Greek philosophy to Roman readers? In a letter to Atticus (ad Att. xii. 52, 3) Cicero wrote the following: ''Ἀπόγραφα sunt, minore labore fiunt, verba tantum adfero quibus abundo'. We shall assume, what cannot be proved,[4] that this remark refers to the philosophical writings. But let us be careful. First, these words were written in 45 B.C. and there is no warrant for applying them (as has been done) to any works except those on which Cicero was then engaged. Secondly, and more important, the self-teasing in the last two words might have served as a warning that Cicero is perhaps not entirely serious. But for long neither point was heeded. The only attention most scholars have paid to Cicero's philosophical work for many years has taken the form of attempting to identify his sources. Little certainty or agreement has been achieved, but the effort has not been wasted provided that the correct conclusion is drawn from the negative results, namely that the basic hypothesis was probably wrong, and that

Cicero did not after all work all the time by translating chunks of Greek handbooks. Instead of basing conjectures on an uncertain hypothesis, let us rather start with what we know.

We know first that all his life Cicero had a great interest in philosophy[5]: he did not come to it in the year 45 as a novice when, as our preface says (*de Div*. ii. 7), 'haec studia *renovare* coepimus'. For years a Stoic philosopher Diodotus had lived in his house. According to a credible tradition, Cicero edited Lucretius's poem for publication. He exchanges philosophical jokes with Varro in 47 (*ad Fam*. ix. 4), and with Cassius (*ad Fam*. xv. 16, 17)—in 45 it is true, but not with the air of a struggling learner—and these jokes, we may observe, argue familiarity with logical and epistemological controversies of a technical kind. What of the works themselves? Though his occasional comments on the problems of finding satisfactory Latin equivalents for Greek technical terms usually show good sense combined with a conscientious respect for *nuance*, the loss of all but a few fragments of the original Greek sources means that we have hardly any prospect of checking his technique and accuracy as a translator.[6] But at all events Cicero is not niggardly in acknowledging his debts.[7] Sometimes he stresses that he is rendering a Greek source verbatim as a defence against any accusation of distortion; frequently he names the source for a whole set of arguments. What is striking here is how frequently the latter passages are those which on broad stylistic grounds one would suspect of being 'unoriginal', that is to say, passages of close or technical argument. Obvious instances are the complex discussions of *Academica priora* and *De Fato*. It is not that he was out of his depth: it is precisely on the topics of these passages that he exchanges pleasantries with Varro and Cassius. But he had nothing of substance to add, 'only the words'.

But the impression—and failing positive evidence, 'impressions' must serve—that elsewhere he ranges more freely in presenting and illustrating his material, conforms with his claim (*de Off*. i. 6) to be no mere translator 'sed ut solemus e fontibus eorum (i.e. Stoicorum) iudicio arbitrioque nostro quantum quoque modo videbitur hauriemus'. We must still not claim for Cicero a degree of 'originality' which he does not claim for himself, yet it is true that reaping where others had sown, selecting, adapting, and above all giving eloquent expression to others' ideas, he made of himself a 'source'—not of philosophical propositions and arguments but of an enlightened and humane outlook, the Roman spirit at its best.

The remainder of the preface to *De Divinatione* II is devoted to Cicero's summary of his writings with some comment on their individual purpose and content. He begins with the dialogue *Hortensius*. This was a work of the kind known as protreptic, designed like a modern introduction to a work or subject to analyse its claims on the enthusiasm and interest of the reader. Thus *Hortensius* was the work in which 'cohortati sumus ut maxime potuimus ad philosophiae studium'. Only quotations from it now survive. Yet it has always claimed a special place in the history of European thought as the work which St. Augustine several times mentions as the one which turned his attention from worldly frivolity to 'philosophia' and the 'studium sapientiae' (*Conf.* iii. 4, 7; viii. 7, 17 etc.).[8]

Like all Cicero's reflective works, except *Orator* and *De Officiis*, *Hortensius* was cast in dialogue form, so that an opportunity presents itself to look briefly at Cicero as a writer of dialogue. It requires little literary perception to make the conventional comment that Cicero in his dialogues is less 'lively' than Plato. The combination of philosophy and fun in Plato's early dialogues is after all unique, and Plato himself increasingly abandoned his early 'artistry' as he came to find it an inadequate vehicle for serious philosophical thinking.[9] But the dialogue form lived on as a convenient if not always realistic means of setting out opposing points of view, and also of course as sugar on the pill of close argument or exposition.[10] A modern writer,[11] otherwise sympathetic to Cicero's aims in his philosophical writings, declares that 'in those opening passages where he tries to copy the conversational style of Plato he fails lamentably'. It seems to me that in such passages, considered *in themselves*, Cicero succeeds admirably. What he could not achieve was the easy transition from conversational 'small talk' to the serious subject of discussion which gives the early Platonic dialogue its unity and is indeed so attractively and convincingly done that many people not having read Xenophon's Socratic dialogues imagine that late fifth-century Athenians actually talked like that. Lacking Plato's genius for this kind of thing, Cicero might have gained by abandoning all pretence at dialogue.

Yet much would also have been lost. For all the artificiality of the form—and Cicero found it by no means easy to transfer it to the Roman environment, as is shown by his difficulties in drafting the *Academica*, mentioned below—a few individual characters come to life, and, what is more important, there *is* an atmosphere of genuine debate in the dialogues, as one may discover by turning to the monologue of the *De Officiis*, and there is a picture of a decorous and civilized side of Roman life which makes a pleasant and useful corrective to the current popular and (alas! too often) pedagogic mythology of brutal, bloodthirsty, and disgusting Romans. Finally, to meet on their own ground those who insist on fun with their philosophy, it would surely be a pity if Cicero had never left us, among many other lively or humorous touches, such things as the close of the *Academica* where the noble disputants take their departure by boat from Hortensius' villa overlooking the Bay of Naples (*Acad. pr.* 147-8), the vignette of the sarcastic and self-confident Epicurean Velleius in the first book of *De Natura Deorum* (especially 16-18), or that of the younger Cato found by Cicero in a friend's library 'multis circumfusum Stoicorum libris' (*Fin.* iii. 8).

But it is not the present object to entice the reader to these works of Cicero with a tempting display of attractive titbits. Such an attempt would only insult the reader by suggesting that he is as much in need of such allurement as the unphilosophical Romans of Cicero's own day. The truth is that all the modern concentration on Cicero's alleged defects as a writer of philosophical dialogue is a product of *parti pris*, that anti-Ciceronianism and naive philhellenism to which we shall unfortunately have to return in discussing Cicero's influence. It is interesting only for its characteristic superficiality and irrelevance[12] and its occasional grotesque results. Thus Hunt[13]—and one regrets again having to speak unkindly of a scholar who has been prepared to take seriously at any rate the substance of these works—suggest that *Hortensius*, being so much admired by Augustine and others, must have been very different in quality from the extant works with 'their unattractive arrangement and uninspired tone which makes pleasurable reading impossible'. But the argument collapses unless it can be shown that earlier ages would accept these strictures: that would be a task indeed. It is not enough to claim the support of an isolated and half-ironical passage in Montaigne (*Essais* ii. 10)[14]:

I want discourses which plunge straight into the heart of the perplexity: his beat feebly about the bush.

Montaigne is here pleading a special and curious case. He 'wants books that offer the results of learning, not those that set it out': it is Cicero's 'logical and Aristotelian orderings of the material' which bore him. Hence too

> even Plato's dialogues drag and stifle their meaning in a plethora of argument. Can I be forgiven for deploring the time that a man who had so many more valuable things to say spent on long and useless preliminary discussions?

But let us leave these melancholy but necessary polemics, and pass with Cicero to the *Academica*, in which he sets out what he calls the 'genus philosophandi minime arrogans maximeque et constans et elegans', that is, the views of the so-called 'New' Academy.

To explain the connexion of this school with the original Academy founded by Plato we have to glance back to Plato himself. His great concern, in an age when traditional morality was under attack, was to find a firm rational basis for the 'good life.' Such a basis, he believed, could rest only on certain knowledge: how can one know how to live without knowledge of the universe in which one plays a part? But there appeared to be two great obstacles to the attainment of knowledge. First, the physical world around us is in constant change, movement, and decay: how can you say anything permanently true, i.e. have permanent knowledge, of what is itself impermanent? At a later stage in his thought, Plato also concerned himself with the problem that has greatly exercised philosophers ever since, the apparent uncertainty even of such 'knowledge' as we think we enjoy of the physical world, for our senses may be the victims of illusion, hallucinations, and other deceptions. From either point of view, the former more important in Plato's own development, the latter in subsequent philosophy, it seems that the world cannot yield certain knowledge. Another 'world', that of the Platonic 'forms' or 'ideas', was believed by Plato to be the only possible source of such certainty: he was led to this by consideration of the ability we have to formulate and understand both the 'eternal' truths of mathematics, which are not physically exemplified in the world, and also our ideals of 'virtue' which equally do not themselves exist in the world around us.

No later school in the period which concerns us followed Plato the whole way with his answers, but the problems he posed remained the fundamental issues of philosophy. Stoics and Epicureans, though differing in much else, agreed in maintaining that our sense-perceptions *are* sufficiently reliable for us to have knowledge of the world around us, and they attempted to evolve moral theories on the basis of their views of the 'nature' of the universe and humanity in particular. The Academics who immediately followed Plato concentrated on mathematics, which the Master had seen as one of the great guides to reality. But the so-called New Academy, founded by Carneades in the middle of the second century B.C., followed out the lead given by the Middle Academy under Arcesilaus a century earlier in stressing the sceptical aspects of Plato's thought, while finding no place for the knowable other-world of ideas. These Academics maintained that no sense-perception was, as the Stoics thought, of self-guaranteeing authenticity—to take a homely example, the Stoics would claim that we sometimes *know* that we are awake, not dreaming: the Academics replied, 'You can never be sure'. Equally the Academics maintained that 'there were two sides to every question': any positive assertion could be refuted, or at least weakened, so that the highest status any assertion could claim was 'probability', not 'certainty'. The ethical teaching of this school followed the same lines. Ethics could not be based on the other-worldly certainty of Plato, nor on the this-worldly certainties of Stoics and Epicureans: it must rest on a choice of the most probable view, and on common sense.

Cicero, by temperament and by training as orator and lawyer, was always ready to see both sides of a question. In his writings he often attacks dogmatism, and he is scathing about those who accept the first view they hear or swallow uncritically the dicta of some authority (cf. *Nat. D.* i. 10). Freedom to change one's mind he also values, even, it has been suggested,[15] showing 'an indifference to consistency which verges on irresponsibility'. The great advantage of this attitude was that it enabled Cicero to set forth a very wide variety of views with as much impartiality as one can expect of mortal man. But he had certain views, though preferring to keep them in the background for fear that they too should be taken as 'authoritative'; and the Academic tradition of the open mind 'suspension of judgement' never debarred a man from assent, if but temporary and conditional, to the 'more probable' view. The Academics claimed that this system of arguing both sides with a summing-up in favour of one was the Socratic method (*ad Att.* ii. 3, 3). Thus Cicero leaned strongly to much of what was valuable in Stoicism: he was distressed at being accused of partisan hostility towards Epicureanism (*Tusc.* iii. 50), but there was in fact scarcely anything in it which he found acceptable.

It was for this reason that Cicero followed *Hortensius* with the *Academica* which sets out the Academic grounds for scepticism. Cicero produced a first draft in two books, but growing dissatisfied with some features of it, in particular regretting the role he had patriotically assigned to some distinguished but notoriously unphilosophical Romans, he redrafted it with a less inappropriate cast, dividing the original two books into four. But accidents of publication and circulation have produced a curious and confusing result. Of the second edition (*Academica posteriora*) in which the doctrines of the New Academy were set in place in an historical survey of all Greek philosophy, we have only a part of the first book and it is most regrettable that what we have lost includes the account of Arcesilaus' and Carneades' own views. Of the earlier edition (*Academica priora*), on the other hand, the whole of the second book survives. In it are expounded with much technical elaboration the Stoic arguments for, and the Academic arguments against the possibility of certain knowledge and the reliability of our sense-perceptions. The work provides an excellent introduction to these problems, but it has never been very popular.

Cicero's survey of his writings now passes to the work we usually call *De Finibus* with these words:

Cumque fundamentum esset philosophiae positum in finibus bonorum et malorum, perpurgatus est is locus a nobis quinque libris, ut quid a quoque et quid contra quemque philosophum diceretur intellegi posset.

The title attempts to render the Greek περὶ τελῶν, that is, it concerns 'the ends aimed at' in the moral sphere, the 'ultimate' good and evil. We have already noticed how morality and the definition of the good life was the fundamental concern (*fundamentum*) of ancient philosophy, and observed the Academic liking

for demolishing theses. So in *De Finibus* the Epicurean argument—
that the ultimate aim of human life, beyond even *virtus*, moral
goodness, is pleasure—is expounded and then refuted. There
follow the exposition and refutation of the more complex Stoic
moral theory of which the central tenet was that *virtus* was not
only the ultimate good, but the only thing which could properly
be called good. Finally Cicero sets out the doctrine expounded by
Antiochus of Ascalon, one of his teachers.

Hunt sees the main purpose of Cicero's philosophical writings
as the exposition and examination of the views of Antiochus.
The difficulty in this view is that it involves stigmatizing large
parts of the works as 'irrelevant', and it is easier to believe that
Cicero's main purpose was somewhat wider, particularly in view
of what he says himself in the present and many other passages.
None the less Antiochus was an important figure whose views
influenced many Romans, including Varro and Brutus. Taking
over the headship of the Academy from Philo of Larissa, a representative of the sceptical trend in the Academic tradition, he
claimed that this scepticism was a deviation from the authentic
tradition of the school amd maintained that on a true view of the
matter many controversies, especially those with the Stoics,
could be disposed of by a return to the fountain head of all the
contending schools, the 'original' Academy. It is important to
realize that Antiochus's claim, like most such claims to restore a
lost ancient 'truth', was unhistorical. The content of Antiochus's
views was a combination of the Stoic belief in certain knowledge
based on reliable sense-perception with the ethical theory of
Aristotle and his followers the Peripatetics, which laid down that
virtue, though the highest good, was not the only good: such
things as health, wealth and a certain length of days were also
necessary components of the absolutely good or perfect life for
man. For his school Antiochus claimed the name of the Old
Academy. He maintained that Academics and Peripatetics had
always taught the same thing, that the argument with the Stoics
about 'virtue' and 'the good' was a mere quarrel over words.
But there was more propaganda than truth in these assertions, and
it is better simply to regard the 'Old' Academy as Antiochus's
creation, and a somewhat unfortunately entitled successor to the
'New' Academy of Carneades and Philo.

Thus it comes about that the fifth book of *De Finibus* takes from

Antiochus its account of Peripatetic ethics. But though such a theory might be expected to appeal to the common sense of the Romans, that is not the end of the story, which is a clear indication from Cicero that in the last resort he favours the Stoic view. This view he himself had undertaken to refute as a character in the dialogue, on two main grounds. First, there must be something wrong with a doctrine, however logically impregnable its exponents think it to be, that produces such absurd corollaries as resulted from the view that nothing but virtue or moral excellence can properly be called good, e.g.—to say nothing of the invention of new outlandish terms to describe the things ordinary people call 'good'—the beliefs that all sins were equal, and that the wise man (the Stoic *sapiens* or sage), because he is wise, has all other desirable qualities; he, and he alone, is not only wise and good, but rich, royal, and eloquent. Secondly, the Stoics' logic is not in any case irrefragable either in the details of the syllogistic arguments they favoured or—a matter of more permanent importance —in the particular form of their attempt to deduce human morality from human 'nature'. There was an awkward gap in their argument when they tried to pass from the 'natural' human instincts, such as those towards the preservation of the self and society, to their purely intellectual sage committed to that *un*natural suppression of *all* emotions for which the Stoics have become a by-word.

Given that Cicero was aware of these objections, how can he waver at the end of the whole work towards the Stoic view? He was, we have observed, anxious to suppress his own views and so appears as a character in the work in a destructive role; yet he was, we have also seen, not excluded by his adherence to the New Academy from deciding which way the balance tilted. Why does it tilt towards Stoicism? He leaves the answer in no doubt.

Whatever its faults in detail, Stoicism alone of the rival schools of Cicero's time, met what seemed to ancient thought one general all-important requirement in any definition of the 'good life', namely self-sufficiency. To the modern reader, influenced by Christianity with its very different presuppositions about human nature, the Stoic sage, proud, independent, and self-regarding, seems not a figure of almost divine stature but a calculating prig. Yet the fault lies not so much in the Stoics' answer to the problem as in the assumptions, shared by them with other ancient schools, on which the answer was based. The first assumption was that the answer can be found by contemplating human nature, not as in Judaeo-Christian thought as something essentially flawed and dependent, but as something like all other things capable of realizing its own appropriate perfection, which we deduce by considering its essential qualities. To use analogies like those of Plato, to maintain that humanity is essentially flawed is like saying that we are living in a world in which knives should not be expected to cut, horses to make good mounts, pilots to be able to navigate, and doctors to heal their patients. Christians maintain that in the ethical sphere we live in just such a world, but to an ancient pagan the idea that it was a man's job or duty to live well and that yet he could not possibly do it by understanding and employing his own strictly human resources was close to self-contradiction. The second assumption is that the truly good life, if it is to have the longed-for quality of permanence and assurance, must be independent of chance and circumstance: again it follows that the ideal life must be that of a man who depends only on his own goodness and strength of character. How is such independence to be achieved except through contempt not only for worldly goods but for all emotional ties as well? Thus we explain the Stoic sage, and his attraction even for a man as humane as Cicero. If it can be demonstrated that *virtus* alone is enough for the *beata vita*, to use the ancient formulation, here is a guarantee that the 'happy life' is attainable and there is a road hard but (in theory) practicable by which to attain it.

To this theme Cicero returned in his next work:

> totidem subsecuti libri Tusculanarum Disputationum *res ad beate vivendum maxime necessarias* aperuerunt. primus enim est de contemnenda morte, secundus de tolerando dolore, de aegritudine lenienda tertius, quartus de reliquis animi perturbationibus; quintus eum locum complexus est *qui totam philosophiam maxime inlustrat*, docet enim *ad beate vivendum virtutem se ipsa esse contentam.*'

Tradition has perpetuated the Englishing as 'Tusculan Disputations' of a title which really means 'Discussions at my country-house at Tusculum'. It is small wonder that few now penetrate beyond covers bearing so forbidding a title into the text of the least demanding of Cicero's larger philosophical writings. The tone and content are in the main Stoic, but in that vein of moderate popular Stoicism which was to be greatly influential in the

Greco-Roman world of the imperial period and much of which was easily absorbed into Christian thought. Now the specious pleas put forward earlier in this chapter will not have concealed from the perceptive reader that the *Academica* and *De Finibus* are in large measure too technical to be amusing, and their attempts at dialogue pathetic. But the perceptive reader will by definition not be so innocent as to draw the wrong conclusion from the absence of any substantial quantity either of technicality or of dialogue in the *Tusculans*, or to be surprised to learn that a weighty body of opinion recommends that they be left on the shelf along with what may be called their senior brethren. For they contain nothing but edifying rhetoric, and our age is suspicious or contemptuous of both rhetoric and edification.

So be it: but let us at least give Cicero the credit for knowing what he is doing. Not only does *De Finibus* II open with an intelligent discussion of the problems of presenting philosophical expositions,[16] but the introduction to the *Tusculans* themselves (*Tusc.* i. 7-8) explains candidly that these will be rhetorical exercises on philosophical themes. This does not mean merely purple passages, though the *Tusculans* contain some fine ones. It implies rather a 'popular' style which proceeds less by spare logical analysis than by example and illustration drawn from a wide range of Greek and Roman myth, history, and literature.

In the same vein of moralizing, genial but often on analysis more demanding in the standards proposed than is commonly realized, Cicero also wrote *De Senectute* and the two extant works not mentioned in our Preface, the *De Amicitia*—long regarded as a natural companion-piece to the *De Senectute*, and the pair seem not to have altogether lost their appeal—and the more substantial and even more influential *De Officiis*, or 'On Duties'—but in this instance the old-fashioned Englishing of the title as 'Offices' has its value so far as it makes clear that we are dealing with a technical term. It was the best Cicero could do—he discusses the difficulty in his letters (*ad Att.* xvi. 11 and 14)—to render the Greek καθῆκον, a Stoic term for the 'obligations' of the ordinary imperfect man, to whose problems Stoicism had, after its early concentration on the totally virtuous 'sage', granted a place in its teachings. So in *De Officiis* Cicero drew on the work of Panaetius, head of the Stoic school and an associate of Scipio Aemilianus and his circle of Roman aristocratic statesmen and

Greek intellectuals. Of the many fruits of that attempt to combine the best in Greek and Roman traditions *De Officiis* is a fine example, even revealing in its last book the extent and limitations of what a Roman could do with a theme for which there was no suitable Greek model.

At all points it has its feet on the ground. For appetites jaded past stimulation except by the spectacular and paradoxical (e.g. such ideas as philosophers as kings, community of women, the expulsion of most poets) it has no savour—naturally, for it is a serious work about real problems. It also illustrates the truth of Aristotle's dictum which has provided much-needed light relief for so many undergraduates busy with the *Nicomachean Ethics*, that moral philosophy is an unsuitable study for the young. For it is usually only with increasing experience, maturity, and above all with the ever-increasing network of ties and responsibilities that life as a member of a family, a profession and a community brings to a man, that the real difficulties of moral decision are felt and understood, and that there comes, if it ever comes, the realization that most people most of the time do not live in a world of chivalric selfless endeavour—but they have their problems of 'what to do' which merit consideration. It is even worth discussing, as Cicero shows in the second book of *De Officiis*, the problems of 'what to do' that have little or no moral content at all. In other words he recognizes that the world of decision-making is not only the world of agonizing moral choice which fills the whole canvas in a certain kind of old-fashioned moral philosophy, the kind whose exclusive concern with 'duties' in the moral sphere is another reason for regretting that there is no more suitable word to render Cicero's *officia*.[17]

It is arguable that the *De Officiis* is the most influential secular prose work ever written; but nowadays few regard it much. Reasons for the general decline in the reputation of Cicero's philosophical works will be advanced and examined at the end of this chapter, but there is a special reason for the decline of this once specially influential work. It is a work, I have suggested, on adult topics for readers with adult tastes, but we no longer live in an age which finds in the classics the natural companions of a man's *adult* life, when problems are complex, and, rarely admitting of a purely intellectual solution, call on all the resources of his humanity. Insensibly our tastes in classical reading have been shaped *and* distorted by concentration on what appeals to the young.[18]

We have digressed to take in *De Officiis* and complete the tale of Cicero's moral writings. Following again the threads of his account in *De Divinatione*, we come to the 'theological' works, *De Natura Deorum* and *De Divinatione* itself, with the subsequently written *De Fato*.

Much of their material is now only of antiquarian interest, though as a rich source of information about Roman religion *De Natura Deorum*, in particular, was well known to early Christian apologists such as Minucius Felix, Lactantius, and Augustine. There are, however, some points to notice. First, the theological enquiry is conducted *after* both the epistemological and ethical enquiries, and they are quite independent of each other, except in the formal sense that Cicero's general scepticism and practice of stating both sides of an argument applies as much to theology as any other sphere of investigation. Thus the philosophy in no way depends on the theology. There is no suggestion that God must be the starting-point. Secondly, the chief interest of *De Natura Deorum* will probably be found in the confrontation of the arguments in favour of and against the belief in a divine providence. The Stoics believed in it, the Epicureans denied it, the Academics raised doubts and difficulties. As we have the work, the argument, often since echoed, 'from design' revealed in the order and beauty of the universe and its utility to mankind is eloquently expressed, but part of the Academic retort is lost. (Can it be mere coincidence that both the *Academica* and the *De Natura Deorum* survive in versions which lack a large part of the sceptics' case?) However, enough survives to show that the justification of God's ways to man was then, as now, no easy or supererogatory task. The optimists had a case to meet. Thirdly, Cicero, as in *De Finibus*, follows a long statement of an Academic case with an indication—here a single phrase (*Nat. D.* iii. 94)—that he favours on balance the Stoic view.

One might reasonably suppose that even in Cicero's day the subject of *De Divinatione* would have had so limited an appeal that the scale of the work is surprising. Two circumstances explain it. First, Stoicism held that all events were predetermined—in what precise sense Cicero discussed in the fragmentary *De Fato*, a work valuable for its record of some of the earliest discussions of 'the problem of free-will', and often strikingly modern in flavour because it treats the issue as primarily a logical one turning on the implications of statements employing terms of futurity, possibility, and necessity. It was thus intellectually respectable to accept augury, omens, and the other paraphernalia of prediction as means made available by divine providence to enable man to discover the future. Secondly, divination by various means was still in Cicero's day an important part of Roman religious practice. Roman 'official' religion is often derided as a set of coldly legalistic and ritualistic forms which, having nothing to offer to the individual, came in time to mean nothing to any intelligent man, surviving only as weapon of political manœuvre. The matter is not so simple. Rome had inherited and preserved the common enough type of primitive religion which is first and foremost concerned with the relationships of the gods and the *community*. It follows that when we regard the political 'entanglements' of Roman religion as *ipso facto* perversions, we are failing to see that these entanglements were in principle, if not in the precise forms they took, natural and inevitable. Further, the intelligent man was not confronted with a clear demand to stake his eternal salvation on assent to a creed: by contrast, though recitation of the Christian creeds is normally a communal act, each there speaks for himself in the first person singular.

These points must be remembered if we are not to misunderstand Cicero's attitude. Though he himself is an augur, he makes clear his scepticism about augury, and yet argues for the maintenance of the traditional religious practices for 'reasons of state'. We may think this attitude inconsistent: what it is not is a cynical perversion of religious for political ends. The Roman religion *existed* for 'political ends', and the long survival of the feeling that the welfare of the *community*—whatever the individual might think or do—was bound up with the worship of the old gods is attested by the persecution of Christianity and, long after Constantine, by the controversy that provoked Augustine's *City of God*. In this light we must read the fine passage from the close of *De Divinatione* (ii. 148) which contains what sounds nearest to a statement of personal belief and amplifies the closing sentence of *De Natura Deorum*:

Nec vero (id enim diligenter intelligi volo) superstitione tollenda religio tollitur. nam et maiorum instituta tueri sacris caeri-

moniisque retinendis sapientis est: et esse praestantem aliquam
aeternamque naturam, et eam suspiciendam admirandamque
hominum generi pulchritudo mundi ordoque rerum caelestium
cogit confiteri.

We now follow Cicero as with a hint of apology and an appeal
to the authority of Plato, Aristotle and Theophrastus, he claims a
place among his philosophical writings for his treatises on politics
and oratory, of which the most important were the *De Oratore*
and *De Re Publica*. Now the subjects of Cicero's later philosophical
works—what a man can know about the universe, and how he
should order his life in society and how face suffering and death—
are, self-evidently, important, however we estimate Cicero's
handling of them. But as we come to *De Oratore* we have to show
that the subject itself is not antiquated and remote, that the
perusal of a long work on oratory and rhetoric is not without its
rewards.

In ancient times, the word 'rhetoric' meant the art of effective
speech. It did not of itself connote empty or deceitful speech.
'Rhetorical' utterance might be empty when used for purposes of
mere display, and throughout antiquity there were audiences
highly receptive of verbal virtuosity for its own sake. It could be
deceitful when effectiveness was interpreted solely in terms of
winning legal cases, and ancient rhetoric both in theory and practice always had over-close connexions with the world of the law-
courts. But many ancient writers were critical of these tendencies,
and none more emphatically than Cicero. A further danger, not
implied in the modern pejorative use of the term 'rhetoric', was
that as the instrument of education which it became in the late
fifth century B.C. and remained to the end of antiquity, it could
be made into something fantastically pedantic, both by being
over-elaborated and by being stereotyped into a formal drill.
But reduced to its simplest terms, rhetoric taught the apparently
obvious but easily overlooked essentials of effective utterance:
the exploration of the subject (*inventio*: Cicero's youthful *De
Inventione* is about this; it is written in the textbook manner), the
arrangement of the material (*dispositio*) and the art of correct and
attractive presentation, 'style' (*elocutio*).[19]

All this is sensible, and Cicero, though in his maturity contemptuous of pedantic technicalities, was not ashamed to use the system as a basis for *De Oratore*, even though it was his intention not

to write just another textbook on rhetoric. Sometimes, it is true, detailed technicalities intrude, almost it seems against Cicero's will. We must make allowance here, as also when we note a curious repetitiveness in parts of the work, for Cicero's position in the history of Roman literature. Could he, even if we grant it to be ideally desirable, emancipate himself completely from the Greek rhetorical tradition? The *De Oratore* shows signs of struggle, not in its style, which is astonishingly fluent, but in its substance. He wishes to find a Roman voice, but the struggle shows in the intrusion of Greek technicalities on the one hand and on the other, as has just been said, in the repetitiveness with which Cicero hammers out the formulation of the ideas that were his own. The method results in certain *longueurs*, but at least the reader can easily see where Cicero wishes his emphases to fall.

In particular, Cicero seeks to overthrow the definition of the 'orator' which limits the term to the forensic advocate with no knowledge except of the tricks of the rhetorical trade. Cicero took the view which identified the 'orator' with the 'statesman', and he also believed that statesmanship is the highest function a man can perform, taking precedence over all merely reflective or theoretical pursuits. For his 'orator' in this sense Cicero repeatedly demands a liberal and humane culture based on a wide general knowledge, especially of law, literature, philosophy, and history. It is this fact primarily which gives the book, rich as it is in valuable detail and digression, its particular value, and it is worth illustrating Cicero's outlook from an illuminating example of his attitude to traditional 'rhetoric', the discussion of 'style' in the third book.

Traditionally, style was considered under the headings of linguistic accuracy, clarity, suitability (to subject, occasion, and audience), and finally elaboration. This last heading, though including euphony and rhythm, matters of great moment to ancient readers, or rather 'hearers'—for all read aloud, even when on their own, and a high proportion of ancient literature was publicly performed, delivered, or recited—dealt mainly with the figures of speech, which offered fine scope for classification, subdivision and exemplification.

Cicero's treatment (*De Or.* iii. 37-212) abandons the text-book tradition both in manner and matter. He begins by asserting that style and content are inseparable, and that style contains an unanalysable element of the individual. As he approaches the traditional formulation he almost by-passes the first two requirements by declaring that every properly educated Roman, not merely the trained orator, should speak grammatically and have no marked eccentricities of pronunciation, and as for clarity, why speak at all if you cannot be understood?[20] But what of *ornatus*? The conventionally trained reader who had survived the earlier shocks now met the biggest shock of all. He was told that the true source of *ornatus* was not figures of speech—he will get a list of them thrown at him at the end of the book, for form's sake (§§ 202-207),[21] but the end is a long way off—it was *probitas* and *prudentia*, high moral and intellectual quality, without which a training in rhetoric was like giving weapons to lunatics. There follows a whole series of attacks on accepted notions. Oratory should not be merely a matter of momentary attractiveness: permanent value is something different and harder to achieve. The breach between rhetoric (practical statesmanship) and philosophy (the theoretic or contemplative life), traceable, according to Cicero, back to Socrates, was a disaster. The ideal man, the perfect orator, will combine philosophy with oratory. Thus, for example, the stereotyped *loci communes*, set pieces on such general and recurrent topics as e.g. patriotism, traditionally taught by rhetoricians, should be used with an awareness of their philosophical background and implications. Even for professional purposes therefore the orator needs a wide education, 'rerum enim copia verborum copiam gignit'. Only thus can the dangers inherent in rhetoric, the temptations to emptiness, deceit, or narrowness, be averted—Cicero makes it clear through the mouth of L. Crassus, the participant in the dialogue who most clearly speaks for Cicero himself, what is the second best to his ideal statesman of lofty moral and intellectual standards: 'malim indisertam prudentiam quam stultitiam loquacem'.

De Oratore is a long and difficult work containing much that is only of technical or antiquarian interest. Yet difficult as it is to extract, the gold is there. It was most evident to the eyes of the Renaissance, the only period when the book has been widely popular. For the Renaissance saw a revival of the ideal of the liberally educated secular administrator or statesman, while the Middle Ages had preferred of all Cicero's works the dry rhetorical precepts of *De Inventione*, or the 'Dream of Scipio', equally though in a very different way, as will shortly appear, uncharacteristic of its author, and in recent times disesteem for 'rhetoric' and loss of the necessary background knowledge of ancient rhetoric has led to renewed neglect. Yet, as I have tried briefly to show, Cicero is dealing with the perennial question 'How are we to educate our rulers so that they will exercise their power effectively but without abusing it?' His answer is not foolish nor contemptible. It is worth considering alongside many that have attracted more attention.

Just assessment of *De Re Publica* is made impossible by the loss of the greater part of it. Apart from its epilogue, the 'Dream of Scipio', which was separately preserved with an elaborate commentary written by Macrobius in the fourth century, we have only fragments, in part quotations, for the work was a great favourite with early Christian writers, especially Lactantius and Augustine, and also contained a number of linguistic oddities which attracted the attention of grammarians, and in part the readable sections of a palimpsest. This last was discovered in 1820. As the original manuscript of *De Re Publica* was not only half-obliterated for re-use but also split up and rebound, the text as recovered is not consecutive for more than a page or two at a time. Some of the later books are still almost totally lost. Yet something emerges of Cicero's political ideals.

The title, like that of *De Legibus*, reveals that, as with *De Oratore*, we have a work that at one and the same time imitates and challenges the Greeks. Many Greek philosophers, and not of course Plato alone, had written their 'Republics', sketches for Utopia. Cicero rejects the theoretical approach. With a Roman's patriotism and a Roman's sense of history and tradition he claims that no one legislator could achieve what the long evolution of Roman institutions had achieved—the ideal of a united society (it was the overriding need for unity which had led Plato to some of his confessedly bizarre conclusions) in the form advocated by Greek theorists after Plato, a constitution, that is, perfectly balanced between the principles of rule by the one, the few, and the many.

Cicero did not claim that this ideal remained fulfilled in the Rome of his own day: he looked back to the age of Scipio Aemilianus in the middle of the second century B.C. Yet it is foolish to dismiss *De Re Publica* as mere nostalgia produced by

Cicero's own political frustrations. Cicero of course over-idealized the Roman past; he failed to see that the Roman Republic was not suffering in his day from a temporary malaise (induced, as he supposed, by the 'seditious' activities of a few 'bad men') but from fatal and incurable maladies, though none of his contemporaries was more perspicacious. Yet, though it is fashionable to reject with scorn any suggestion that the principles and practice of the imperial period owed something to direct acquaintance with Cicero's work (and the *De Re Publica* was, as the numerous quotations show, well known), it is undeniable that, clinging at a time of personal disappointment and political chaos to the ideals of a humane, rationally based society, he succeeded in foreshadowing much of the best in the age that was to follow. In particular, as several fine and familiar passages reveal, his patriotism, though profound, was not narrow. He imbibed from the Hellenistic Greeks and transmitted to Western Europe the ideal of a *world* in harmony, for all human beings, as the Stoics in particular had taught, are linked by their common humanity to each other and to the divine, and are subject to a law that transcends the separate laws of individual states (cf. especially *Rep.* iii. 33).

The 'Dream of Scipio' which concludes the work contains much outdated cosmology with its universe of concentric spheres centred round the earth, producing by their revolutions that 'music of the spheres' familiar in literary allusion. But its main and surprising message, which accounts for the great popularity of the work and a consequent very false picture of Cicero in the Middle Ages, is the comparative triviality of earthly matters. The soul is immortal (Cicero borrows a 'proof' of this from Plato), and while a man may not seek eternal bliss (by suicide) but must wait until God summons him, and must devote himself to *res optimae* defined as *curae de salute patriae*, he must at the same time not lose sight of what lies beyond; the souls of those who do otherwise will be earthbound after death. The commentators throughout the ages have emphasized the unexpected otherworldliness of this passage: it is important not to overlook that in essence the central ideal is the same as the philosopher-statesman of *De Oratore*, though with a new dimension added.

Such then were Cicero's philosophical writings, described, so far as possible, in such terms as will explain the vicissitudes of their subsequent reputation, the theme to which we now turn.

Cicero tells us himself in the preface which has been the guiding thread of our survey that he was gratified by the number of readers he found among his contemporaries, but the younger generation was not interested. The prudent scepticism of the New Academy, which was Cicero's starting-point, was not fashionable (*Nat. D.* i. 9), and to the young in particular must have seemed the very authentic voice of the established and elderly. We know that the dogmatism which youth demands was supplied to the young Virgil, for instance, by Epicureanism. In the century or two that followed the establishment of the imperial system, 'philosophy', when it did not mean eccentric charlatanry of the kind mocked by Quintilian or Lucian, generally amounted to little more than Stoically tinged moralizing of a kind which makes even the *Tusculans* seem by comparison an intellectual feast.

But early Christianity was of tougher fibre, and the early Christian writers recognized in Cicero a master of exposition whose technique and style some writers like Minucius Felix and Lactantius were glad to borrow, and whose analysis of 'duties' was closely followed by St. Ambrose in his *De Officiis Ministrorum*. Others fought against the siren songs of pagan literature. A famous passage in St. Jerome's letters (xxii. 30) tells how, in a grave illness, he seemed to himself to be taken before the heavenly judgement-seat and, on claiming to be a Christian, to receive the answer, 'Mentiris: Ciceronianus es non Christianus; "ubi thesaurus tuus, ibi et cor tuum".' In consequence he foreswore, if but temporarily and ineffectually, the delights of the pagan authors. It is curious to see the early Christian caught in a tension so closely analogous to that of the Roman centuries before when confronted with Greek literature. Both struggle, the one for patriotic, the other for religious reasons, to find his own voice, when of sheer necessity he must borrow the very means of expression, even of thought, from the source he would gladly reject.[22] The result was much the same. A new amalgam is created with its own character and value, in one case the literature of pagan Rome, in the other the literature of Christian humanism, that is first the literature written by Christians to speak across the gulf to their pagan contemporaries—the tone of early apologetics is often noticeably different from that adopted in commentaries, homilies, or devotional works intended for fellow Christians—and secondly the writings of those who throughout the ages have interpreted liberally Augustine's defence of the exploitation of the riches of pagan thought as a form of 'spoiling the Egyptians'.

If we cross beyond the Dark Age to the 'Carolingian Renaissance' we find Cicero sharing in a renewed interest in pagan literature generally. Familiar signs are Einhard's quotation from the *Tusculans* in the preface to his *Life of Charles the Great* and Servatus Lupus's acquisition of manuscripts of the *Tusculans* and *De Oratore*. Ciceronian excerpts appear in florilegia; the remarkable *Excerpta Hadoardi* (ninth or tenth century) has a truly astonishing array of quotations from his writings, especially again the *Tusculans*. All Cicero's extant philosophical works survive in Carolingian manuscripts. How significant are these phenomena? Some see in them evidence of a wide acquaintance with Cicero: these surviving pieces of evidence are but the visible part of an iceberg. Others see in them the rare exception, evidence of unusual interest and learning in a handful of individuals. We must of course make allowance not only for the chance and scanty nature of the evidence, but also for the fact that in Carolingian times and most of the succeeding mediaeval period the whole educated class was limited in number and had but limited access to books; many of its members, since it was mainly ecclesiastical, might either be not especially concerned with pagan literature or even actively hostile to it.[23] Others had, along with the convictions that Christianity had made all things new, a strong feeling of continuity with the ancient past of Rome; the effect of this, however, shows itself not so much in enthusiasm for 'classical' literature as in the lack of a modern distinction, introduced at the Renaissance, between 'classical' and 'mediaeval' Latin. Hence in mediaeval curricula Virgil and Ovid rub shoulders with writers of the fifth to twelfth centuries, and the contents of mediaeval manuscripts are likely to shock (quite unreasonably) the modern scholar by what seems to him an outlandish hotch potch. It would then be foolish to expect a wide diffusion of interest in one author such as Cicero, in the sense in which we should nowadays use the words. Yet it seems that Cicero was not, even within the appropriate limits of the phrase, an especially 'popular' author in the Middle Ages.

First, Cicero never enjoyed, even with those well-read in the classics, the popularity of the poets—not only Virgil and Ovid, but Terence, Horace, Lucan, Persius, and Statius were all more prominent in educational curricula and literary allusion. Secondly, even among prose writers, though Cicero retained a respected reputation as a master of Latin style, and of oratory in particular, the respect so accorded was somewhat distant. Cicero was not in fact much read. Sallust was often found more readable, and being given to epigram, quotable. What mediaeval writers wanted from antiquity was nothing so large as an outlook on life, which is what Cicero's writings offer, but pithy examples and quotations to adorn their own productions with an air of antique authority. But Cicero is the least quotable of all great writers. When he is quoted, the quotations are nearly always at second-hand, from anthologies, grammars, or earlier writers such as Jerome or Augustine. Thirdly, we can also discern how at a popular level 'Cicero' was just a great name of shadowy prestige, useful for the adornment of a sermon or tale, but what was said of him was liable to be blatantly unhistorical.[24]

If we turn to the positive side of mediaeval knowledge of Cicero we find it generally confined to a few works, which were, with one exception, short. The exception was the rhetorical textbook *De Inventione*. Another rhetorical textbook, the *Rhetorica ad Herennium*, wrongly attributed to Cicero from before Jerome's time to the fifteenth century, was also well known from the twelfth century onwards. The extraordinary multiplication of manuscripts of these works shows that we must not exaggerate the inaccessibility of books through scarcity of copies and difficulties of communication, different though conditions were from our own day. 'Where there's a will there's a way', and as in the obvious case of the scriptures and liturgy, what the mediaevals wanted badly enough they obtained. Beyond this, the essential mediaeval Cicero consisted of the *Dream of Scipio*, interpreted with the support of Macrobius's commentary as a defence of the contemplative life, and *Topica*, a small quasi-philosophical (really rhetorical) treatise on which Boethius had written a commentary. Of the treatises more properly classed as philosophical, there were always some who knew the *Tusculans* and especially the *De Officiis*, but far the most popular were the two short essays on friendship and old age. It is certainly true that Cicero's philosophical writings were more widely known than the speeches and letters, but then these were hardly known at all.

Before seeking to justify these assertions from the evidence of the well-documented 'Renaissance of the Twelfth Century' in which literary studies reached their mediaeval peak, it is perhaps as well to indicate that this emphasis on the limitations of mediaeval knowledge of Cicero is not intended as a denigration of the Middle Ages. What the Middle Ages read, as well as the kind of Latin they wrote, was their own business. But a certain kind of modish scholarly 'mediaevalism' tends to exaggerate the evidence for mediaeval knowledge of the classics apparently in an attempt to confer respectability on a period for long regarded as barbarous —and it is worth remembering that in the language of popular politics and journalism 'mediaeval' is still a term of abuse. I believe it to be better to take the Middle Ages on their own terms. What is valuable in the mediaeval outlook must be in the main what was mediaeval in it. Secondly the modish and not so scholarly philhellenism of recent times has naturally seen the main importance of the Renaissance in the recovery of Greek in Western Europe, and it has been easy to slide into the assumption that (in effect—I ask indulgence for the crude formulation) Cicero was all very well in the Middle Ages, but the Renaissance brought back Plato. That is not what happened. The Renaissance was primarily the recovery of ancient Rome, and above all, Cicero.[25]

But now for some bald, bare facts. Hildebert of Lavardin (1050-1133) wrote a treatise *De Honesto et Utili* owing much to Cicero and Seneca. Marbod of Rennes (1035-1123) included in his moralizing hexameters, the *Liber decem capitulorum*, two chapters, *De Senectute* and *De Vera Amicitia*, parts of which are paraphrases of Cicero's essays on these themes. Conrad of Hirschau, of the early twelfth century, in the curriculum set out in his *Dialogus super Auctores* mentions alone of Cicero's writings the same two opuscules, though Meinhard of Bamberg before the end of the eleventh century had recommended the *Tusculans* as an excellent work, valuable as a propaedeutic to Christian philosophy. Abelard, who died in 1142, cites only in addition to *De Inventione* and *Topica*, *De Officiis* and the *Paradoxa Stoicorum*, a not very seriously intended set of brief elaborations of the Stoic paradoxes referred to above, and some others. Now little read, it was once much more popular. The historian Otto of Freising who died in 1158 shows debts to *De Officiis*. About 1160 Ailred of Rievaulx wrote a dialogue *De Spirituali Amicitia* indebted in matter and manner to Cicero's *De Amicitia*, as is the *De Amicitia Christiana* of Peter of Blois

(? 1130 to after 1204); and about the same time Harbord of Michelsberg quoted verbatim substantial parts of *De Officiis*. The same work was the basis of an influential *Moralium dogma philosophorum* attributed, probably wrongly, to William of Conches, who was tutor to both Henry II and John of Salisbury. Philip of Bayeux died in 1164, and bequeathed to the abbey of Bec an unusual collection of books which included Cicero's three theological treatises, the *De Legibus* and the *Tusculans*: is this evidence that these works were 'known', or that they were scarce and desirable?

John of Salisbury (c. 1115-1180) stands acknowledged as the greatest of the twelfth-century 'humanists', on the grounds both of the 'purity' of his Latinity and on the width of his interests and of his classical reading. Of Cicero's works[26] he probably knew neither speeches nor letters, but he almost certainly knew all the philosophical works except the *Academica, De Divinatione, De Fato*, and *De Re Publica. De Oratore* he not only knew but owned, bequeathing it at his death to Chartres, with his copy of *De Officiis*, and he was profoundly indebted to these two works, finding in them support for his own ideals of statesmanship, for his natural love of 'letters', and for his antipathy to dogmatism and specialism.[27] But he remains 'mediaeval', taking from antiquity what he needs within the context of his time. He exemplifies at its best that mediaeval sense of continuity with the Roman past to which reference has been made. He is not like the Renaissance humanist, whose return to the Roman past involves the rejection of the intervening 'Middle Age'.

John of Salisbury saw with foreboding the impending triumph of 'scholasticism'. The study of the 'arts', of logic and of theology, was to become dominant over the 'authors', literary studies. Grammar and Rhetoric, which had provided the framework and the excuse for literary studies, lost prestige. These generalizations remain true even if we accept the view[28] that literary studies were quantitatively more flourishing than ever before in the thirteenth century, just as it is true that the middle twentieth century is a 'technological' age even though classical and other literary or historical studies are being pursued more vigorously and effectively than ever before. Alexander of Neckam towards the end of the twelfth century recommends a curriculum which includes the *De Oratore* and *Tusculans* as well as the more familiar *De Officiis* and *Paradoxa* and the inevitable 'Old Age' and 'Friendship'. But reading lists often err towards optimism. One may have doubts, too, about the authenticity of the range of Ciceronian (and other) knowledge claimed by thirteenth-century encyclopaedists like Vincent of Beauvais. To find 'humanism' we do better to look south of the Alps where the impact of scholasticism was late and (comparatively) slight. There, to take the best known example, we find Geremia da Montagnone (c. 1300) compiling a *Compendium moralium notabilium* showing much out of the way knowledge —of Catullus, for instance, and of Cicero's *De Fato* and *Philippics*. In terms both of time and place we are within hail of the Italian Renaissance, but we do not leave the late Middle Ages without mentions of its greatest name. Dante cites or alludes to Cicero some fifty times, and almost always as a philosopher. He knew *De Finibus*, *De Officiis*, *De Senectute*, and like so many of his age owed most to *De Amicitia*. But for Dante Aristotle was the 'Master of those who know': Cicero was Rome's 'best Aristotelian'.[29] The arrangement of sins in the Inferno owes most to Aristotle, a little to Cicero.

So we come to the Renaissance. Once thought of as a sudden shattering of a confining prison of mediaeval superstition and scholastic pedantry, the whole conception has been subjected to such careful analysis and redefinition as to have been at times in danger of dissolving quite away. But most, including those who would reject the pejorative description of mediaevalism in the above formula, now concede that a significant and unusually rapid change in habits of thought and modes of expression began in Petrarch's lifetime and that Petrarch himself had much to do with it. I shall therefore assume that the Renaissance 'happened'. Yet the old idea is certainly too simple. Not only did mediaevalism not disappear overnight: the Renaissance was in its origins not merely a straightforward rebellion against all that we regard as typically mediaeval. Petrarch's contempt for scholasticism, though vigorously expressed, is only a small part of the story. Scholasticism was essentially a phenomenon of Northern Europe, of France, of Paris. Petrarch was Italian, and what he rejected was above all the Italian tradition of education and learning which was primarily legal, while at the same time he was habituated to a climate in which secular learning and also worldly success were respectable, and in which the appeal to ancient secular authority in the shape of Roman lawyers was no novelty. Nor, for all the divisions of Renaissance Italy and passionate local loyalties, must we ignore the part played by an Italian and Roman patriotism in the Renaissance attempt to recover the tradition of Roman antiquity. Hence Petrarch's pride in his Latin epic *Africa* rather than his vernacular poetry, and the revival of the Ciceronian contempt for 'Greeklings'. Finally, Italian political conditions in the Renaissance period were very different from those in the regal and imperial North of Europe. City-states flourished and provided an environment in which statesmen of the old Roman type could re-emerge.

All these considerations are relevant to the Renaissance attitude to Cicero. There was a renewed interest in his letters, as revealing his personality, and in his speeches as a testament to his republicanism and patriotism.[30] The philosophical works were at first sight in no very changed position. But as has been said, 'what Petrarch exemplified and propounded was a different attitude to letters, not in itself a new curriculum'.[31] The 'different attitude to letters' was a different attitude to life. We can give it various names, 'humanistic'—but the term is now frowned on for its ambiguity and vagueness—'secular', even 'pagan'—though Petrarch wrote 'cave male dicas' against Cicero's statement in *Nat. D.* iii. 86:

> hoc quidem omnes mortales sic habent; . . . omnem denique commoditatem prosperitatemque vitae a dis se habere: *virtutem autem nemo deo acceptam rettulit.*

At all events a renewed interest in humanity and this world gave Cicero a new place as a guide to life. We no longer find writers under a necessity to 'christianize' or 'spiritualize' the *De Amicitia*.

Thus, familiar as the world after the Renaissance became with Cicero's speeches and letters, the philosophical works, with which must be included the now influential *De Oratore*—the education of the secular statesman was an important matter—more than held their own. A few random illustrations must suffice. Coluccio Salutati cites Cicero more often than any other classical author, and in fact as often as the New Testament (but there is less of the New Testament). Of those citations far the greater number come from the philosophical writings, especially the *Tusculans* and *De Officiis* and the two essays. A list of early vernacular translations[32] reveals the predominance of the same philosophical works with the addition of the *Somnium Scipionis*. Though it is true that in

Italy translations of the speeches have some early prominence, generally only the *pro Archia*, most of which is a discourse on the value of literature, was popular. The list of datable first printings of classical authors begins with two editions of *De Officiis* (1465 and 1466) and *De Oratore* had been printed twice by 1469.

For three more centuries it was the same story. Here or there the Ciceronian influence is more marked, more explicit. The eighteenth century with its cool rationalism and scepticism (and the growth at that time of political ideas which, though like Cicero's, were liberal, were, like his, not democratic) had an especial affinity with Cicero.[33] But throughout these centuries every educated man had studied something of Cicero's philosophical writings at school or university.[34] His influence is past calculation or analysis. It is true that many quotations or allusions, as in all times, were second-hand or traditional. It is also true that he was only one of many 'authoritative' classical writers, and that as in mediaeval times, reason was commonly held inferior to revelation. But among the pagan classics Cicero's philosophical writings held a high and apparently unassailable position.

Yet the nineteenth century saw a collapse of Cicero's whole reputation, and nothing of his suffered so much contempt or neglect as his philosophical writings. How did such a change come about? It could not in the first place have come about at all but for the healthy growth of the critical spirit which led to a reassessment of the classics—they were no longer authoritative, the secular counterpart of Holy Writ, which too was beginning to be critically examined, and in a very similar way. Not only were questions of attribution and authenticity investigated but distinctions of value and relevance began to be sharply drawn. But when traditional authority ceases to be the criterion, the criteria which replace it are not themselves exempt from criticism. They may turn out to be after all only prejudices and presuppositions. So it seems to be when we try to find out why Cicero's philosophical works suddenly declined in esteem. It may be that the judgement of the last century was right, and that of earlier ages wrong. It may be at least that Cicero's works ceased to be relevant, though once they had been, and our own age is doubtless as much entitled as the Middle Ages to decide what it wants to read. Yet the question 'Why was there this change?' has not thereby been answered, and the answer may affect our judgement of the change.

It is sometimes said that Cicero's philosophical writings suffered from the general attacks on Cicero as man and politician especially associated with the name of Mommsen. Yet the letters continue to be read—if only as historical documents—and so do the speeches—if only for the same reason, and with no widespread interest in their merits as literature. The philosophical works have declined far more sharply. The reason is curious and tells us more about the age which saw this happen than the works themselves. The root of the matter is simply that it suddenly became overwhelmingly important that Cicero's works were copies, and copies from Greek sources. This half-truth became the most important thing to be said about them, the first, and often enough the last piece of information any one normally acquires about them. No one has shown Cicero's views to be false or pernicious: it is enough that they are 'unoriginal', for the modern age will always prefer originality, however shallow, bizarre, or perverse, to tradition, however sane, wise, and true. Or if it is not enough, the balance is provided by that naive and romantic philhellenism which, despite frowns and disclaimers from per- ceptive Greek scholars of our time, still flourishes at popular and pedagogic levels, taking as axiomatic that the Greeks were superior in all respects, except government and engineering, to the Romans. But justice is not done to Cicero's philosophical writings by point- ing out their dependence on Greek sources, still less by simply murmuring 'Plato',[35] as if life were not for most of us long enough to read both.

For, at the simplest level, Cicero's subject-matter is not the same as that of Plato and Aristotle. We should not neglect his presentation of the Hellenistic philosophers, those acute and thoughtful men, engaged on problems of perennial human interest. As I have tried to show, there is a Roman contribution too, hard to disentangle because the very technique and lan- guage of ratiocination was Greek, and the Roman element is a form of life, eluding the kind of formulation which would enable it to be transmitted like the multiplication table. Those who wish may call it nebulous. It is there, and I have tried to indicate where it is to be looked for.

There is one other element in the temper of the last century which must be taken into account. It cannot be denied that Cicero's philosophical works are 'edifying', and it is no coincidence that the decline in their reputation was contemporaneous with a similar decline in the reputations of such other improving moralists (even though two of them wrote in Greek) as Seneca, Plutarch and Marcus Aurelius. There is a curious notion abroad that such writers are 'dull'. The literature of edification like any other kind may be bad or good, dull or interesting. In my own view the charge of dullness levelled against such authors as those I have named is mere evasion. The truth is that such writers come near to a reader, to *any* reader, in a way that metaphysical or Utopian speculations do only to a few; and we do not nowadays like to be made uncomfortable about our way of life.

Some reaction against these attitudes has already set in. 'Tradition' is no longer a rude word. There is again a real concern about moral problems. The nineteenth-century belief that the traditional wisdom could be taken for granted,[36] and that what moral problems remained 'progress' would solve has been shattered. But the reaction has been very largely to new dogmatisms, a neo-scholasticism or neo-fundamentalism. Even yet the time seems hardly propitious for a renewed hearing for the cautious voice of liberal common sense, combined with a warm concern for the welfare of man in society, which is the characteristic voice of Cicero.

APPENDIX

De Divinatione, ii. 1-7

1. Quaerenti mihi multumque et diu cogitanti, quanam re possem prodesse quam plurimis, ne quando intermitterem consulere rei publicae, nulla maior occurrebat, quam si optimarum artium vias traderem meis civibus; quod conpluribus iam libris me arbitror consecutum. Nam et cohortati sumus, ut maxime potuimus, ad philosophiae studium eo libro, qui est inscriptus Hortensius, et quod genus philosophandi minime adrogans maximeque et constans et elegans arbitraremur, quattuor Academicis libris ostendimus. 2. Cumque fundamentum esset philosophiae positum in finibus bonorum et malorum, perpurgatus est is locus a nobis quinque libris, ut, quid a quoque, et quid contra quemque philosophum diceretur, intellegi posset. Totidem subsecuti libri Tusculanarum disputationum res ad beate vivendum maxime necessarias aperuerunt. Primus enim est de contemnenda morte, secundus de tolerando dolore, de aegritudine lenienda tertius, quartus de reliquis animi perturbationibus, quintus eum locum conplexus est, qui totam philosophiam maxime inlustrat; docet enim ad beate vivendum virtutem se ipsa esse contentam. 3. Quibus rebus editis tres libri perfecti sunt de natura deorum,

in quibus omnis eius loci quaestio continetur. Quae ut plane esset cumula-
teque perfecta, de divinatione ingressi sumus his libris scribere; quibus, ut
est in animo, de fato si adiunxerimus, erit abunde satis factum toti huic
quaestioni. Atque his libris adnumerandi sunt sex de re publica, quos tum
scripsimus, cum gubernacula rei publicae tenebamus. Magnus locus philo-
sophiaeque proprius a Platone, Aristotele, Theophrasto totaque Peripateti-
corum familia tractatus uberrime. . . . Interiectus est etiam nuper liber is,
quem ad nostrum Atticum de senectute misimus. . . . 4. Cumque Aristoteles
itemque Theophrastus, excellentes viri cum subtilitate, tum copia, cum
philosophia dicendi etiam praecepta coniunxerint, nostri quoque oratorii
libri in eundem librorum numerum referendi videntur. Ita tres erunt de
oratore, quartus Brutus, quintus orator. . . . Quod enim munus rei publicae
adferre maius meliusve possumus, quam si docemus atque erudimus iuven-
tutem? his praesertim moribus atque temporibus, quibus ita prolapsa est,
ut omnium opibus refrenanda atque coërcenda sit. 5. Nec vero id effici posse
confido, quod ne postulandum quidem est, ut omnes adulescentes se ad haec
studia convertant. Pauci utinam! quorum tamen in re publica late patere
poterit industria. Equidem ex iis etiam fructum capio laboris mei, qui iam
aetate provecti in nostris libris adquiescunt; quorum studio legendi meum
scribendi studium vehementius in dies incitatur; quos quidem plures, quam
rebar, esse cognovi. Magnificum illud etiam Romanisque hominibus glorio-
sum, ut Graecis de philosophia litteris non egeant; quod adsequar profecto,
si instituta perfecero. 6. Ac mihi quidem explicandae philosophiae causam
adtulit casus gravis civitatis, cum in armis civilibus nec tueri meo more rem
publicam nec nihil agere poteram nec, quid potius, quod quidem me dignum
esset, agerem, reperiebam. . . . 7. Tum pristinis orbati muneribus haec studia
renovare coepimus, ut et animus molestiis hac potissimum re levaretur et
prodessemus civibus nostris, qua re cumque possemus. In libris enim sententiam dicebamus, contionabamur, philosophiam nobis pro rei publicae pro-
curatione substitutam putabamus.

NOTES

[1] A few other works are absent; of these much the most important is *De
Legibus*; its date of composition and publication is uncertain. Of extant works
mentioned, *Brutus* and *Orator*, both of 46 B.C., will not be discussed in the
present survey, but the *De Oratore*, also in form a rhetorical work, is important for our purpose.

[2] On the effect on Plato and Aristotle's moral philosophy of the survival
of ideas drawn from a more primitive state of society cf. A. W. H. Adkins,
Merit and Responsibility (Oxford, 1960).

[3] For a modern statement of this view (couched in more cynical terms)
see Louis MacNeice *Autumn Journal* (1939), xiii. Had his classics not been, as
other parts of the poem reveal, so completely dominated by Greek, he might
have known where to find a philosophy for grown men. The point will recur.

[4] Cf. D. R. Shackleton Bailey, *Towards a Text of Cicero ad Atticum* (Cambridge, 1960), pp. 61-2.

[5] On this point and the whole subject of these paragraphs P. Boyancé 'Les méthodes de l'histoire littéraire: Cicéron et son oeuvre philosophique', *RÉL* xiv (1936), 288-309, is lively and penetrating.

[6] See P. Poncelet, *Cicéron traducteur de Platon* (Paris, 1957), for a subtle and rigorous investigation of what can be discovered; see also my reservations about some of his views in my article 'Platonis Aemulus?', *Greece and Rome* 2nd ser. ix (March 1962), 48-50.

[7] He is unusually generous by ancient standards, surprisingly so if we remember that the very limited circulation of books in antiquity and the actual form of the book (the manuscript roll) made the kind of detailed references we nowadays expect in scholarly works impracticable, or even when practically feasible, of very little use to the reader.

[8] As Augustine's various references show, the work was still a normal part of the student's curriculum.

[9] Cf. H. C. Baldry, *Greek Literature for the Modern Reader* (Cambridge, 1951), pp. 281-3.

[10] The method survived in Victorian works of edification and instruction and seems to be enjoying a renewed vogue as a means of advertising or conveying official information to a public which cannot be expected to comprehend more straightforward modes of exposition.

[11] H. A. Kinross Hunt, *The Humanism of Cicero* (Melbourne, 1954), p. 9.

[12] Modern criticism dwells far too much on the question of Cicero's dialogue technique. In the ages when these works were admired, the most popular were the *Tusculans*, the *De Amicitia*, *De Senectute* and *De Officiis* in which dialogue is at its most formal or (in the last case) altogether absent.

[13] *Op. cit.* p. 11.

[14] Translation by J. M. Cohen for the Penguin Classics (Harmondsworth, 1958), pp. 166-7.

[15] M. L. Clarke, *The Roman Mind* (Cohen & West, 1956), p. 64.

[16] *De Legibus*, iii. 26, contains a delectable pleasantry at the expense of a traditional device of philosophical dialogue, the assumed agreement of the interlocutor.

[17] As Adkins has shown (cf. n. 2 and his article 'Friendship and Self-Sufficiency in Homer and Aristotle', *CQ* (N.S.), xiii (1962), 30-45), Greek 'moral philosophy' is unintelligible if we suppose it to be only concerned with 'moral' questions in the narrow sense. 'Expediency' plays a large part.

[18] Erasmus and Montaigne are two distinguished examples of men whose youthful distaste for Cicero later turned to admiration.

[19] 'Elocution' in our sense was part of 'delivery' (*actio*). Memory-training (*memoria*) was also part of the traditional system. Both are appropriate in training in the use of the spoken word. But Cicero says little, and we shall say nothing, about them.

[20] His treatment of 'fitness' (§§ 210-212) is equally cursory.

[21] Of the traditional means of *ornatus*, Cicero was most interested in rhythm, which he discusses (§§ 173-195) at length, and probably with a good deal of originality, though his account is confused by his excessive reverence for Greek authorities.

[22] H. Guite, 'Cicero's Attitude to the Greeks', *Greece and Rome*, 2nd ser.

ix (1962), 142-59, draws a most illuminating parallel with the struggles of the Europeanized Asian and Africans of our own day to 'find their own soul'. It is a pity that the rest of his article is marred by the typical modern conviction among scholars that Cicero has to be scored off by any possible means including the misinterpretation of evidence.

[23] For a brief account of this tendency down to the twelfth century see the well-known work of C. H. Haskins, *The Renaissance of the Twelfth Century* (Cambridge, 1927), pp. 94-8.

[24] It is impossible to give within a reasonable compass documentation for the statements in this and the following paragraphs, but an amusing illustration of the last point can be found in B. Smalley, *The English Friars and Antiquity* (Oxford, 1960), p. 166.

[25] Many people suppose that the 'traditional' classical education in Britain was a Renaissance creation. But the early enthusiasm for Greek of the period round 1500 soon waned, and M. L. Clarke, *Greek Studies in England 1700-1830* (Cambridge, 1945), reveals the thinness of the tradition in Greek studies in his period. Our literature almost to Clarke's terminal date owes far more to Rome than Greece. The classical education which demands as high proficiency in Greek as in Latin and inculcates as axiomatic the superiority of things Greek over things Roman is a nineteenth-century creation.

[26] Cf. C. C. J. Webb's introduction to his edition of John's *Policraticus*, p. xxix.

[27] See H. Liebeschuetz, *Mediaeval Humanism in the Life and Writings of John of Salisbury* (London, 1950), ch. vi, and esp. p. 88, for an analysis of a detailed borrowing by John from *De Oratore*.

[28] Advanced by E. K. Rand, 'The Classics in the Thirteenth-Century', *Speculum*, iv (1929), 249 ff.

[29] Cf. P. Renucci, *Danti disciple et juge du monde greco-latin* (Clermont-Ferrand, 1954), p. 331.

[30] H. Baron, 'Cicero and the Roman Civic Spirit in the Middle Ages and Early Renaissance' (*Bull. John Rylands Library*, xx (1938), 72 ff.), showed that Petrarch himself at first believed in the mediaeval picture, based on parts of the *Tusculans* and the *Dream of Scipio*, of Cicero as a philosophical recluse. His famous letter to Cicero on the discovery of the letters to Atticus reflects shock not so much (as is usually thought) at the revelation of Cicero's general instability of character as at the particular discovery of Cicero's return to politics after the death of Caesar. Later Petrarch 'accepted' this new Cicero, but it is with Salutati and Vergerio that we find a full civic humanism which recognizes in Cicero the 'ideal union of political action and literary creation'.

[31] D. Hay, *The Italian Renaissance in its Historical Background* (Cambridge, 1961), p. 86. He continues 'Wherever (in the Middle Ages) there was a grammarian, we can find some Cicero, Virgil, Ovid'. But is it accidental that in the example he chooses ('Chioggia, not a famous centre') only the *poets* are referred to as the Latin curriculum?

[32] R. R. Bolgar, *The Classical Heritage and its Beneficiaries* (Cambridge, 1954), pp. 526 ff.

[33] Details can be found in Th. Zielinski's *Cicero im Wandel der Jahrhunderte* (Leipzig, 1912), ch. 16.

[34] Cf. M. L. Clarke, *Classical Education in Britain 1500-1900* (Cambridge, 1959), *passim*.

[35] On the ineptitude of the comparison (as old, it is true, as Quintilian) see my article cited in n. 6. above.

[36] So J. W. Mackail, *Latin Literature* (John Murray, 1895), p. 73: 'If his philosophy seems now to have exhausted its influence, it is because it has in great measure been absorbed into the fabric of civilized society.' A recent writer (W. Rüegg, *Cicero und der Humanismus*, Zürich, 1946) had a different perspective, seeing in Mommsen's attack on Cicero no spent force, as Mackail had done, but the beginning of the long and disastrous decline of German liberalism.

VII

Cicero the Man

J. P. V. D. BALSDON

BEYOND the quite remarkable coincidence that they both came from Arpinum and were very distantly related, the only two 'new men' of real distinction in the late Republic had no other common trait than their 'newness'. In personality two men could hardly be more different. Marius was a soldier, and little else; while, even if Cicero had achieved his coveted triumph on his return from governing Cilicia, it would still be true that he was nothing of a soldier at all. Marius was lucky in the time when he lived; for it may be doubted whether, except in a period of severe military crisis, he would have risen to the top. Cicero, too, was lucky in the circumstances of his consular election; yet he might well have become consul at any time at all when the Roman world was, generally, at peace. Both men worked hard for their success. For, limited as his talents may have been, Marius took his soldiering very seriously indeed. And Cicero, whose talent displayed itself early when he was a schoolboy (and, however wrongly, he was thought to be a poet of genius in the making[1]), worked unsparingly in his preparation for a public career.[2] Under a series of talented teachers, Roman and Greek, he devoted himself between the ages of fifteen and twenty-nine, first in Rome and then in Greece, to the study of oratory and of philosophy; and he displayed an infinite capacity for taking pains in such tedious but important matters as learning to identify by sight anybody whom it might at any time be useful to recognize, and acquiring information about the man's family background: how rich he was, and where in Italy his property lay. It was said that, when Cicero travelled by any main road, he could speak in familiar terms of the owners of every estate that he passed.[3]

His home life and upbringing was of the happiest kind, and
left no scars. The family was rich enough, with its property at
Arpinum and its town house in the Carinae at Rome, which,
when Cicero inherited, he made over to his brother Quintus.
With Quintus (four years his junior) Marcus was on the best of
terms. They shared the cultural tastes which both their father and
their kind uncle Lucius—'homo humanissimus'[4]—fostered;
yet they differed sufficiently in personality to avoid rivalry and
conflict. Marcus had not his brother's quick temper; he was the
more promising scholar, while Quintus, with his greater bent for
the practical, was the better equipped of the two for administrative
life. Marcus was the brilliant boy, and Quintus did not complain of
taking second place. All through his life, indeed, his interests were
to be subordinated to those of his brother. Their father Marcus
is mentioned often by his elder son, always with gratitude and
affection[5]; of his mother Helvia he had left no record at all. From
the fact that she is mentioned once—as an extremely canny
house-keeper—in a letter of Quintus to Tiro,[6] it would be over-
imaginative to suggest that Marcus was his father's favourite,
Quintus his mother's. Though the family was not in politics, it
had connections with those who were. Uncle Lucius had been
taken out as a youth to Cilicia—which his nephew was one day
to govern—on the staff of M. Antonius in 102, an experience
which he owed to the influence of one of Antonius's prefects,
M. Gratidius of Arpinum. And this Gratidius, brother-in-law to
the grandfather of Marcus and Quintus, himself had the great
Marius for brother-in-law; and his son, the ill-fated M. Marius
Gratidianus,[7] was adopted by Marius's brother. Marcus and
Quintus were brought up with two first cousins, both of whom
they greatly liked: L. Cicero, the son of uncle Lucius, and C.
Visellius Varro, a friend and associate of Julius Caesar. Visellius's
mother Helvia was sister to the mother of Marcus and Quintus.[8]

They were, perhaps, a delicate family; and Cicero's friends
feared, he tells us, that the arduous exercise of an orator would
place too heavy a strain on his physique. But he survived. His
eyes often gave him trouble; but his letters are not those of a man
who was frequently troubled by bad health, and Asinius Pollio
reasonably considered him fortunate in that, surviving until
his sixties, he retained good looks and good health too.[9]

No less satisfactory over a long period of time was the family life which he himself created. He married well. Terentia was a woman of tough character, good breeding and not inconsiderable private means.[10] She is said—though there is little evidence of this in the Letters—to have taken a livelier interest in her husband's political life than he took in her domestic problems,[11] but this was probably a not abnormal state of affairs. There is a colourful story that it was Terentia who provoked Cicero, however indirectly, to the fatal act of antagonizing Clodius in the Bona Dea scandal of 62/1.[12] For she is said to have interrupted a compromising correspondence between Cicero and one of Clodius's sisters; and so, according to the story, he went out of his way to abuse Clodius in public, in order that, by so doing, he might re-establish himself in his wife's eyes as a faithful husband. That Terentia supported Cicero's action in 61 and that she and Clodius disliked one another, is not improbable[13]; but the rest of the story is unlikely to be more than gossip.

There were two children of the marriage—Tullia, born in 79, and young Marcus, born in 65, both adored and consistently spoilt by their father. Tullia's death in February 45 was, without doubt, the greatest personal tragedy in Cicero's life; suddenly, indeed, as he reached sixty, the whole stable foundation of his private life disintegrated. The strain of the Civil War had taken its toll, combined, perhaps, with the emotional instability which sometimes besets the sexagenarian. He developed quite fantastic obsessions about his wife Terentia: that she should have come from Rome to join him at Brindisi in the winter of 48/7; that she was stealing his money.[14] So he divorced her in winter 47/6 and married—whether, as Terentia said, for her looks or, as Tiro affirmed, for her money—a girl forty-five years younger than himself; and a few months later, because (according to Plutarch) she did not grieve sufficiently over the death of her thirty-five-year-old step-daughter, he divorced her too.[15] Only his spoilt son was left, living beyond his means at the University in Athens in 44 and unimproved by the *De Officiis*, which his fond father dedicated to him in that year, intending it to supplement the teaching in Morals which young Marcus was receiving from his tutors. It was not, perhaps, the boy's fault that, after the vicissitudes of the civil war and his father's murder, he became a boor and a sot. And it was not altogether his father's fault either.

On the propriety of Cicero's continuing to be on good relations with Tullia's third and most unsatisfactory husband, P. Cornelius Dolabella, from whom she had been divorced shortly before her death, it is presumptuous to pass judgement. Dolabella was an unstable politician, and his private life was deplorable. But it is not difficult to understand from the surviving letters why Terentia and Tullia in the early days were captivated by him and why, until the last months of their lives, Cicero himself thought him not beyond redemption.[16]

The marriage of his brother Quintus to Pomponia, sister of his close friend, publisher and banker, T. Pomponius Atticus was arranged, perhaps, rather to suit the interest of Marcus and Atticus than that of the two contracting parties.[17] There was a son, another Quintus; but, for the rest, it was as unhappy as a marriage could be. Pomponia was both older and richer than her husband, and she was a jealous woman, alert always to take offence. Yet, somehow, the marriage survived for a long time—until they were divorced at the end of 45. In the interval it was a subject of common interest to Cicero and his friend, Cicero's reasonable and loyal sympathy being always for his brother; and, indeed, despite a period of estrangement in the twelve months after Pharsalus, when, with his son, Quintus endeavoured to re-establish himself in the favour of Caesar and the Caesarians by maligning Marcus to an intemperate degree,[18] Marcus died, as for nearly all his life he had lived, his brother's very close friend.

How self-centred and inconsiderate Cicero was, by the standard of his times, in the hardships which he imposed on his relations and in the demands which he made of them, is hard to know. It was not only to serve Marcus's interest, but to make money for himself, that Quintus spent an uncomfortable and dangerous two years on Caesar's staff in Gaul[19] and a cold winter before that on Pompey's staff in Sardinia. Whether Cicero made proper arrangements for his wife and boy—his daughter was married—when he left home in a panic in 58, we do not know. But his family seems to have been left to its own devices as he himself moved from villa to villa, debating whether or not to follow Pompey overseas, in the first five months of 49. Yet women did not normally go overseas with their husbands, and Brutus and Cassius, admittedly after discussion with them, left their women-folk at home when they sailed from Italy in 44. Tullia (but not, it seems, Terentia) journeyed to Brindisi to greet Cicero on his triumphant homecoming in 57, and Terentia was at Brindisi in the early winter to greet him when he landed in 50. But Terentia did not come south to spend the winter with him on his return to Italy in 48, and, by failing to do this though she was in fact obeying his own instruction, she appeared to him to have deserted her duty as a wife. Tullia paid him a short visit, to discuss her divorce, in the summer of 47.[20]

Family life was not only a question of relations. There were also slaves. It has often been marked as a point of difference between Marcus and his brother that, at the grim finish, Quintus's slaves co-operated in his murder, but Marcus's slaves struggled to the end to secure his escape.[21] That Marcus was a generous master cannot be doubted. His letters show his interest in his own slaves, and in Atticus's slaves too. And Tiro, a man of very nearly his own age, whom he freed and whom he had to leave behind ill at Patras on the way home from Cilicia in 50, was less a servant than a talented and loyal friend. Everyone in the family loved him: Marcus, Quintus and their two sons. And Tiro's loyalty did not end when Cicero died. This was the moment when his most important work, the publication of much of Marcus's literary material, began.[22]

Tireless energy and a disinclination for idle relaxation were qualities of many outstanding Romans, and nothing is more remarkable about Cicero than the fact that he was never idle.[23] His life, whether in Rome itself, in his suburban villa at Tusculum or in one of his country houses further south, was devoted to the same intense concentration of interests. The problems and engagements of public life ranked highest[24]: speaking, whether in the Senate or on a public platform; pleading in the Courts (whose cases were so often a part of politics); competition to secure his own election at the earliest legal age to the successive curule magistracies, and canvassing for the election of his friends. Up to the end of his consulship in 63 his public life followed an ideal course, and there can be no part of it that he would have wished to be different. Had Fortune continued to smile on him in his old age—which for a Roman started in his forties—he would, with occasional appearances in the Courts, have enjoyed, in a stable political society, the life of an elder statesman, 'cum dignitate otium'.[25] An ageing consular, he would have been invited to speak at an early stage in every important debate. 'Dic, M. Tulli.' With all the wisdom of experience he would, particularly to the younger generation, have been an inspiration and a guide.

As it happened, however, except for the winter following his return from exile in 57 and the fatal twelve months after Caesar's murder, that Indian summer of his political career, events did not follow this desirable course. Immediately after his consulship, in 62 and 61, there were second thoughts—in other people's minds, but not in his own—about the execution of the Catilinarians in 63. The years from 59 to 49 lay under the heavy shadow of the Dynasts. From 48 to 44 there was the Dictator.

In these years, therefore, Cicero's unbounded energy required some other outlet. Not for him, even if he could have afforded it, the life of an 'otiosus', a man content to turn his back on the world and on serious pursuits, and to devote himself to idle retirement. Worse still was the self-indulgent life of such pluto-crats as Hortensius and L. Lucullus, who squandered money on their parks and pleasures, their fishponds and their food. Until 52 the Courts functioned in a traditional way. For the rest, there was his pen. Already he had published monographs and poems on his own achievements, and versions of a number of his speeches. From 54 to 51 and from 46 to 44 he wrote furiously[26]: dialogues on constitutional history, on oratory, on religion, on philosophy. He toyed with the idea of writing a history of Rome and he was a tremendous letter-writer. To his freedman Tiro, on a single day, 7th November 50, he wrote three letters, none of them of any substance.[27] All this was evidence, not only of indefatigable energy but also of indomitable spirit. And when Caesar's death once more unlocked the door to active political life, Cicero returned and, undaunted by twenty years of disappointment and frustration, showed all the sanguine vigour of his younger days.

All these interests of his could be pursued, often by letter, as long as he was in Rome or within easy reach of Rome. A long period of residence at a single one of his villas would have been tedious—almost as tedious as that long winter of 48/7 which he was forced to spend at Brindisi; for, though part of his income must have come from land,[28] and though, when Quintus was in Gaul in 54 and he was supervising his property at Arpinum, he showed good sense and expertize,[29] he had, like Sallust,[30] no interest at all in farming. Nor could he adapt himself to the un-familiar conditions of life outside Italy, in the provinces. Twice he was forced to endure what he called 'the insufferable tedium' of provincial administration: first in 75 when, instead of one of the urban quaestorships, he drew by lot the quaestorship of western Sicily; and a second time in 51 when, in consequence of Pompey's law of the previous year, he had no option but to go out for a year to govern the potentially dangerous province of Cilicia. He was home-sick for Rome from the moment when he left it. As soon as he arrived in Cilicia, he ticked off the days like a schoolboy, until the year was over and he could come home. 'Omnis peregrinatio obscura et sordida est iis, quorum industria Romae potest inlustris esse.'[31] When his time was up, and no successor came, he did not remain in the province (though he knew well enough that he should have done so). He left it in the charge of a quaestor, freshly arrived from Rome, a young man whom he believed to be both irresponsible and corrupt.[32]

If, even with the *dignitas* and *auctoritas* of a proconsul, with lictors in attendance on him, life in a province was no life at all, how much less endurable was provincial existence for Cicero as an exile in winter 58/7. He was utterly cast down, plunged into what seemed an eternity of tedium, discomfort and danger. Even his pen did not help him; nearly hysterical letters were as much as he could manage.[33]

Contrast the stern letters which he wrote to other men who chafed at being out of Rome: to Quintus in Gaul in 54 (he must remember the importance to Marcus as well as to himself of Caesar's favour); to Trebatius, the young lawyer, in Gaul (this was a great opportunity, which he must not throw away); and, during Caesar's dictatorship, to those of his friends, less fortunate than himself, who had not been pardoned, and who must therefore remain in exile. He came near to telling them that they were lucky to be where they were; for his own life in Rome under Caesar's dictatorship—so he assured them—was so disagreeable as not to be enviable at all.[34]

Cicero was not only not a 'noble'; he had no politicians at all among his ancestors, and he was as 'new' as a 'new man' could be. His father had been told by the great M. Scaurus that he should have gone in for politics; but that was all.[35] In ordinary life, of course, no stigma attached to a man from the mere fact that he was not a senator. Caesar's equestrian friend C. Matius and

Atticus, who was everybody's friend, were both far richer than many senators, and met senators socially on equal terms. Naturally a senator with his own way to make, even if he did not bribe heavily and did not feel bound, as aedile, to give expensive games, still had to spend large sums of money on his public career. We have Cicero's word that the expense of his aedileship was not substantial,[36] and he did not bribe heavily, for he would certainly have been brought to court on this charge, had there been the slightest chance of a conviction. Yet he was embarrassed all through his life by the fact that he was not rich enough to cut the figure which he wished to cut. His 'dignitas', he felt, demanded a good address in Rome, the expensive house on the Palatine which he acquired with the help of P. Sulla in 62. He needed a good suburban villa at Tusculum. And, apart from his villa at Arpinum, he acquired country houses in the south at Formiae and on the bay of Naples, with what his contemporaries regarded as foolish extravagance. These villas gave him status, he felt; and he resented what seemed to him to be callous criticism. For, when on his return from exile in 57, he claimed, as public compensation, the sums necessary to restore his Palatine house and his Tusculan villa, which Clodius's rowdies had destroyed, there were people who said bluntly that he would be far wiser to sell the sites and, they implied, live on a less expensive scale.[37]

Cicero did not inherit the necessary instrument for easy political success—a strong and reliable *clientela*, such as was attached to every noble family and, for anyone who had been a general, was constituted by those who had fought under his command. Like any 'new man', when he entered politics, he was conscious of new inferiorities: the fact that there were no death masks of distinguished ancestors in the *tablinum* of his hall; difficulty of securing admission to one or other of the great priestly Colleges. For an augurship, as he said himself, was the one bait with which Caesar, Pompey, and Crassus might have hooked him in 59,[38] and his eventual election to be augur in 53 gave a great fillip to his self-esteem. But the world of politics and politicians has never in any country been a kindly world. The patricians in Rome had once fought hard against plebeian invasion; and since the great wars the 'nobility'—'Appietas' and 'Lentulitas'[39]—had resisted the intrusion of the newcomer. So 'new men' who rose to the top were rare. The latest in time were C. Coelius Caldus, consul in 94, and

L. Gellius, the elderly consul of 72.[40] The last of any real distinction was Marius.

Up to his consulship Cicero never made a false move. He opposed the Sullan settlement even while Sulla was still alive. He identified himself—though with a tact and diplomacy which shines through every line of the *De Imperio Cn. Pompei*—with Pompey's triumphant career. He was a *popularis*. And then, having the luck to be pitted against men who were either insignificant or, from their past careers, suspect, he was elected consul with strong Optimate support.[41] Without doubt he had their backing, and that of all other sections of the people, in his strong action against Catiline's supporters. Q. Catulus, the most deeply entrenched Optimate alive, hailed him as 'Father of his Country[42]'. In such circumstances stronger men than Cicero would have sighed with happy relief, confident, as he was confident, that he had 'arrived', that the *Boni* accepted him as one of themselves.

Hardly had the applause died down before he was sharply reminded of the realities. The act of Metellus Nepos, one of the new tribunes, in forbidding him to make a public speech when out of office as consul, was clear evidence that his behaviour in 63 was likely to be challenged.[43] Metellus evidently behaved with gross ill manners,[44] and Cicero remonstrated politely through the women of Metellus's house, Clodia, his sister-in-law, and Mucia, his half-sister, Pompey's wife. He cannot have expected a letter of the kind which he received in January from Nepos's brother, Metellus Celer, who as praetor had been a loyal coadjutor in the troubles of the previous month. Cicero was told that, in his public criticism of Nepos, he had forgotten the status of the Metelli ('familiae nostrae dignitas'); he had, in fact, behaved with the discourtesy of the *arriviste* ('nec maiorum nostrorum clementia').[45] Worse than this, once danger threatened, his powerful friends of 63 were prepared to leave him to face the music alone. He realized his isolation. 'I am abandoned on all sides. I can relax only in the family, with my wife, my little girl and the boy, who is a honey ('mellito Cicerone'). My grand connections are no real friends at all; they put on a show in public, but in private life their friendship amounts to nothing. My house is full in the morning, and my friends flock round me when I walk to the forum; but there is not one of the whole lot with whom I can joke freely or sigh with the smallest intimacy.'[46] Atticus was his only intimate friend, and Atticus was in Greece.

Of other 'new men', Cicero was a friend of L. Murena, whom he defended in 63. He disliked P. Vatinius and Q. Fufius Calenus, both for their politics and for themselves. For L. Afranius, consul in 60 on Pompey's insistence, he had outspoken contempt. Milo, whose merits he so grossly exaggerated, had no claim to nobility either as a Papius of Lanuvium (the family of his birth) or as an Annius (the family into which he was adopted); but Cicero did not, either in his case or in anybody else's, show the smallest inclination to crusade on behalf of the claims of 'new men' as such. He was immodest enough to see his own success as a purely personal affair.[47] Indeed, like so many other *parvenus* in Rome, and in other countries too, he showed an exaggerated respect for nobility as such. When the governor of Asia had to leave a deputy when he returned from his province in 50, Cicero considered that the 'nobilitas' of his quaestor L. Antonius constituted an outstanding qualification for the appointment.[48] And, no less interestingly, he liked (apart from Atticus and Quintus) to use distinguished figures as speakers in his fictional dialogues. If Atticus had not stressed the absurdity of making men as unphilosophic as Catulus and L. Lucullus the spokesmen in the *Academica* in 45, the dialogue would never have been re-written and would have been published with Cicero's full approval in its original form.[49]

Cicero was not alone among Roman politicians in the importance which he attached to his self-esteem, his *dignitas*; for Caesar himself claimed, as sufficient reason for his invasion of Italy in 49, the need to defend his *dignitas* against Optimate insult.[50] But for Cicero after his exile and after the interruption of his independence in politics in 56, the preservation, even the enhancement, of his formal standing was a vital matter. He would have liked to be censor in 55.[51] He was overjoyed in 53 at election to the augurate. And it is to be hoped that, embarrassed by their long-withered laurels, the lictors who accompanied him home from Cilicia as the Civil War broke out knew how much, to their proconsul, a triumph would have meant.

Where the personal side of political life was concerned, Cicero was condemned—like Pompey—to perpetual solitude; for men who change from one side to the other in politics are subsequently trusted by neither. And Cicero had not even, as Pompey had, a

cluster of satellites, the 'familiares Pompei'. An occasional Optimate, like Lentulus Spinther admired and was kind to him.
He patronized a number of younger men with intemperate
enthusiasm (Octavian the last of them), conscious of their failings,
but wilfully blind to the significance of those failings. As so
often in life, Cicero saw only what he wanted to see. Even Milo
—except when he squandered money[52]—could do no wrong.

Of his relations with his outstanding contemporaries, his
attitude to Pompey, by whom he was mesmerized, is hardest to
understand. He had admired Pompey's achievements from the
start and in the early sixties, to a degree, he was useful to him.
In the moment of his own declining political stature, after
Pompey's return from the East in 62, he dreamed dreams of a
strong *amicitia*, which would somehow put the Roman political
ship once more on an even keel. Pompey he cast for the part of
Scipio, himself for Laelius.[53] Pompey would be at the helm, and
Cicero would chart the course.

There were difficulties in such a project, for Cicero's opinion
about the execution of the conspirators was evidently not
Pompey's; and it may well be inferred from Cicero's silence on
the subject, that he did not back Pompey's arrogant claim that
the Senate should ratify his eastern settlement without even
discussing it in debate. None the less, Cicero had the illusion that
he might succeed.[54] But Pompey was not interested. If there was
to be a political alliance, he looked for strength, not weakness—
to Cato and his friends (who declined his overtures[55]) or to Caesar
and Crassus, whom in the end he joined. Hence Cicero's bitterness
with Pompey in the early months of 59. In the fifties Cicero no
more shared the secrets of Pompey's enigmatic mind than did
anyone else in Rome.[56] In the crisis of 58 Pompey gave him neither
help nor advice. Indeed, if Plutarch is to be believed, he was too
much of a coward even to give him a hearing.[57] Yet—and his
critics justly taunted him on this account—Cicero cherished no
resentment, but only remembered Pompey's service in securing
his recall.[58] And, when the storm broke in 49, his personal feeling
for Pompey in the end determined the action which he
took.[59]

To Caesar he was attached by more than one link. In youth
Caesar had been a close friend of the young Ciceros and their
cousin, C. Visellius Varro.[60] Not only had he received the same

kind of education as Cicero and his brother (including a period of further education in Greece) but, more than this, he was, like both of them, a man of deeply humane interests. Like Marcus, he attracted notice as a young man in the Courts and he could, like Marcus, have made a brilliant orator. Like Marcus, he wrote well; as far as their writings went, their admiration was reciprocal.[61] When their relations were close, as in 54, at least one work of Cicero's was posted out to Caesar in Gaul in advance of publication: his poem *De temporibus suis* (the beginning of which Caesar professed to have enjoyed, but after that it evidently sent him to sleep[62]). And when Quintus crossed to Britain in 54, Marcus importuned him for local colour, because he wanted to write about the Conquest, and to send it to Caesar.[63] Even when their relations were cold in 46, Caesar showed discriminating judgement in sifting the true from the false, as he assiduously collected the latest reported Ciceronian *mot* and recorded it in his Book of Jests.[64]

In 45, when Munda had been won and, even though Sextus Pompeius was still alive, the Civil War was at last concluded, Cicero longed to write Caesar an important letter, an essay full of suggestions for the solution of the problems of the day. Had not Aristotle and Theopompus written such letters to Alexander— letters by which, Cicero knew enough history to realize, Alexander had not been greatly impressed? But by this time Caesar could only be approached through his agents in Rome, men like Hirtius, Cornelius Balbus and C. Oppius. One draft after another was rejected by these agents, who at least understood Caesar's intentions; and perhaps they acted with kindness in killing the project. It is tempting to wonder how much about all this Caesar himself knew.[65]

Yet, even so, there was still a *vinculum amicitiae*. When Caesar descended on Cicero at Puteoli in December 45 with, as it seemed, a whole army in his train, all needing to be fed, and when— because, politically, at that moment they had nothing in common —they could not talk, as Cicero would have liked to talk, about Caesar's political plans for a new Rome, they could still spend an animated evening in literary conversation.[66]

Quintus, who tossed off four tragedies in sixteen days when he was in Gaul,[67] was another link. He had been Caesar's colleague as aedile and as praetor; he was on Caesar's staff from 54 to 52, and in resisting the attack on his camp in winter 54 he performed a distinguished service to which Caesar paid a warm tribute.[68]

Moreover, in politics Marcus had a useful potential. Caesar would have liked an effective *amicitia* in 60.[69] He secured it in 56 and confirmed it when, among other things, Quintus joined his staff two years later.[70] He was generous, and lent Cicero money.[71] And all the time he went out of his way to flatter him. Fully aware of the triviality of Cicero's military success in Cilicia, he none the less wrote to congratulate him on its recognition by the government at Rome.[72] In 49 he recognized Cicero's unique qualification as a negotiator between himself and Pompey and, when the possibility of negotiation had vanished, he badly wanted Cicero to stay in Italy and to be one of his senators. Cicero was approached directly by Caesar, and also through Cornelius Balbus and Oppius.[73] There was, indeed, only one occasion on which it was possible to pretend that Caesar acted in any but a friendly way towards Cicero. That was in early 58, when he stayed outside Rome with his troops, delaying his departure for Gaul until Clodius's sinister purpose was accomplished and Cicero was in flight. But is it inconceivable that Caesar stayed because he mistrusted Clodius and, if there was violence, he wanted to be on the spot to act in the interest of Cicero's safety? After all, in the previous year when the danger from Clodius first threatened, he had offered Cicero a way of escape, which Cicero had not accepted —a post on his own staff in Gaul.[74]

Here was Caesar's attraction, an almost irresistible force. Yet there were two opposing forces, whose combined power in the end was stronger—the integrity of Cato, and the mesmerism of Pompey, neither of them men with even a portion of Caesar's personal attractiveness. Each in his heart of hearts despised Cicero as much as Caesar respected him. With neither had Cicero any cultural affinity. There was little to attract him in the rigid Stoicism of Cato. Pompey—though he was capable of writing a clear letter—had little culture.[75] Yet in public life Cato had an integrity to which Cicero could make no claim. Cato was impolitic (in his opposition to the *Equites*, which destroyed the *concordia* in 61[76]); he was self-centred and conceited (in the matter of his Cyprus mission[77]); he was high-principled to the point of absurdity in 52 when he declined to propose the election of Pompey as sole consul, but was happy to second the proposal when it was made by his son-in-law Bibulus[78]; he was mean and disingenuous (when in 50, after disparaging the military achievement of Cicero in Cilicia, he proposed extravagant honours in recognition of Bibulus' trifling successes in Syria[79]); he was not without responsibility for one of the most crooked financial transactions of the period (his nephew Brutus' loan to the Salaminians of Cyprus[80]); in his family and married life one is tempted to wonder whether he had any human feelings at all; and, as Cicero showed so amusingly in the *Pro Murena*, he was an outsize prig.[81]

Yet, except in the case of the honours which Cato proposed for Bibulus in 50, a matter which touched him to the bone, Cicero never referred to Cato with any malice. Neither during nor after his exile did he reproach Cato with perfidy. There was a coldness, naturally, when, on his return from Cyprus, Cato defended the legality of Clodius's *acta*. But, in general, Cicero respected Cato, and with a genuine respect. And for once considerations of expediency meant nothing to him when in 46 he published his eulogy of Cato, a work which provoked, in Caesar's *Anticato*, an acrid retort.

Cato was never worried, as Cicero was worried, by the problem as to when a man may legitimately put aside thoughts of right and wrong, and allow considerations of expediency to guide his conduct. This was a question which had long worried philosophers. Panaetius of Rhodes in the second century had started, but never finished, a book on the question. After Caesar's death Cicero took the book, made a Roman version of it, and supplied the missing conclusion. This was the *De Officiis*; and its astonishing and convenient conclusion was that the good man might pursue the right ('honestum') and the expedient ('utile') indifferently because, in the end, they were the same. So, whether or not with such conscious high-mindedness, Cicero unashamedly pursued expediency when, in conflict with Cato, he favoured the making of concessions to the business men in 60[82]; and he followed this same policy in 56 when—because, he claimed, of the spineless ineffectiveness, the jealousy and the dishonesty of those who had been his political associates—he surrendered his independence and accepted the party ticket of the Three. In a changing world, he claimed, there was no particular virtue in consistency. 'Temporibus adsentiendum.' One must move with the times.[83]

For in public life a man must be a realist and accept the facts of the situation. When there was no prospect of success in the course which he believed to be right, then, like a ship-captain who could not make harbour, he must change course.[84] 'Mutare sententiam turpe est' was the creed of the Stoic Sapiens; to accept realities was the behaviour of the Ciceronian Sapiens. This was how Cicero explained his own submission in 56; and it was how he justified his return to Italy and acceptance of Caesar's domination after Pharsalus in 48. To follow Pompey in opposition to Caesar had been, morally, the right course, as long as the issue was in doubt. When, after Pharsalus, it was clear that Caesar was invincible, it was stupid to continue to oppose him. Pompey, he thought, was doomed. No personal tie bound him to Cato, as he had been bound to Pompey. The other republican leaders who survived were men about whose integrity he had no illusions at all. So, in returning to Italy, Cicero convinced himself that he did what was right.[85]

Only one anecdote survives to illustrate even the smallest intimacy in Cicero's relations with Pompey—the story of their joining in an attempt (which their host ingeniously defeated) to find how simply L. Lucullus fed when he was alone at home, and unexpected visitors arrived to take pot-luck.[86]

If Pompey once behaved with generosity to Cicero, apart from working belatedly for his recall from exile, history has left no record of the fact. His conceit was inordinate; and his behaviour suggests that he regarded Cicero as a small man, a person to be encouraged only in as far as he was useful to himself. Yet, except in the first alarming months of his association with Caesar in 59, Pompey had 'gravitas' and, like Cato, a moral integrity which Caesar lacked. 'Hominem enim integrum et castum et gravem cognovi', Cicero wrote, when he heard that Pompey was dead.[87] Those three epithets hold the key to Pompey's attraction.[88] They were epithets which Cicero could not at any time have used of Caesar.

In public life, in fact, Cato and Pompey were to be trusted; and Caesar was not to be trusted at all. Cato would never have tried to overthrow the republic which, with its traditions, Cicero loved as well as he loved life itself. While republicanism survived, harmless filibustering was as far as Cato would go in the way of political protest; though, if his opponents were prepared to use force against him, he was not afraid to face it, as when he was thrown off the platform in the passage of Caesar's land bill in 59, and sent to prison (as the only means of stopping him from orating) by Caesar in 59 and by the tribune Trebonius in 55.[89] And, despite bitter remarks in 49/8 like, 'Ita sullaturit animus eius',[90] Cicero never feared an attempt to overthrow the republic on Pompey's part. Caesar's behaviour in 59 was something of which neither Cato nor Pompey could have been capable—an unauthorized use of force which, as later comments in the *De Legibus* show, was intolerable. Intolerable, too, however great the provocation, was Caesar's invasion of Italy in 49. The conduct of Caesar as dictator was more intolerable still, and Cicero's conscience could never be reconciled to Caesar's public behaviour. In public life he was the typical villain of the whole of that Greek philosophy which was Cicero's bible.

In a world of cold ideas, the warmth of human personality counts for nothing at all. So the murder of Caesar brought Cicero nothing but satisfaction.[91] He was in exultation over the senatorial decree of 17th March, which abolished the dictatorship —an ideological triumph which did not begin to touch the realities of political life[92]—and he was acutely embarrassed when Caesar's friend C. Matius, with whom he was spending the evening, had the bad taste to talk about Caesar not as a repulsive idea but as a generous, lovable, intelligent and outstanding man. This, Cicero wrote, was talk which a 'good man' ('quisquam bonus') could not but find offensive.[93]

Even had fortune been kind, and had active politics engrossed the whole of Cicero's adult constructive life, his social existence would have been singularly arid if it had been spent in the company of politicians alone. A philosopher needs the company of other philosophers; a poet needs the society of poets. Cicero was fortunate in that Atticus[94] and Quintus, the two men nearest to him, had affinities with every one of his far-ranging interests.

In their love of Greece, of its literature and thought (even though, like so many of his other friends, Atticus was an Epicurean), they shared a common culture. Atticus, for all the power that his wealth gave him, typified the sort of society in which Cicero had been brought up—a society in touch with politics, but not perilously involved in them.

Close on four hundred letters survive, to illustrate the intimacy of their friendship. But it is a one-sided picture, for all the letters which survive were written by Cicero. Whether or not Atticus published the correspondence after Cicero's death, he certainly co-operated with Tiro in preparing it for publication[95]; and, cunning as a fox, he ensured that no letter should survive which might in any way incriminate his own reputation. Cicero's letters were a mixture of business (for Atticus was, in a sense, both his banker and his publisher), of politics, of social and family affairs and of cultured humanity. In politics Atticus was Cicero's confidant, a knight flatteringly invited to advise a consular, and phlegmatically unirritated by the chill response which he so often received. If his advice in 58 was no more constructive than that of others, Cicero left him in no doubt about the fact.[96] When Atticus criticized the intemperance of Cicero's public jubilation over the destruction of a pro-Caesarian monument in the forum by Dolabella after Caesar's death, he was told bluntly that he was himself the cause of Cicero's behaviour.[97] And when (after the plan had been abandoned) he criticized Cicero's plan to go to Greece in the summer of 44, Cicero retorted with a positive torrent of abuse.[98] But Atticus was not easily perturbed. That was why he remained Cicero's close friend, and the close friend also of most other men of prominence in Roman public life.

Even without his Letters, we should know of Cicero's interest in bright and talented young men, many of them his pupils at the Bar. In Cornelius Nepos he shared a common friend with Catullus.[99] Catullus cannot have sympathized with Cicero the poet, any more than Cicero himself sympathized with the work of the new school of young poets; yet Catullus's lines

> Tanto pessimus omnium poeta
> quanto tu optimus omnium patronus,

alive as they are with irony and amusement, are not unfriendly.[100] Young Licinius Calvus was not Cicero's type of orator; yet 'de ingenio eius valde existimavi bene'.[101] Cicero had a genius for interesting himself in promising young men of intelligence: in C. Cassius Longinus[102]; in the slightly comic Trebatius Testa (who evidently had the makings of a really good lawyer[103]); in young Curio, who was so much more talented than his dotard of a father[104]; and in his former pupil, M. Caelius Rufus, who may have lacked balance, but who was infinitely witty and intelligent.[105]

Outside politics, again, his letters introduce us to a number of other men too, whose friendship gave him the greatest satisfaction, for the diversity of Cicero's talents gave him the *entrée* to a whole variety of social worlds. The wit and gaiety of a letter from Volumnius Eutrapelus lifted the curtain for a moment on the humanity of civilized life, when the mail arrived to break the tedium of relegation to distant Cilicia.[106] And in Naples there was L. Papirius Paetus, a rich old gourmet, to whom it was possible to talk or write intelligently about literature or about philosophy, whose leg could be pulled about his claim to pretentious ancestry, and who could be amused by a letter on obscenity, and the absurdity of Stoic doctrine on the subject.[107] At Pompeii, prostrated by gout but an excellent conversationalist all the same, was M. Marius, a distant relative, a man who found as little enjoyment in the public games and shows as did Cicero himself.[108] There was the elderly Caerellia, the passionate enthusiast of philosophy, who secured a pre-publication copy of the *De Finibus* in 45.[109] A. Caecina, an associate in the happier days before the civil war broke out, was author of an authoritative book on Etruscan augury, which gave Cicero much of the material which he needed for the *De Divinatione*[110]; and, a close friend in the late sixties and early fifties, there was Nigidius Figulus, the Pythagorean, who dabbled in the occult.[111]

With the learned M. Terentius Varro, on the other hand, he consorted and corresponded on terms of strained politeness, but never of intimacy. Both he and Cicero were Pompey's friends and, on their return to Italy after the Civil War, they both were battered men, who owed their survival to Caesar's clemency. They were drawn together by this common experience and also by Atticus, a common friend. Cicero dedicated the second version of the *Academica* to Varro in 45, and Varro returned the compliment. Both were scholars, but scholars of a very different sort. Varro was a researcher, an antiquarian, a 'curiosus', a man who had been projected by Pompey's instigation rather than by his own impulse into public administration. His mind had not the breadth of Cicero's, and he had none of Cicero's rich imagination. For Varro scholarship was a preferable alternative to public life; for Cicero it was an enforced substitute.[112]

'Amicus' in Latin was an ambivalent word. The 'amicitia' about which Cicero published a little dialogue was friendship in the fullest sense, a relationship which was ideally achievable only between two morally perfect men (such as we are invited to believe Scipioand Laelius to have been[113]). In the *De Amicitia* Cicero stated that true friendships were very difficult to achieve in public and political life.[114] Yet those very politicians had so abused and coarsened the word 'amicus' that, in the language of the Lobbies, as has been observed, '*Amicitia* was a weapon of politics, not a sentiment of congeniality.'[115] In politics a man's 'amici' were those who voted on his side of the House, his 'inimici' those who voted against him. His own association with his partners was a 'societas', an 'amicitia'; the association of his opponents constituted a 'factio'. The inner ring of his 'amici' were his 'familiares'. Cornelius Balbus was Caesar's 'familiaris'[116]; the fifties were haunted by the 'familiares Pompei'.[117]

Cicero's opponents and traducers appeared to him to fall into one of two categories; either they were enemies, morally bad men ('inimici' or 'improbi') or they were jealous of him ('invidi').[118] This latter conception is interesting for, literary distinction apart, it is hard to detect much that was enviable after 63 in Cicero's public career. Yet Cicero scented jealousy everywhere; he was even capable of believing in 61 B.C. that Pompey was jealous of him.[119]

In his own case, jealousy of other men's success had no part in his constitution, and Plutarch did well to emphasize the fact.[120]

In politics men changed sides; so the 'amici' of yesterday might be the 'inimici' of tomorrow. Caesar lost 'friends', whose support he never recovered, when he associated with Pompey in 59. And conversely the 'enemies' of yesterday might become the 'friends' of tomorrow.[121]

Despite the virulence with which Cicero abused both Catiline and P. Clodius in their lifetimes, he was ready to state in public a few years after Catiline's death that there had been much good in the man;[122] and only a year after Clodius was dead, he excused him generously on two grounds, firstly that behind Clodius's opposition to him a really important political principle was at stake, and secondly that, under the impulse of others, Clodius had been driven to more uncompromising hostility with Cicero than he would himself have desired.[123] Seven years later he wrote in a letter that, were Clodius still alive, there was no reason why they should not be living on friendly terms.[124] The two consuls of 58 were the targets of Cicero's unqualified vituperation; yet the monster of the *In Pisonem*, 'the man who had lost an army' was, in the autumn of 44, a politician of whom Cicero approved[125]; and Gabinius, 'the man who sold his army', was perhaps less ardently hated by Cicero after he had been driven, however unwillingly, to defend him in the Courts in 54.[126] Vatinius, the unspeakable tribune of 59, was a friend, and an amusingly critical friend, of Cicero in 44.[127] There were, perhaps, only three men for whom Cicero felt genuine hatred. He hated M. Crassus, not only because he saw an utter lack of integrity in his avarice[128] but also, surely, on some deeper ground. His hatred of Caesar during his dictatorship and after his death had an ideological basis; Caesar was a man who had deliberately suppressed and trampled on free republicanism, on liberty. And, probably from the winter of 48/7, he and Antony entertained the deepest hatred for one another.[129]

Together with the news of Cicero's murder in late 43, there arrived his severed head and hands, as Antony had commanded, for nailing up on the Rostra at Rome: the hands because they had penned the Philippic orations.[130] Perhaps the tongue alone would have sufficed, that tongue in whose activity—naturally enough, in a comparison of Cicero's Life with that of Demosthenes —Plutarch interested himself so greatly.

In the Courts Cicero prosecuted Verres in 70 and T. Munatius Plancus Bursa, tribune of 52, in early 51, both times successfully[131]; but we know of no other occasions when he prosecuted in the Courts. He spoke always for the Defence and among the Defending Counsel he usually spoke last, because he had to an unparalleled degree the faculty of rousing the jury's pity and sympathy for the prisoner. In the Courts, therefore, he was not primarily engaged in castigation and abuse. It was mainly in the cross-examination of witnesses in Court and in the antecedents of cases (public meetings, *contiones*) or in their aftermath (an 'altercatio', perhaps in the Senate), that he moved in to the attack. Cicero was famous for his wit on such occasions, but he admits himself that of the jokes which he made some were less good than others.[132] Often on such occasions he showed himself capable of an outspoken vehemence which outstripped the bounds of legitimate abuse, and he had cause more than once, in a cooler

moment, to regret what he had said. We can read the *In Pisonem*
and the *In Vatinium*. We do not possess the text of his intemperate
abuse of P. Clodius at a *contio* before Clodius's trial in 61, which
(and not what Cicero deposed as a witness in the trial itself) made
Clodius his enemy.[133] We have specimens of his subsequent
abuse of Clodius and Curio in an *altercatio* in the Senate. So far
from being witty, it is coarse and rather puerile.[134]

Mockery of the physical defects and peculiarities of his opponent was in antiquity a legitimate indulgence for the orator, just
as today, even with the grossest savagery, it is practised, as we
think rightly, by the cartoonist. None the less, in Plutarch's view
and in the view, no doubt, of many of his own contemporaries,
Cicero often went beyond what was legitimate.[135] Often, Plutarch
thought, he did this in order to raise a laugh.[136] That was 'levitas',
surely—a charge which Cicero would have been deeply shocked
to have made against him.

In the public discharge, whether on the platform or in the
Courts, of premeditated invective and elaborate jokes (like saucy,
porcine punning on the name of Verres), the orator took a cal-
culated risk. If the abuse returned like a boomerang, he could not
complain. When Cicero polished up the violent attack which he
delivered on Curio and Clodius in the Senate in 61 and, by an
act of indiscretion, his publisher allowed the finished version to
circulate in 58, just when Cicero needed Curio's help for his
restoration, it was disingenuous to think that its authorship
might be disclaimed: 'posse probari non esse meam'.[137]

More dangerous was the private discharge of the sudden inspiration of a quick wit and a mischievously venemous tongue.
The more offensive a witticism, the greater the certainty that
it will circulate. Sooner or later 'the boy' Octavian was bound to
hear that he was to be praised, provided for, and then polished
off: 'laudandum, ornandum, tollendum'.[138] In moments of
epistolary excitement, discretion vanished. In the bitter first six
months of 59 Pompey was the Nabob—'Alabarchus', 'Sampsicer-
amus'.[139] In 61 the young Curio, suspected of Catilinarian sym-
pathies, was 'Little Miss Curio', 'Filiola Curionis'.[140] In the same
year M. Piso the consul had not invited Cicero to open the senatorial debate on 1st January, and then made it evident that he
disapproved of the prosecution of Clodius. So, though he was an
old friend, a companion in Greece eighteen years earlier, a bene-

factor (in that he had successfully defended Terentia's relative at the trial of the Vestal Virgins in 73), he was 'the funny fellow with the funnier face' 'the perfect image of a ham actor'—'Facie magis quam facetiis ridiculus', 'Deterioris histrionis similis'.[141]

After he reached Pompey's camp in 49, at a time when men were both irritable and anxious, Cicero's *sottises*, in one clever and destructive criticism after another, were more than they could stand. When a new arrival reported that there was a rumour in Rome that Pompey was under siege, Cicero said, 'So that is why you have come: to see for yourself'. When Labienus reported portents of victory for Pompey, Cicero said, 'Losing our camp, then, was a stroke of genius for a start'.[142]

If he made a lot of bad jokes, he also made a number of good ones; for not without justification he prided himself on a quick wit and a sense of ironical humour.[143] The defence of an elected magistrate who was charged with bribery by one of his unsuccessful rivals (L. Murena in 63, Plancius in 54) showed Cicero at his best, mocking the prosecutor's immodest conviction that nothing but bribery could explain his own failure to secure election. And in ordinary speech he was capable of a pretty wit. When he saw Tullia's husband, a very small man, wearing a very large sword, he said, 'Who has been buckling my son-in-law on to a sword?'[144] At the end of Crassus's second consulship in 55, pressure was put on Cicero to agree to a public reconciliation with him; so, for evidence, Crassus invited himself to dinner with Cicero before he left for the East. When, later, Cicero was told that Vatinius wished for better relationship with him, he said, 'Surely Vatinius does not want to be asked to dinner too'.[145] And, when he was pestered as governor of Cilicia to send a consignment of panthers home to Caelius in Rome, there was a coy elegance about the manner in which he took the opportunity to reflect on the integrity of his own administration. He answered, 'Our panthers have crossed into Caria; why, they complain, should they alone be victimized?'[146] His good jokes were a part of his *festivitas*, his *urbanitas*. Caesar collected them. Tiro published three books of them when Cicero was dead.

For many years after 44 a bare reference to the 'Ides' was easily understood as a reference to Caesar's murder on the Ides of March 44. For Cicero, but not for many others, a bare reference to 'the Nones' meant the execution of the Catilinarian prisoners on the

Nones of December 63. It was the outstanding mark of Cicero's egotism that he never concealed his belief that this was the outstanding historical event of his own lifetime. It was also, of course, a mark whether of obstinacy or of firm principle that, disastrous as the consequences were for himself, he never thought that the execution had been a mistake.

Pompey was the first to suffer: in a letter—'as long as a book'—which reached him at a moment when, with Mithridates dead, the eastern world was at his feet. It was a letter which he could hardly bring himself to acknowledge and one about which on more than one occasion Cicero was publicly mocked.[147] Jury after jury in the Courts listened to the bombastic story. The reading public was offered Cicero's own version of the events, in Greek and in Latin, in prose and in verse.[148] The leading historians of the day—Posidonius and L. Lucceius—were invited to write monographs on the subject.[149] Brutus referred bitterly to this obsession of Cicero's in a letter to Atticus after Caesar's death.[150] As Plutarch said, there was absolutely no limit to this egotistical conceit.[151] Psychologically it is not difficult to understand. It was his desperate and only way of fighting against the recognition of his subsequent political unimportance.

That there was real danger in the plans of the conspirators inside Rome in 63 as well as in the marshalling of the Catilinarian army in Etruria was never doubted, and most people would not have disagreed with what was probably the opinion of Brutus (in his lost account of the conspiracy) and was certainly the opinion of Sallust, that Cicero deserved the highest praise for neutralizing his untrustworthy colleague and for convincing a reluctant senate that the danger existed. He was, as both Brutus and Sallust said, an excellent consul—'optimus consul'.[152] The question which many people must have asked was this: 'Would the Senate have voted as it did, and would Cicero have executed the conspirators, on the Nones, if Cato's speech in the Senate had never been made?' Brutus's answer to both parts of the question, and Sallust's also, would certainly have been 'No'.

When the blow fell in 58, however, Cicero felt no inclination at all to shelter behind Cato. After 57 he felt less inclination still for, while others no doubt regarded his recall from exile as a judgement on the lawless procedure which Clodius had followed in 58, Cicero himself regarded it as a public vindication of the propriety of his execution of the conspirators in 63. He was extremely angry, therefore, when, writing in 45, Brutus made Cato responsible for the critical decision that the prisoners under arrest should be put to death.[153]

The execution was right, and it was Cicero's responsibility. Never to the time of his death did Cicero question these, to him, self-evident truths.

He was also convinced that the origin of the Civil War lay in the association of Pompey and Caesar in 59. He blamed Pompey and he was convinced that, in taking this fatal course, Pompey had disregarded advice which he had received from Cicero himself. He went further and stated that he had advised Pompey against making concessions to Caesar in 55, and again in 52.[154] It is impossible in the absence of explicit evidence to estimate what slender element of truth may be contained in these monotonous claims. The man who claims always to have been right, but whose advice was never heeded: among politicians in all ages he is a familiar and—to his contemporaries—a highly irritating figure.

In reviewing historical crises, once they lay in the past, Cicero saw himself all too often in the centre of the stage, when he had in fact been in the wings. When at the end of 54 he had to explain to Lentulus Spinther, who had been out of Rome since 57, why he had capitulated to the Dynasts and surrendered his own political independence after the Conference of Luca in 56, he painted a splendid picture of his own heroic resistence to the last, even suggesting it was fear of Cicero which had brought the three together again in 56. But his picture was not a true picture. His imagination was better than his memory.[155]

In smaller matters it was the same. In 63 he resigned the consular province of Cisalpine Gaul. By 50 B.C. it was not a province but 'the certain hope of a triumph' which he had viewed with indifference.[156] In 59 he had revealed to Atticus his interest in the possibility of election to the augurate; by 50 a priesthood was something which he could at any time have achieved without difficulty, but something in which he was not interested at all until he received the augurate in 53.[157] At the end of 50 he would like a triumph for the sake of 'dignitas', because Bibulus was claiming a triumph, and for no other reason.[158] But what of the letters which he had written before anything was known of Bibulus's claim? And when he had left Cilicia and told Atticus in

August 50 that he had made up his mind—'statueram'—if any danger still threatened from Parthia, to leave Quintus in charge or else to stay on in the province himself, had he forgotten what he had written on the subject to Atticus at the end of May, when war did threaten, 'cum bellum esse in Syria magnum putetur, id videatur in hanc provinciam erupturum, hic praesidi nihil sit'?[159] And even though his influence in politics was greater from 54 to 51 than it was in 45, it was a not inconsiderable exaggeration to state that he wrote the *De Republica* 'cum gubernacula reipublicae tenebamus'.[160] It is an act of imaginative vanity to fictionalize the past in this way; but it is perhaps not a very serious weakness, and it is one to which in all ages men in public life are singularly liable.

It is hard to distinguish between instability and extreme sensibility in the emotions; and the criticism was justly made of Cicero that he was too easily elated and too easily depressed. In moments of humiliation he did not spare himself. He ought, he felt in 56, to have taken Atticus's advice and to have made his political submission to Caesar earlier: 'Scio me asinum germanum fuisse'.[161] In the unhappy winter of 48/7 which he spent at Brindisi, uncertain of the verdict which Caesar would pronounce on his return, he deplored the mistake ('peccatum') which he had made in joining Pompey two years earlier. 'It was all my fault'; 'Meo vitio pereo'.[162] Worst of all was the gloom of exile in 58/7. He ought never to have fled from Rome; 'Caeci, caeci fuimus'. He should have killed himself rather.[163] His exile, however, unlike some of his other disasters, had a happy ending. After his recall and his triumphal and garlanded march on Rome, when—in his own proud expression, which others later were to mock[164]—'Italy carried him home on its shoulders', he changed his mind in his mercurial way. He said time and time again, and doubtless believed, that, in leaving Rome, he had trampled on his own wish and inclination, which was to stay and face the danger; he had gone because, had he remained, there would have been fighting. Lives would have been lost, and he was not prepared to countenance such sacrifice on the part of others.[165] Metellus Numidicus was already one of his heroes, and now he had the satisfaction of depicting himself as a second and more illustrious Metellus; for the circumstances of Metellus' recall were by no means as glorious as the circumstances of his own.[166]

He was only human in that a blow to his pride was something

which he found it very difficult to sustain. As long as it seemed likely in early 61 that Clodius would be tried satisfactorily, and be condemned for his alleged intrusion on the *Bona Dea* celebrations in Caesar's house, letter followed letter to Atticus, who was out of the country.[167] When, contrary to his expectation, Clodius was acquitted, Cicero had not the heart to write. The news reached Atticus from some other source, and it was only in response to Atticus's enquiry that Cicero wrote, two months after the case was over, to describe its outcome.[168] Again, when he made his political capitulation in 56, it was only when Atticus asked for the facts that Cicero wrote to tell him.[169] And in the first case, though he cannot have failed to realize the danger which impended from his antagonizing of Clodius, he tried to give the impression—and, indeed, tried even to persuade himself—that, as a result of the whole business, he had strengthened his own political standing.[170] He was easily cast down, and as easily revived; in particular, he exaggerated, both in his own case and in that of others, the significance of popular demonstrations, whether favourable or unfavourable, at the games, at the theatre and in the streets.[171]

Courage is a hard quality to estimate in others, even in oneself. Cato was lauded in antiquity for his courage; Cicero was maligned as a coward. Ostentatious Stoicism then as later in the Empire was the stuff of which heroes were made, and Cicero was no Stoic. As Brutus wrote, 'We are far more frightened by the thought of death, exile and poverty than we ought to be; but for Cicero these are the last word in disaster'.[172] It is hard to believe that in Cato's position he could have endured so lightly the hardships of the North African desert and, despite everything that he wrote in the first book of the *De Officiis* about bravery, it is certain that Cicero could not have lived—indeed would not have had the selfless imagination to live—those splendid last days at Utica. Cato's *dignitas*, which was the mainspring of every Roman's action in public life, precluded surrender to Caesar; his philosophy inspired him to die well.

Cicero, on the other hand, never showed any inclination to die of his own free will for a cause. The feeling in exile in winter 58 that he should have killed himself rather than flee from Rome was a passing thought, quickly banished. After Pharsalus he saw no point in martyrdom; nor, after all, did Cassius or Brutus. The reflection in the following years that it was a mistake for him to remain alive was singularly half-hearted; and when in the *De Officiis* he stated that, while suicide was Cato's duty, it was not, in the same circumstances, the duty of men whose fibre was less tough than Cato's, he was clearly not forgetting about himself.[173] In the first book of the Tusculan Disputations,[174] published in 44, he reflected that, with Tullia dead and the way to public distinction barred, death would have been a boon. But he continued to live. Until the autumn of 43 the moment for Cicero to contemplate suicide never came; it would certainly have come if the Republicans had won the battle of Thapsus.

There were times, of course, when Cicero displayed political cowardice. More than once he worked himself into a frenzy in debating the speech which he should make at a critical meeting of the Senate; and then he failed to attend the meeting. This was the case on 1st January 59; it was the case again on 1st September 44.

But he was not altogether a coward. It is easy to be amused by the casual display of armour under his toga when he presided at the consular election in 63. Yet during much of that year his life must have been in great danger. In 54 he kept away from the Senate because he did not think it safe.[175] On the other hand, he was one of only three ex-consuls who braved the stone-throwing of Clodius's gangsters to attend the important meeting of the Senate on the food situation on 7th September, directly after his return from exile in 57.[176] And, though he may have lost his nerve in Court, he showed great courage in persisting in his defence of Milo in 52, in what was in effect a military court, with the prisoner as good as condemned before the proceedings started, and a strong rumour current that, if Cicero proceeded with the case, he would himself be the next to face prosecution.[177]

It does not require great exercise of the historian's imagination to understand the dilemma which confronted Cicero in the first three months of 49. Pompey and Caesar were both, in a political sense, his 'amici'. Pompey, for whatever reason, was also his friend. Yet Caesar (to whom he owed money) had since 56 treated him and his friends with the utmost generosity.[178] The issue was not a simple one of Right and Wrong. Caesar was technically the aggressor; yet, Cicero realized, he acted under provocation.[179]

Civil war was an unutterable disaster in itself and could be fatal to republicanism, whatever its outcome. When Cicero criticized Pompey as a strategist, because of his decision to abandon Rome and Italy, he was silly; the fact has never been in doubt.[180] If there was hysteria in many of the letters which he wrote at this time, it is understandable hysteria. More important by far is the decision which Cicero eventually reached, and the manner in which he reached it. He decided not to commit himself until he had spoken to Caesar. After the consuls and Pompey had left Italy, the meeting took place. For Caesar, intensely anxious to collect as 'republican' a Senate as he could at Rome, Cicero's support had great potential value. When they met, Cicero propounded his conditions. He would come to Rome and attend the Senate, provided he was allowed to propose that Caesar should not carry the war into Spain, and that he was allowed to speak in extenuation of Pompey.[181] 'I was pleased with myself,' he wrote to Atticus after the interview, 'and that is something which has not happened before.' It is wilful not to see in this the most resolute moment of Cicero's life.[182]

The episode is one which Plutarch did not record. For him as for Livy, Cicero's one moment of courage was his last, when the assassins arrived, and he did not flinch.[183]

Vicariously and at second-hand, it must be admitted, Cicero was a great killer. Greek history and Greek philosophy alike taught the lesson that a tyrant needed killing. Anybody who sought to overthrow the republican constitution in favour of a personal *dominatio* was, clearly, a tyrant.

It was for Cicero one of the lessons of Roman history that subverters of republicanism, aspirants to personal domination, were struck down with comforting regularity: Tarquinius Superbus, Spurius Cassius, Spurius Maelius, M. Manlius Capitolinus and then, after an interval, the Gracchi, Saturninus and Livius Drusus.[184] His views on this subject were notorious, and the mere mention by an informer in 59 of 'a consular who said that Rome needed a second Servilius Ahala, a second L. Iunius Brutus' was enough for identification purposes.[185] M. Brutus was thought to inherit the blood both of L. Iunius Brutus and of Servilius Ahala; so when in 46, at the conclusion of the *Brutus*,[186] he was invited to emulate his two great ancestors, the meaning was clear enough.

Caesar had not been a tyrant in 59 or, indeed, in 49. But when in 45 he was in a position to emulate Sulla by restoring the republic and retiring into private life, and failed to do so, the descendant of Iunius Brutus and of Ahala knew his duty, and Cato's worthy daughter knew hers.[187] Brutus, himself as humane as Cicero, knew that the strain of conspiracy might be too much for Cicero, and wisely refrained from inviting him to join in the murder. Once it was achieved—at a meeting of the Senate which, for whatever reason, Cicero did not attend—Cicero was in an ecstasy.[188] He himself, after all, had executed the Catilinarians, men who were on fire to destroy the constitution if given half a chance.

Yet there was a difference between murdering Caesar for what he had already done and murdering other people for what, given the opportunity, they might well proceed to do. Men in a less unequivocal position than the dictator Caesar could be brought before the Courts; for it was a bastion of Roman law that no citizen could be executed without a trial. But Cicero's mind worked differently. The case of the constitutionalists—indeed Caesar's case in 63—that the Catilinarians should have been held and tried in a constitutional manner, presented Cicero with no dilemma at all. The conspirators could not, as citizens, claim the protection of Roman law because they were in fact not citizens at all; they were self-confessed *hostes*. So compelling is logic to the academic mind.

In 44 Cicero's mind worked in just the same way. It was not long after the Ides before he was saying that the tyrannicides had left a good deed half done. 'I wish I had been invited to the dinner; in that case there would have been no leavings.'[189] Antony should have shared Caesar's fate. And the tragedy of the winter of 44/3 from Cicero's point of view was that Antony was a self-confessed *hostis*, and the Senate wilfully refused to recognize the fact. Not Antony only, but his brother. When Brutus held C. Antonius prisoner in Macedonia in early 43, Cicero had no doubt at all that he should be executed. Brutus, who had killed Caesar, knew better. Romans were Romans, and it was for the Senate and People to decide their fate.[190] You could not simply announce that, by your own definition, they were not Romans but *hostes*, and so proceed to kill them. 'Voluntas mea, Brute, de summa re publica semper eadem fuit quam tua, ratio quibusdam in rebus paulo fortasse vehementior.'[191] A curious sentence to write to a tyrannicide.

The leading politicians of the late Roman republic were men of such versatile genius as, perhaps, no country has ever produced.

Many of them were elaborately trained in the art of public speaking. Their education in political philosophy and in the history both of their own country and of Greece was, in a great many cases, a living companion to the whole of their adult life. They were familiar with the literature of Greece as well as with the not as yet very extensive literature of Rome. Greek was for all of them a second language which they both read and spoke. As quaestors they had acquired practical experience of public finance. They had an expert knowledge of Roman law for, apart from considerable practice as a barrister, each of them, as praetor, had sat on the Bench for a year. They often had practical experience of diplomacy (through service on embassies to foreign parts) as well as of provincial administration. At Rome they lived in a world of politics and politicians. Some farmed estates with interest and skill. A great many of them were priests, familiar with complicated formalities and ritual. They had all done military service, and many of them had commanded armies in war.

They lived, in Cicero's time, in an age in which everything, it seemed, had gone wrong. Armies were loyal to their individual commanders, no longer to the State; and armies, under their commanders, were often in a position to coerce civil government. Bribery—which involved extensive borrowing from moneylenders, and debt—had corrupted free elections and justice in the Courts alike and, despite a spate of legislation, the abuse was impervious to correction. In the city there was gangsterdom and, in the fifties, often a state of anarchy.

A hundred years earlier Polybius had admired the Roman state for its harmonious and balanced constitution. The tribunate of Tiberius Gracchus had split that state into two parts.[192] For a short and deceptive moment Sulla seemed to have restored stability. Ten years later the correction, as it seemed, of Sulla's mistakes resulted, again, in a certain optimism. Then for Cicero it seemed that out of the tragedy of the Catilinarian conspiracy a new promise was born in the display, at the moment of crisis, of the solidarity, in defence of law and order, of all ranks of the State ('concordia ordinum'), with the loyal backing of the inhabitants of the Italian countryside ('consensus Italiae').[193] Yet as soon as the crisis was surmounted, the concord vanished. Cato's intransigence was, clearly, no solution at all. Worse things followed: the first disorderly consulship of Caesar, the mischief of

Clodius. After his return from exile Cicero made one more stirring appeal for Unity, claiming in an eloquent, but far from convincing passage in the *Pro Sestio* in early 56 that the common qualities of the rival parties in politics (the *Optimates* and the *Populares*) were far stronger than their disagreements[194]; that both stood for law and order, against the violence of disruption. They were brave words—and, in public as a politician, until Caesar's death, almost his last. His capitulation followed and, instead of speaking, he put his ideas on paper. In the *De Republica*, written between 54 and 51, Cicero recognized that the Republic could not function without the support of a single strong man, a 'moderator' or a 'gubernator'; but not enough of the book survives to show what he intended.[195] From 51, perhaps for the rest of his life, he was writing the *De Legibus*, constructing an ideal republic which first the domination of Caesar and, a few months after Caesar's death, the all-importance of the soldiery (the legions and the veterans of Caesar) showed to be nothing better than a blue-print for a dead world. So that he was not at any time a constructive political thinker, ready to face the real problems of his time: the creation of an effective machinery for the preservation of law and order in Rome and Italy, the subordination of the armed forces to the civil government, and the need to see in the provinces of the Empire a great problem and a great potential, something more than a collection of large-scale public estates—'quasi praedia populi Romani'. This failure does not rank him below his contemporaries. It simply means that he had not Augustus's political genius—just, of course, as he had not Augustus's political opportunity.

As Augustus rightly said, he was a great patriot.[196] He loved his country and, in particular, he understood and loved its distinguished past. Had it ever been written, his history of Rome would have underlined the moral lessons of the past as heavily as Livy was to underline them; though perhaps, if the *De Divinatione* is any guide, it would not have wasted space on prodigies and the irrational, and would have been no treasure trove for Obsequens to plunder. He had other intense interests: the practice and history of Roman oratory, the practice and history of Roman religion, and the political and moral philosophy of Greece. As far as the majority of Greeks of the contemporary world was concerned he shared the opinions of the ordinary Roman. They were shifty,

dishonest, unreliable people, characterized by 'levitas'.[197] But
Greek thinkers, ancient and modern, he admired without limit,
and he believed that he was doing a great service to his country
in introducing a large amount of Greek thinking in morals and
politics to Roman readers by his writing[198]; and in doing this he
was in fact, though he could not know it, an inestimable benefactor to a world of the future far larger than that of Rome. He
wrote dialogues, though he had, as he himself recognized, none of
Plato's mastery of the subtlety of dialogue as an expression of
living and constructive thought. But when he wrote, as when he
spoke, it was not easy for him to be dull.

In having such resources on which to fall back, so as to satisfy
his need for uninterrupted occupation, when the active life of an
effective politician was denied him, he was inestimably lucky, and
he was himself fully conscious of his good fortune.[199] He wrote as
a scholar, no less conscious than Lucretius of the difficulty of
turning technical Greek into satisfactory Latin[200]; painstaking in
research, so as to avoid inaccuracies in the historical settings of his
dialogues[201]; and gifted with an acute sense of the dramatic, as
he showed by placing the *De Republica* and the *De Amicitia* at
different dates in 129 B.C., and the *De Oratore* in 91.

He knew that usually he wrote, as he spoke, well. He was
pleased with himself, often bombastic and, if criticism was
anything but blatant, it failed to touch him. When Posidonius
declined the invitation to write of Cicero's consulship, stating
that, after reading Cicero's own effort on the subject, he was ter-
rified by the thought, it did not occur to Cicero to think that the
remark might not be a compliment.[202] 'I have confounded the
Greeks', he wrote more than once, when he thought that he had
improved on his model.[203] But these were outbursts of temporary
exuberance, and should be treated as such.

Serious vanity, indeed, was perhaps not as large an element in
Cicero's composition as is often thought. He was self-centred,
certainly. He did not hesitate to take credit, after the event, for
a wise prescience—for instance in 59, that Pompey's association
with Caesar, and in 50 that his rupture with Caesar would lead
to disaster.[204] Yet the only surviving letter in which he forecasts
the line which future events may follow, written at the end of
December 50,[205] proved in the event to be uncannily accurate.
The real evidence for his vanity lies in his obsession with the

importance of his consulship, an obsession which, so far from being dimmed, was enhanced by the passage of time. But for this, as has already been seen, there is an easy psychological explanation. He was not conceited about the quality of his published work, and the *Brutus*, with its account of his own oratorical career, was anything but immodest.[206] There is, it is true, one letter—a letter of which he was extremely proud[207]—which has done him harm. It was written in the late spring or early summer of 56, and was an invitation to the historian L. Lucceius to write a monograph on the period which Cicero himself covered in his autobiographical poems; it was to start with his consulship and to end with his triumphal return to Rome in August 57. The letter contains what, by the standards of modern taste, are shocking passages: 'Once a man oversteps the boundaries of modesty, he must be well and properly shameless. And so I beg and beseech you to write the subject up with an exuberance which you yourself may well not feel. Forget about strict historical accuracy ('leges historiae'). There was, I remember, a charming passage in the introduction to one of your books in which you wrote that you could no more be deflected by partiality than Xenophon's Hercules by Pleasure. Well, make an exception on this occasion. We are friends; so in friendship's name go just a little further than strict truth will allow.' The whole letter is written in the same vein. Yet, to be judged fairly, it must be seen in the context of ancient historiographical convention. The distinction between 'panegyric' and 'history' was accepted in the Hellenistic world; it was observed by Polybius when he wrote of Philopoemen[208]; and it is indicated elsewhere by Cicero himself.[209] Though Lucceius did not accept Cicero's invitation, he was perhaps less deeply horrified by its expression than is a reader in the modern world.[210]

In every field his instincts were wholly conservative. In rhetoric the excesses of both the Asian and the modern Attic styles were to be avoided by making the style of Demosthenes a model.[211] In philosophy, under the influence of his tutor Antiochus, he took his stand with the Old Academy, sympathizing neither with extreme scepticism nor, at any point, with Epicureanism nor with the greater part of Stoicism. Of poets, the Roman Ennius was the model whom he chose to improve on, and he was out of sympathy with the elegant polish and perfection of

Alexandrian verse. Whatever his personal view about divination, he respected the tradition of the Roman state religion. Above all, in the public life of the State he stood for the traditional constitution—not excluding the tribunate, from whose onslaught he had suffered such deep personal loss. For when Quintus challenged its value in the *De Legibus*,[212] Cicero spoke with great strength and conviction in its defence; and in this he showed himself a wiser man than Sulla.

Both Livy and Asinius Pollio found in Cicero a lack of manliness[213]. For the rest, the spirit of contemporary criticism is preserved in the pseudo-Sallustian invective and in Fufius Calenus's attack on Cicero in 43, as recounted by Cassius Dio[214]. The normal stock in trade of invective can be disregarded: a sordid upbringing, and an irregular sex-life. So can allegations against the sources of his income, and the mockery of his poetry—which amounts to little more than the repetition of two unhappy lines of his verse, in both of which, alas, Cicero himself took considerable pride.[215] The main attack on his public life was on the ground of his inconsistency, his ingratitude to his benefactors, his inclination to turn and snarl at his friends. He was 'levissimus transfuga'.[216] Yet he never deserted Pompey until Pharsalus was lost; and it is absurd to pretend, as Calenus did, that Antony had ever been in any sense at all a benefactor of Cicero. It was not Cicero who was responsible, in his relation to Antony, for the disruption of the *Homonoia* proclaimed in the Temple of Tellus on 17th March 44. For only a month had passed since that reconciliation when Antony wrote Cicero a letter which survives, on the subject of the restoration of Sextus Cloelius.[217] The letter is a poisonous piece of bullying.

Finally, his political ineffectiveness—the poverty of his achievement, when contrasted with the vanity of his pretensions. Yet was he completely ineffective in public life? A man must be susceptible, indeed, to the lure of paradox before he believes, with Fufius Calenus, that the Catilinarian conspiracy was an invention of Cicero's, a diabolical device on Cicero's part for 'framing' good citizens and honest men. And anyone who criticizes his policy in the twelve months after Caesar's death, because it proved disastrous, should show what other policy could possibly have saved republicanism and averted further civil war. What is remarkable is the authority and prestige which in those months Cicero so easily and naturally assumed.

'What,' Cicero once asked himself, 'will history say of me six hundred years hence?'[218] What would it say in two thousand years time?

As far as the judgement of posterity has been concerned, Cicero, in his writings, has been his worst enemy. Because of his occasional vanity, because he was not a poet as good as Virgil or a philosopher as good as Plato,[219] it has been tempting to deride his literary achievement; and because in politics he was a failure, he can be written off as a failure all round, the tremendous contribution of his writings to European thought can be neglected, and the fact can be forgotten that he was perhaps the most civilized man who has ever lived. You can, in fact, dismiss him as Fufius Calenus and Mommsen dismissed him. Asinius Pollio showed better balance. 'Opera mansura in omne aevum', was his correct estimate of Cicero's writing.[220]

Alternatively it is possible to take a magnifying-glass to his letters. Nobody will deny that they reflect, in every mood and circumstance, the whole man. 'Te totum in litteris vidi,' as Quintus wrote—and wrote with reference to the happy act of Tiro's emancipation.[221] Approached with venom and without *integritas* the Letters can be shown to reflect an unbalanced and, by modern European standards, a not wholly admirable personality. But those letters were not written for the historian. Some, it is true, were written in the expectation, indeed in the hope, that they would be published. Cicero tells us so himself.[222] Others, and we have Cicero's word for it, were written with that privilege of privacy with which we all write letters to our friends. It is true that in the modern world a man of prominence should not write letters even to his tailor without the thought that, behind his tailor's shoulder, a journalist or a biographer may well be lurking. But Cicero did not write in modern times. Indeed it may well have been a very original thought indeed of Cornelius Nepos that Cicero's Letters to Atticus could be used as if they were a history book.[223] And what, in fact, do they reveal to his discredit which the private letters of his great contemporaries—of Cato, Caesar, and Pompey—would not have revealed to their writers' discredit, if anybody at all had thought such letters—as people thought Cicero's letters—worth preserving? It is meanness, indeed, to judge a great man not by his bearing and expression, but by the stain on his coat lapel, where he spilt his soup.[224]

NOTES

[1] Plut. *Cic.* 2. Writing poetry was a diversion of which throughout his life he never tired. His first considerable poem was about Marius. The longest surviving fragment of his poetry comes from his by no means despicable translation of Aratus, *Phaenomena*, which Lucretius is thought to have read: see *P.L.M.* i. 3-28. Where lengthy fragments of Greek verse are quoted in his dialogues in Latin (e.g. *Tusc. Disp.* 2, 20-5), the versions are his own. See on him as a poet, Schanz-Hosius, *Geschichte d. röm. Literatur*[4] (Munich, 1927), i. 535-8, and *R.E.* vii. A, 1236-67 (K. Büchner).

[2] Plut. *Cic.* 3 f. Cf. *Brutus*, 313-16, for his own account of his early education in rhetoric.

[3] Plut. *Cic.* 7, 1 f.

[4] *De Or.* ii. 3; *R.E.* vii. A, 822 f. (no. 25).

[5] *De Or.* ii. 1; *De Legg.* 2. 3; *R.E.* vii. A, 824-7 (no. 28). He died during Cicero's canvass for the consulship (Asc., *In Tog. Cand.* 82 C) and not earlier (for in *Ad Att.* i. 6, 2 'frater' must certainly be read instead of 'pater': see *R.E.* vii. A, 823 f.

[6] *Ad Fam.* xvi. 26, 2.

[7] *R.E.* xiv. 1825-7 (no. 42).

[8] Cousin Lucius, *R.E.* vii. A, 823 f. (no. 26). He died young, in 67 (*Ad Att.* i. 6, 2, reading 'frater'). C. Visellius Varro (104-58 B.C.), *R.E.* ix. A, 355-8 (no. 3).

[9] *H.R.R.* ii, p. 69, F.5 (=L. Seneca, *Suas.* 6, 24). Delicacy in the family, *R.E.* vii. A, 823; *De Legg.* 2, 3; of Cicero in youth, *Brutus*, 313-16; Plut., *Cic.* 3, 7.

[10] Terentia, *R.E.* v. A, 710-16 (no. 95, S. Weinstock); Plut., *Cic.* 29, 4, τοῦ Κικέρωνος ἄρχουσα', cf. 20, 3.

[11] Plut. *Cic.* 20, 3.

[12] Plut. *Cic.* 29, 2-4.

[13] Plut. *Cic.* 29, 3; 30, 4; [Sall.], *In Cic.* 2, 3.

[14] Plut. *Cic.* 41, 2 f. (though he himself told her not to come to Brindisi, *Ad Fam.* xiv. 12); *Ad Att.* xi. 16, 5; xi. 24, 3; *Ad Fam.* iv. 14, 3, to Plancius (very offensive language).

[15] Publilia (*R.E.* xxiii. 1917 f., no. 17); Plut. *Cic.* 41, 4-8.

[16] Letters from Cicero to Dolabella (45-4 B.C.), *Ad Fam.* ix. 10-14; *Ad Att.* xv. 14, 2 f.; from Dolabella to Cicero, *Ad Fam.* ix. 9 (48 B.C.). 'Ab eo qui mihi amicus numquam fuit' in *Ad Att.* xi. 9, 1, must, in my opinion, refer to Antony, not to Dolabella. Dolabella's attractiveness in 50 to Terentia and Tullia, *Ad Att.* vi. 6, 1, 'mulieres delectari obsequio et comitate adulescentis'. J. Carcopino is deeply shocked by Cicero's continuing friendship with Dolabella after Tullia's death, *Cicero, the Secrets of his Correspondence* (London, 1953), i. 177-88.

[17] Corn. Nepos, *Atticus*, 5, 3.

[18] Refs. in *R.E.* vii. A, 1302 f., esp. *Ad Att.* xi. 9, 3 ('I wish Quintus had never been born'); xi. 13, 2: xi. 21, 1 ('Quinti scelus'); xi. 22, 1 ('illius in me odium'). Carcopino (*Op. cit.*, n. 16) i. 188, n. 1, utterly misrepresents the behaviour of Quintus in 47.

[19] Marcus's interest in Quintus's appointment to Gaul, *Ad Q. Fr.* ii. 14 (13), 1; iii, 6 (8), 1. Financial advantage to Quintus, *Ad Q. Fr.* ii. 15 (14), 3; *Ad Att.* xi. 9, 2; Quintus in Sardinia, *Ad Fam.* i. 9, 9.

[20] Brindisi, 57 B.C., *Ad Att.* iv. 1, 4, *Pro Sestio* 131; 50 B.C., *Ad Att.* vii. 2, 2; 48 B.C., see note 14 above; 47 B.C., *Ad Att.* xi. 17 and 17a, 1.

[21] Plut. *Cic.* 47, 4 and 10; Livy, F. 60 (=L. Seneca, *Suas.* 6, 17).

[22] Letters from Marcus, Quintus and their sons to Tiro, *Ad Fam.* xvi. 1-15, 17-27; from Quintus to Marcus, on Tiro's emancipation, *Ad Fam.* xvi. 16. On Tiro, *R.E.* vii. A, 1319-25, no. 52.

[23] *Ad Q. Fr.* ii. 13 (12), 1, 'quiescere non possumus', (54 B.C.); *Pro Plancio* 66, 'Ecquid ego dicam de occupatis meis temporibus, cui fuerit ne otium quidem umquam otiosum'; *Topica* 4; *De Div.* 2, 6, 'Nec nihil agere poteram'; *Ad Fam.* vii. 1, 5, 'Molestissimae occupationes.'

[24] *De Offic.* i. 69-73 on the superiority of public life to even the best and most usefully occupied retirement.

[25] *Pro Sest.* 98; *Ad Fam.* i. 9, 21; *De Or.* i. 1. On the phrase, see Ch. Wirszubski, 'Cicero's *Cum Dignitate Otium*: a Reconsideration', *J.R.S.* 1954, 1-13; J. P. V. D. Balsdon, '*Auctoritas, Dignitas, Otium*', *C.Q.* 1960, 43-50.

[26] Most important: the *De Oratore*, published in 55; the *De Republica*, published in 51; the *Brutus, Paradoxa* and *Orator*, in 46; the *Hortensius, Academica* and *De Finibus*, in 45; the *Tusculan Disputations, De Deorum Natura, De Divinatione, De Senectute, De Amicitia, Topica* and *De Officiis*, published in 44. The *De Legibus*, started in 51, may not have been published in his lifetime. In 54 he wrote, 'Multa mihi dant solacia. . . . Me refero ad litteras et studia nostra', *Ad Att.* iv. 18, 2. On his activities after 56, *Orator*, 148; on speaking and writing as a second-best to politics, *Ad Q. Fr.* iii. 5, 4; *De Officiis*, ii. 2-4; iii. 1-4.

[27] *Ad Fam.* xvi. 4-6.

[28] His 'praediola' at Arpinum, and the 'mercedulae' from them (neither diminutive need be taken too seriously), *Ad Att.* xiii. 9, 2; xiii. 11, 1.

[29] *Ad Q. Fr.* iii. 1, 1-6 (54 B.C.).

[30] 'Servile officium', *Cat. Coniur.* 4, 1.

[31] *Ad Fam.* ii. 12, 2; cf. *Ad Att.* v. 10, 3; v. 11, 5 ('haec ἀνεξία'); vi. 3, 2 *Ad Fam.* ii. 11, 1 ('Totum negotium non est dignum viribus nostris').

[32] C. Coelius Caldus: ' "Puerum" inquies "et fortasse fatuum et non gravem et non continentem". Adsentior,' *Ad Att.* vi. 6, 3; cf. *Ad Fam.* ii. 15, 4, to Caelius, ' "Puerum" inquis. At quaestorem, at nobilem adulescentem.'

[33] There are 34 letters in all, Tyrrell and Purser i, 56-89.

[34] *Ad Fam.* v. 17, 3, to P. Sittius in 57, 'Te ut hortarer . . . ut et hominem te et virum esse meminisses'; *Ad Q. Fr.* iii. 6 (8), 1 (54 B.C.); *Ad Fam.* vii. 8, 1; vii. 17, 1, 'Levis in urbis urbanitatisque desiderio . . . videbare' (54 B.C.); v. 18, 1 (to T. Fadius in 52), 'Rogo atque oro, te conligas virumque te praebeas'; *Ad Fam.* iv. 13, 7 (to P. Figulus in 46); vi. 6 (to A. Caecina in 46); 7, 3 (to M. Marius in 46).

[35] *De Legg.* 3, 36.

[36] *De Offic.* 2, 59.

[37] *Ad Att.* iv. 5, 2. For criticism of his purchase of his Palatine house, *Ad Att.* i. 13, 6; i. 16, 10; and, for scathing criticism of Cicero's expenditure, J. Carcopino, *O.c.* (n. 16), i. 43-55.

[38] *Ad Att.* ii. 5, 2.

[39] *Ad Fam.* iii. 7, 5 (to Appius Claudius).

[40] *Novitas* of Coelius Caldus: *De Or.* i. 117; *In Verr.* ii. 5, 181; *Pro Mur.* 17. Cicero never refers to this aspect of L. Gellius; indeed he overlooks it in passages like *De Leg. Agr.* ii. 3, 'Me perlongo intervallo prope memoriae temporumque nostrorum primum hominem novum consulem fecistis.'

[41] And elected, as no 'new man' before him, 'anno suo', in the first year in which the law allowed him to compete, *De Leg. Agr.* ii. 3.

[42] *Pro Sest.* 121; *In Pis.* 6.

[43] *Ad Fam.* v. 2. 7 f. Metellus in fact had shown his colours even before the execution on 5th December: *Pro Mur.* 81. See *R.E.* vii. A, 891 f.

[44] Plut. *Cic.* 26, 9.

[45] *Ad Fam.* v. 1.

[46] *Ad Att.* i. 18, 1.

[47] In *Pro Mur.* 15-17 he speaks of 'new men'; in *De Leg. Agr.* ii. 3 f. he emphasizes his own unique success as a new man.

[48] *Ad Fam.* ii. 18, 2 f. Cf. n. 32 above.

[49] *Ad Att.* xiii. 13, 1, 'Totam Academiam ab hominibus nobilissimis abstuli; xiii. 19, 5, 'Sane in personas non cadebant; erant enim λογικώτερα quam ut illi de iis somniasse umquam viderentur.' *M. Tulli Ciceronis Academica*, ed. J. S. Reid (London, 1885), 28-35.

[50] *B.C.* i. 8, 3; i. 9, 2; *Ad Att.* vii. 11, 1.

[51] *Ad Att.* iv. 2, 6.

[52] *Ad Q. Fr.* iii. 6 (8), 6, 'Stulte bis terque'.

[53] *Ad Fam.* v. 7, 3.

[54] *Ad Att.* i. 16, 11; i. 17, 10, 'Utor Pompeio familiarissime'; i. 19, 7 (cf. i. 19, 3, 'Nos duo quasi pignora reipublicae').

[55] Plut. *Pomp.* 44.

[56] *Ad Att.* ii. 16, 2, 'Gnaeus quidem noster iam plane quid cogitet nescio' (59 B.C.); iv. 15, 7, 'Utrum fronte an mente dubitatur' (54); *Ad Q. Fr.* i. 3, 9; ii. 2, 3 *Ad Fam.* viii. 1, 3 (Caelius).

[57] Plut. *Cic.* 31, 2 f.; *Ad Att.* iii. 15, 4; x. 4, 3.

[58] *Ad Att.* x. 8A, 2, 'Ut beneficium daret, prius iniuriam fecit.'

[59] *Ad Att.* viii. 2, 4, 'Ego pro Pompeio libenter emori possum; facio pluris omnium hominum neminem.' (Feb. 49).

[60] *De Prov. Cons.* 40.

[61] On Caesar's distinction as an orator and writer, and on the mutual admiration of Caesar and Cicero, *Brutus* 251-62; *Phil.* 2, 116 Suet., *Div. Iul.* 55 f. 'Caesaris humanitas', *Ad Fam.* i. 9, 12.

[62] *Ad Q. Fr.* ii. 16 (15), 5.

[63] *Ad Q. Fr.* ii. 14 (13), 2; iii. 6 (8), 3.

[64] *Ad Fam.* ix. 16, 4.

[65] *Ad Att.* xii. 51, 2; xiii. 1, 3; xiii. 26, 2; xiii. 27, 1; xiii, 28.

[66] *Ad Att.* xiii. 52, 2, 'φιλόλογα multa'.

[67] *Ad Q. Fr.* iii. 5 (6), 7.

[68] *B.G.* 5, 52.

[69] *Ad Att.* ii. 3, 3; cf. *Ad Att.* ix. 2A, 1.

[70] On the advantages to Marcus and Quintus from Quintus's presence on Caesar's staff: *Ad Q. Fr.* ii. 14 (13), 1; ii. 15 (14), 3; iii. 6 (8), 1; *Ad Att.* xi. 9, 2.

[71] 'Caesaris liberalis', *Ad Fam.* i, 9, 12 (54 B.C.); the loan, *Ad Att.* vii. 8, 5 (50 B.C.).

[72] *Ad Att.* vii. 1, 7; vii. 2, 7.

[73] Letters from Caesar: *Ad Att.* ix. 6A; ix. 16, 2; x. 8B; from Oppius and Balbus, *Ad Att.* viii. 15A; ix. 7A; ix, 7B. Antony wrote in his normal unpleasant tone, *Ad Att.* x. 8A.

[74] *Ad Att.* ii. 18, 3; *De Prov. Cons.* 42; *Ad Att.* ix. 2A, 1.

[75] *Ad Att.* vii. 17, 2, 'Scriptor luculentus'. He is discussed very shortly in *Brutus* 239.

[76] *Ad Att.* ii. 1, 8; *Pro Mur.* 62.

[77] Plut., *Cato mi.* 40; *Cic.* 34, 2; Dio Cass. xxxix. 22, 1.

[78] Asc. 35 f. C; Plut. *Pomp.* 54, 6 f.; *Cato mi.* 47, 3 f.

[79] *Ad Fam.* xv. 5, Cato to Cicero: a priggish letter of which Cicero at first approved (*Ad Att.* vii. 1, 7), but of which he afterwards thought differently (*Ad Att.* vii. 2, 7), and which E. Meyer, *Caesars Monarchie*[3] (Stuttgart-Berlin, 1922), 221, thought the finest letter in the whole of Cicero's correspondence. Cato's proposal of a *supplicatio* for Bibulus of 20 days (the longest ever granted, even to Julius Caesar), *Ad Att.* vii. 2, 6 f.

[80] *Ad Att.* v. 21, 10-12; vi. 2, 7-9.

[81] *Pro Mur.* 60-68.

[82] *Ad Att.* ii. 1, 8; cf. ii. 16, 4.

[83] *Ad Fam.* i. 9, 21; *Pro Planc.* 91-4, pursuit of 'reipublicae utilitas salusque', which is 'quaedam moderatio'. Cf. *Pro Mur.* 60-66 for a pastiche of Cato's rigidity.

[84] *Ad Fam.* i. 9, 21; cf. *Pro Sest.* 98 f.

[85] *Ad Fam.* ix. 6, 3, to Varro; ix. 16, 5 f., to Paetus.

[86] Plut. *Lucull.* 41, 4-7.

[87] *Ad Att.* xi. 6, 5.

[88] In *Tusc. Disp.* 1, 72, the good souls after death are those 'qui se integros castosque servavissent, quibusque fuisset minima cum corporibus contagio'.

[89] Cato's filibustering: Plut. *Cato mi.* 5, 4; 31, 5; 43; *Caesar* 13, 2; *Praec. Reip. Gerend.* 804 C. In 59, Plut., *Cato mi.* 32 f. Imprisonment in 55, Plut. *Cato mi.* 43, 6; Dio Cass. xxxix. 34, 4.

[90] *Ad Att.* ix. 10, 6.

[91] *Ad Fam.* vi. 15, congratulations to one of the assassins.

[92] E.g. *Phil.* 1, 3; 1, 32; 2, 91.

[93] *Ad Att.* xiv, 1.

[94] Cf. *Ad Att.* i. 17, 6 on the intimacy of their friendship; iv. 18, 2 (54 B.C.), 'Nemo in terris est mihi tam consentientibus sensibus.'

[95] Carcopino (*O.c.*, n. 16), 1-37, 411-563, showed that the case for first

publication at the time of Nero was not unassailable. His own view was that they were published as a propaganda work in the interest of Octavian in 34/3 B.C. (and followed immediately by the hurried publication of the letters *Ad Familiares*.) More attractive is the suggestion of A. Piganiol, *Revue historique* cci. 1949, 224-234, that they were published with the approval of Octavian as an act of repentance for the murder of Cicero in the proscriptions.

[96] *Ad Att*. iv. 1, 1.

[97] *Ad Att*. xiv. 18, 1; cf. *Ad Fam*. ix. 14.

[98] *Ad Att*. xvi. 7.

[99] *R.E.* iv. 1408 f. (no. 275).

[100] Cat. 49, 6 f.

[101] *Ad Fam*. xv. 21, 4.

[102] Correspondence: letters from Cicero, *Ad Fam*. xii. 1-10; xv. 14-18; from Cassius to Cicero, *Ad Fam*. xii. 11 f.; xv. 19.

[103] Correspondence: from Cicero, *Ad Fam*. vii. 6-22; from Trebatius and C. Matius to Cicero, *Ad Att*. ix. 15. On Trebatius, Hor. *Sat*. ii. 1.

[104] Letters from Cicero to Curio, *Ad Fam*. ii. 1-7. No letters survive from Curio to Cicero. On the elder Curio, *Brutus* 216 ff.

[105] *Pro Caelio* 9; Quint. xii. 11, 6. Letters from Cicero to Caelius, *Ad Fam*. ii. 8-16; from Caelius to Cicero, *Ad Fam*. viii. 1-17.

[106] *Ad Fam*. vii. 32.

[107] *Ad Fam*. ix. 15-26 (esp. 21 and 22). Stoic and Cynic views on obscenity were a stock joke, *De Offic*. i. 128.

[108] Letters of Cicero to M. Marius, *Ad Fam*. vii. 1-4. On the Games, vii. 1 (but cf. *Tusc. Disp*. ii. 41, for admiration of gladiators' courage).

[109] *Ad Att*. xiii. 21A, 2; xiii. 22, 3; xv. 1, 4.

[110] Letters to Caecina, *Ad Fam*. vi. 5 f. and 8; from Caecina, vi. 7.

[111] *Ad Fam*. iv. 13; *R.E.* xvii. 200-212.

[112] Letters to Varro, *Ad Fam*. ix. 1-8; on the dedication of the *Academica*, *Ad Att*. xiii. 22, 1; xiii. 25, 3.

[113] *De Amicit*. 15; 82.

[114] *De Amicit*. 64.

[115] R. Syme, *The Roman Revolution*[2] (Oxford, 1951), 12.

[116] *Ad Att*. ii. 3, 3.

[117] *Ad Fam*. i. 1, 3 f.; *Ad Q. Fr.* ii. 2, 3.

[118] *Pro Mur*. 17; *Ad Att*. iii. 9, 2 (from exile in 58), 'Nos non inimici sed invidi perdiderunt'; *Ad Fam*. i. 9, 16; ii. 9, 3; *Pro Planc*. 1 (cf. Quint. xii. 10, 13). On 'invidi', *Ad Att*. iv. 5, 2; *Pro Planc*. 59; *Ad Fam*. vii. 2, 3. 'Improbi et invidi', *Ad Att*. vii. 17, 4; as critics of his poem *De Consulatu Suo*, *De Offic*. i. 77. In 46 he thought 'invidia' a danger no longer, for what was there in his position that any one could envy, *Ad Fam*. ix. 16, 5 f.?

[119] *Ad Att*. i. 13, 4.

[120] Plut. *Cic*. 24, 4-7, 'ἀφθονώτατος.'

[121] *B.C.* 1, 4, 'Ipse Pompeius, ab inimicis Caesaris incitatus, . . . totum se ab eius amicitia averterat, et cum communibus inimicis in gratiam redierat.' Cic., *De Amicit*. 33, on the abandonment of 'friendship' because of changed political alignment.

[122] *Pro Caelio*, 12-14.

[123] *Ad Fam.* vii. 2, 3.

[124] *Ad Att.* xiv. 13B, 4.

[125] *Phil.* i. 10, 14; v. 19; xii. 14- even if he was not ready to follow Cicero's policy against Antony to extremes (cf. *Ad Fam.* xii. 4, 1).

[126] Admittedly there is no evidence. The only references in letters of 54/3 are to Gabinius's previous trial for *maiestas* (*Ad Q. Fr.* iii. 7 (9), 3 being the latest). There are no references to him in letters or writings of Cicero after this date (except, of course, the purely factual reference to his condemnation for *repetundae* in the *Pro Rabirio Postumo*, and a scornful allusion to his recall in 49 in *Ad Att.* x. 8, 3).

[127] *Ad Att.* xi. 5, 4 (48 B.C.); *Ad Fam.* v. 9-11 (45/4 B.C.).

[128] *De Offic.* i. 109; *Paradoxa* vi. 46; Cicero was, however, a warm admirer of Crassus' elder son Publius, *Brutus* 281 f.

[129] *Ad Att.* xi. 9, 1, written early in January 47, 'Iam quid sperem ab eo qui mihi amicus numquam fuit', refers, I suspect, to Antony. Oppius and Balbus were more friendly: *Ad Att.* xi. 6, 3; xi. 7, 5; xi. 8, 1.

[130] Plut. *Cic.* 48, 6-49, 2.

[131] *Ad Fam.* vii. 2, 2 f.

[132] *Pro Planc.* 35, with Schol. Bob., p. 159 St.

[133] *Ad Att.* i. 16, 1; i. 18, 2. His evidence at the trial was, by comparison, scarcely offensive at all; 'contraxi vela', *Ad Att.* i. 16, 2.

[134] *Ad Att.* i. 16, 9 f.; Schol. Bob. 85-91 St.

[135] He was 'φιλοσκώπτης', Plut. *Cic.* 50, 6. For Cicero's own discussion of the nature of humour and wit, see *De Or.* ii. 235-90.

[136] Plut. *Cic.* 27, 1; 50, 4. Contemporary critics judged him 'in salibus aliquando frigidus', Quint. xii. 10, 12. Quintilian vi. 3, 3 admits the charge, but confesses himself biassed in Cicero's favour in this matter. A number of jokes for which he was not responsible were fathered on him even in his own lifetime: *Ad Fam.* vii. 32, 1 f. ix. 16, 3 f. C. Trebonius made a collection of his *mots* in 47 (*Ad Fam.* xv. 21, 2) and Caesar in 46 (*Ad Fam.* ix. 16, 4). Cicero's posthumous reputation was not helped by Tiro's publication, in three books, of his jokes, for the selection was anything but discriminating (Quint. vi. 3, 5). Cf. Macrob. *Sat.* 2, 3 for specimens of his humour.

[137] *Ad Att.* iii. 12, 2, 'Puto posse probari non esse meam'; iii. 15, 3. Cf. *Ad Att.* xiii. 22, 3 on Cicero's relation with his publisher, as concerned the publication of his work.

[138] *Ad Fam.* xi. 20, 1.

[139] *Ad Att.* ii. 9, 1; ii. 14, 1; ii. 16, 2; ii. 17, 1 ff.

[140] *Ad Att.* i. 14, 5.

[141] *Ad Att.* i. 13, 2 i. 16, 12.

[142] Plut. *Cic.* 38; Macrob. *Sat.* 2. 3, 7 f.

[143] *Ad Fam.* vii. 32, 2; *Pro Planc.* 35; *Ad Fam.* ix. 16, 3 f.; Macrob. *Sat.*, 2, 3 has collected a number of his brighter witticisms.

[144] Macrob. *Sat.* 2. 3, 3.

[145] Plut. *Cic.* 26, 2.

[146] *Ad Fam.* ii. 11, 2; Plut. *Cic.* 36, 6.

[147] *Ad Fam.* v. 7; cf. *Pro Sulla* 67; *Pro Planc.* 85; Schol. Bob. 167 St.

[148] R.E. vii. A, 1245-50.

[149] Ad Att. ii. 1, 2; Ad Fam. v. 12.

[150] Ad Brut. 25 (1, 17), 1.

[151] Plut. Cic. 51, 'ἀμετρία τῆς περιαυτολογίας'.

[152] Ad Att. xii. 21, 1; Sall. Cat. Con. 43, 1.

[153] Ad Att. xii. 21, 1.

[154] Ad Fam. vi. 6, 4; Phil. ii. 23 f. ; cf. Ad Att. vii. 6, 2; viii. 3, 3.

[155] Ad Fam. i. 9, 8 f., on which see J. P. V. D. Balsdon, J.R.S. 1957, 18 f., T. A. Dorey, C.R. 1959, 13.

[156] Ad Fam. xv. 4, 13.

[157] Ad Att. ii. 5, 2; Ad Fam. xv. 4, 13 (to Cato).

[158] Ad Att. vii. 2, 6.

[159] Ad Att. vi. 6, 3; cf. vi. 3, 1 f.; vi. 4, 1.

[160] De Div. 2, 3.

[161] Ad Att. iv. 5, 3; cf. 'In isto homine colendo tam indormivi diu,' Ad Q. Fr. ii. 14 (13), ii. (54 B.C.).

[162] Ad Att. xi. 9, 1; xi. 15, 2; Ad Fam. xv. 15, 4.

[163] Ad Att. iii. 15, 5; Ad Q. Fr. i. 4, 4.

[164] Post Red. in Sen. 39; [Sall.], In Cic. 7; mockery of Vatinius, Macrob. Sat. 2. 3, 5.

[165] Pro Sest. 44-50; Post Red. in Sen. 4; Pro Planc. 86 ff., 'Esset pugnandum cum consulibus'; Ad Fam. i. 9, 13.

[166] Ad Att. i. 16, 4; Ad Fam. i. 9, 16.

[167] Ad Att. i. 12-15, 1st Jan. to 15th March.

[168] Ad Att. i. 16 (July).

[169] Ad Att. iv. 5.

[170] Ad Att. i. 16, 9 and 11.

[171] Ad Att. ii. 19, 3; iv. 1, 6; iv. 15, 6; Ad Q. Fr. ii. 15 (14), 2.

[172] Ad Brut. 25 (1, 17), 4.

[173] Ad Fam. iv. 13, 2; vii. 3, 4; De Offic. i. 112.

[174] i. 84.

[175] Ad Q. Fr. ii. 16 (15), 2.

[176] Ad Att. iv. 1, 6.

[177] Ascon. In Milon, 38 C.

[178] Ad Att. vii. 8, 5; Ad Fam. i. 9, 18, 'Commemoranda quaedam et divina Caesaris in me fratremque liberalitas.'

[179] As he said, 'Quem fugiam habeo, quem sequar non habeo,' Ad Att. viii. 7, 2; cf Macrob., Sat. 2. 3, 7, Plut. Cic. 37, 3.

[180] Ad Att. vii. 11, 3; viii. 16, 1 (January-March 49). Yet by May Cicero had changed his mind: 'Cuius (sc. Pompei) omne consilium Themistocleum est', Ad Att. x. 8, 4.

[181] Ad Att. x. 18.

[182] Cicero met Caesar on 28th March. Caesar left Rome for Spain on 6th- or 7th April. Cicero left Italy on 7th June. In seeking to controvert the reasonable account of Plutarch (Cic. 37 f.), Carcopino (Op. cit., n. 16, i. 218-225) makes great play of the interval between 6th April and 7th June. He does not mention Cicero's interview with Caesar at all.

[183] Plut. Cic. 48, 3 ff.; Livy F. 61 (=Sen. Suas. 6, 22).

[184] See J. P. V. D. Balsdon, 'The Ides of March', *Historia*, 1958, esp. 88 f.

[185] *Ad Att.* ii. 24, 3.

[186] *Brutus* 331.

[187] See Balsdon, *Historia*, 1958, 93 f.

[188] *Ad Fam.* vi. 15.

[189] *Ad Fam.* x. 28, 1; cf. *Ad Att.* xv. 11, 2.

[190] *Ad Brut.* iii. (2, 3), 2; x. (1, 3A); Cicero's retort, *Ad Brutum* v (2, 5), 5, 'Video te lenitate delectari.'

[191] *Ad Brut.* v. (2, 5), 1.

[192] *De Rep.* i, 31.

[193] The phrase 'concordia ordinum' appears only twice in Cicero's writings, *Ad Att.* i. 17, 9; i. 18, 3. On the general concept, see H. Strasburger, *Concordia Ordinum* (Leipzig, 1931; reprinted Amsterdam, 1956). 'Consensio Italiae', *Ad Att.* i. 14, 4.

[194] *Pro Sest.* 96 ff., on which, J. P. V. D. Balsdon, *C.Q.* 1960, 47 f. (criticized by W. K. Lacey, *C.Q.* 1962, 67-71).

[195] *De Rep.* i, 63; ii. 15; ii. 51, 'Quasi tutor et procurator reipublicae'; v. 5-9, 'Moderator rei publicae'; vi. 1, 'Rector'.

[196] Plut. *Cic.* 49, 5.

[197] *Ad Q. Fr.* i. 1, 16; i. 2, 4; *Pro Flac.* 9 f.

[198] *De Div.* ii. 1-7 is an admirable statement of his writing, its background and purposes; *De Offic.* i, 1; *Tusc. Disp.* i. 1.

[199] *Ad Fam.* vi. 12, 5; vii. 3, 4; *De Div.* ii. 6.

[200] Though in *Tusc. Disp.* ii. 35; iii. 10 (cf. *De Fin.* iii. 5; *N.D.* i. 8) he claimed that for philosophical purposes the vocabulary of Latin was superior to that of Greek.

[201] *Ad Att.* xiii. 4, 1; v. 1; 6A; xxx. 2; xxxii. 3; xxiii. 3.

[202] *Ad Att.* ii. 1, 2.

[203] *Ad Att.* ii. 1, 2; cf. xiii. 13, 1.

[204] See above, n. 154.

[205] *Ad Att.* vii. 9.

[206] *Brut.* 301-324.

[207] *Ad Fam.* v. 12. 'Valde bella' is how, writing to Atticus, he described the letter, *Ad Att.* iv. 6, 4.

[208] Polyb. x. 21, 5-8.

[209] *Ad Att.* i. 19, 10.

[210] See B. L. Ullman, 'History and Tragedy', *T.A.P.A.*, 1942, 44-53.

[211] *Brutus*, 284-91; *Orator*, 20-32.

[212] iii. 19-26.

[213] L. Sen., *Suas.* vi. 14 f. and 24 f.

[214] Dio Cass. xlvi. 1-28.

[215] *In Cic.* 5 f.; cf. *In Pis.* 72; *De Offic.* i. 77; Quint. ix. 4, 41; xi. 1, 24.

[216] *In Cic.* 7; Dio Cass. xlvi. 22.

[217] *Ad Att.* xiv. 13A; on the name 'Cloelius', D. R. Shackleton Bailey, *C.Q.* 1960, 41 f.

[218] *Ad Att.* ii. 5, 1; cf. *Tusc. Disp.* i. 33.

[219] As he knew and said, *Tusc. Disp.* i. 24.

220 L. Sen., *Suas.* vi. 24.
221 *Ad Fam.* xvi. 16, 2.
222 *Ad Fam.* xv. 21, 4.
223 Corn. Nep., *Atticus*, xvi. 3.
224 I refer, of course, to Carcopino, *Op. cit.*, n. 16.

Index